Complete Math WORKOUT

5

Copyright © 2007 **Popular Book Company (Canada) Limited**

15 Wertheim Court, Units 602-603, Richmond Hill, Ontario, Canada L4B 3H7
E-mail: ca-info@popularworld.com   Website: www.popularbook.ca

Printed in China

 Contents

Section 1

Overview

In Grade 4, fraction skills were introduced. In this section, these skills are practiced and expanded upon.

Concepts of equivalent fractions, improper fractions, and mixed numbers are consolidated. Students learn how to add and subtract fractions with like denominators. Ample practice in converting fractions to decimals and adding and subtracting decimals are provided.

Other skills include multiplying and dividing decimals by whole numbers.

1 Operations with Whole Numbers

E X A M P L E S

1. Find the sum of 4,297 and 970 and the difference between them.

$$\begin{array}{r} {}^{1}\ {}^{1} \\ 4{,}2\,9\,7 \\ +\ \ \ 9\,7\,0 \\ \hline \end{array}$$
sum ⟶ 5,2 6 7

$$\begin{array}{r} {}^{3}\ {}^{12} \\ \cancel{4}{,}2\,9\,7 \\ -\ \ \ 9\,7\,0 \\ \hline \end{array}$$
difference ⟶ 3,3 2 7

2. Find the product of 296 and 4.

$$\begin{array}{r} {}^{2} \\ 2\,9\,6 \\ \times\ \ \ 4 \\ \hline 4 \end{array}$$
↑
6 x 4 = 24

⟶

$$\begin{array}{r} {}^{3}\ {}^{2} \\ 2\,9\,6 \\ \times\ \ \ 4 \\ \hline 8\,4 \end{array}$$
↑
9 x 4 + 2 = 36 + 2 = 38

⟶

$$\begin{array}{r} {}^{3} \\ 2\,9\,6 \\ \times\ \ \ 4 \\ \hline 1{,}1\,8\,4 \end{array}$$ ⟵ product
↑
2 x 4 + 3 = 8 + 3 = 11

3. Find the quotient when 511 is divided by 7.

$$\begin{array}{r} 7\,3 \\ 7\,\overline{)5\,1\,1} \\ 4\,9 \\ \hline 2\,1 \\ 2\,1 \\ \hline \end{array}$$

7 3 ⟵ quotient
49 ⟵ 7 x 7 = 49
51 – 49 = 2 ⟶ 2 1 ⟵ bring down 1
21 ⟵ 7 x 3 = 21

INTS:

- Align all numbers on the right-hand side when doing vertical addition, subtraction, and multiplication.

- In doing addition or multiplication, remember to carry groups of 10 to the column on the left if the sum or product of a column is greater than 10.

- In doing subtraction, borrow 10 from the column on the left if you can't take away.

- Continue to divide until the remainder is smaller than the divisor.

- Multiplication and division are done in order from left to right.

Find the answers mentally.

① 2 x 7 x 50 = _____

② 5,700 ÷ 10 = _____

③ 5 x 8 x 20 = _____

④ 2,000 x 35 = _____

⑤ 5 x 29 x 2 = _____

⑥ 27,000 ÷ 300 = _____

⑦ 1,000 x 20 ÷ 100= _____

⑧ 2 x 62 x 5 = _____

⑨ 2,000 ÷ 100 x 5 = _____

⑩ 30 x 100 ÷ 10 = _____

⑪ 500 ÷ 50 x 100 = _____

⑫ 400 ÷ 100 x 10 = _____

Do the calculation.

⑬ 2,784 + 3,796	⑭ 999 − 888
⑮ 2,784 + 4,370 − 401	⑯ 4,983 + 3,974 − 728

⑰ 595 ÷ 7	⑱ 314 × 8	⑲ 438 ÷ 6

⑳ 5 ⟌ 3 2 5	㉑ 3 ⟌ 8 7 3	㉒ 8 ⟌ 7 3 6

㉓ 5 3 7 × 9	㉔ 8 5 4 × 6	㉕ 2 1 3 × 5

Find the answers.

㉖ The sum of seven thousand two and four hundred ninety-nine

_____

㉗ The difference between nine hundred eighty-four and five hundred seventy-eight

_____

Write your answers in the puzzle below.

A	7 x 30
B	208 ÷ 4
C	270 ÷ 9
D	30 x 69
E	48 ÷ 12
F	5 x 150

DOWN

A	225 ÷ 9
C	5 x 75
E	322 ÷ 7
F	19 x 4
G	366 ÷ 3

㉘
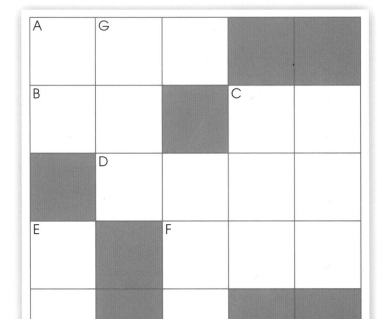

Do the division and write down the remainder in each case. The sum of the remainders is equal to the number of coconuts in the tree.

㉙   218 ÷ 3   remainder   = _____

㉚   497 ÷ 7   remainder   = _____

㉛   100 ÷ 3   remainder   = _____

㉜   200 ÷ 5   remainder   = _____

㉝   124 ÷ 8   remainder   = _____

㉞   874 ÷ 4   remainder   = _____

㉟   Sum of remainders   = _____

There are _____ coconuts in the tree.

Solve the problems. Show your work.

㉧ Jane is 7 years older than Jeff. Jane is 11 years old. How old is Jeff?

Jeff is _____ years old.

㊲ What is the perimeter of the flag?

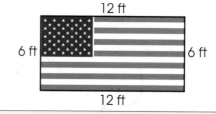

㊳ Dan's heart beats 66 times a minute. How many times does it beat in an hour?

㊴ Farmer Fred's chickens lay 240 eggs per day. If Fred gets $2 for one dozen eggs, how much does he earn per day?

Just for Fun

Solve the problems.

① Write the next 3 numbers in each of the following sequences.

    a. 77 88 99 _____ _____ _____

    b. 72 84 96 _____ _____ _____

② A number is divisible by 3 if the sum of its digits is divisible by 3. Using this fact, circle the numbers which are divisible by 3.

    1,234   5,790   2,927   9,980   4,563

Introducing Decimals

EXAMPLES

1. $0.94 = \frac{94}{100}$ or $\frac{9}{10} + \frac{4}{100}$ = 9 tenths and 4 hundredths

2. $0.4 = \frac{4}{10}$ or $\frac{40}{100}$ = 4 tenths or 40 hundredths

3. $0.02 = \frac{2}{100}$ = 2 hundredths

4. $1.43 = 1 + 0.43$

   $= 1 + \frac{43}{100}$

   $= 1$ and 43 hundredths

HINTS:

ones

↓ ← decimal point

- **2.94** is a decimal number.

  ↑ ↑ ← hundredths

  tenths

It is read as two point nine four.

- 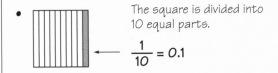 The square is divided into 10 equal parts.

  $\frac{1}{10} = 0.1$

- 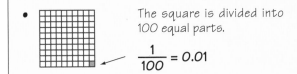 The square is divided into 100 equal parts.

  $\frac{1}{100} = 0.01$

- 1 tenth is the same as 10 hundredths.

- Deleting the zero(s) at the end of a decimal number will not affect the numerical value of a decimal number.

  e.g. 2.30 = 2.3

- When rounding decimal numbers, round up if the last digit is 5 or more; otherwise, round down.

Complete the chart below.

	Decimal	Fraction
①	0.52	
②		$\frac{5}{100}$
③		$\frac{3}{10}$
④	0.09	
⑤		$7\frac{2}{10}$
⑥	4.1	

Place the numbers on the number line below.

⑦

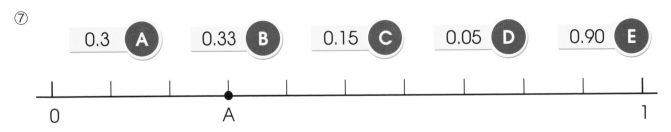

0.3 **A**   0.33 **B**   0.15 **C**   0.05 **D**   0.90 **E**

0   A   1

3 1833 05262 5388

Write the numbers in order from least to greatest.

⑧   0.2, 0.15, 0.1, 0.02, 0.01

_____

⑨   1.45, 1.50, 1.4, 1.54, 1.05

_____

Write the numbers in order from greatest to least.

⑩   5.08, 5.80, 5.885, 0.58, 0.55, 0.50

_____

⑪   2.9, 2.09, 3.2, 2.39, 2.93, 2.3

_____

Write the quantities in decimal form.

⑫   5 cents   = $ _____   ⑬   2 nickels = $ _____

⑭   3 quarters = $ _____   ⑮   4 dimes   = $ _____

⑯   316 cm   = _____ m   ⑰   37 mm   = _____ cm

Write True (T) or False (F) in the (   ).

⑱   0.7 = 0.70   (   )   ⑲   1.02 = 1.2   (   )

⑳   3.0 = 3   (   )   ㉑   0.5 = .5   (   )

㉒ $9.1 = 9\frac{1}{100}$ (   )   ㉓ $2.3 = 2\frac{3}{100}$ (   )

Complete the expanded forms using decimals.

㉔ $7 + \frac{2}{100}$ = _____   ㉕ $3 + \frac{5}{10} + \frac{7}{100}$ = _____

㉖ $\frac{1}{10} + \frac{6}{100}$ = _____   ㉗ $2 + \frac{3}{10} + \frac{5}{100}$ = _____

Write an approximate decimal value for each of the numbers on the number line below.

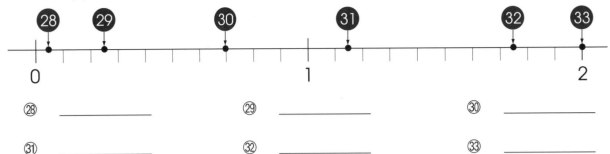

㉘ _____ ㉙ _____ ㉚ _____

㉛ _____ ㉜ _____ ㉝ _____

Write the place value and meaning of each underlined digit.

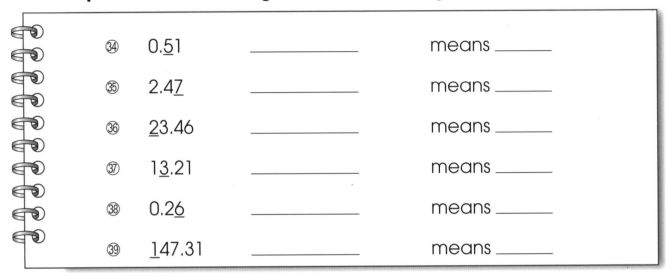

㉞ 0.5̲1 _____ means _____

㉟ 2.4̲7 _____ means _____

㊱ 2̲3.46 _____ means _____

㊲ 13̲.21 _____ means _____

㊳ 0.26̲ _____ means _____

㊴ 1̲47.31 _____ means _____

Round each of the following numbers to the nearest tenth.

㊵ 5.72 _____   ㊶ 0.88 _____

㊷ 1.99 _____   ㊸ 12.34 _____

Round each of the following numbers to the nearest hundredth.

㊹ 5.938 _____   ㊺ 2.704 _____

㊻ 3.097 _____   ㊼ 6.006 _____

Place < or > between each pair of decimal numbers.

㊽ 0.3   0.32   ㊾ 0.09   0.9

㊿ 0.22   0.2   51 23.1   23.01

Answer the following questions.

52   Ron finished a marathon race in 3 hours 57.8 minutes. It took John 0.7 minute longer.

     a. How long did it take John to finish the race?   _____

     b. Did they both finish under 4 hours?   _____

53   Ann spent $47.99 on a pair of jeans and $15.75 on a T-shirt. How much did she spend to the nearest dollar?

_____

54   Janice paid $0.80 for a chocolate bar. Write 2 different ways she could pay with 8 coins.

     a. Use ____ ____ ____ ____

     b. Use ____ ____ ____ ____

55   Ming spent $195.55 at the mall. Write this amount in words.

_____

Determine the value for each symbol. Each symbol has a different value. Write down all the possible solutions.

■ = _____   ♠ = _____

◆ = _____   ♥ = _____

$$
\begin{array}{r}
\blacksquare\ \blacklozenge\ .\ 9 \\
+\ \ \spadesuit\ \ 8\ .\ \heartsuit \\
\hline
5\ \ 6\ .\ 7
\end{array}
$$

Adding Decimals

E X A M P L E S

1. 57.23 + 85.9 + 0.78 + 30
    = 173.91

align the decimal points

```
  57.23
  85.90 ←  write "0"s
   0.78     to fill the
+ 30.00 ←   empty
          places
 173.91
```

2. Write 219.57 in expanded form.
    219.57 = 200 + 10 + 9 + 0.5 + 0.07

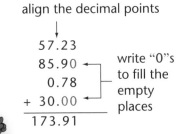

H INTS:

- Align the decimal points when doing vertical addition.

- Write zeros to fill the empty places.

- Add decimal numbers the same way we add whole numbers.

- Don't forget to put the decimal point in the answer.

Add these decimals in tenths.

①
$$
\begin{array}{r}
0.7 \\
+\ 0.8 \\
\hline
\end{array}
$$

②
$$
\begin{array}{r}
1.9 \\
+\ 8.7 \\
\hline
\end{array}
$$

③
$$
\begin{array}{r}
30.2 \\
+\ 16.6 \\
\hline
\end{array}
$$

④
$$
\begin{array}{r}
23.4 \\
+\ 41.6 \\
\hline
\end{array}
$$

⑤ 10.2 + 12.7 = _____

⑥ 0.9 + 12.8 = _____

Add these decimals in hundredths.

⑦
$$
\begin{array}{r}
50.93 \\
+\ \ 7.28 \\
\hline
\end{array}
$$

⑧
$$
\begin{array}{r}
6.54 \\
+\ 27.69 \\
\hline
\end{array}
$$

⑨
$$
\begin{array}{r}
27.84 \\
+\ \ 3.07 \\
\hline
\end{array}
$$

⑩
$$
\begin{array}{r}
100.30 \\
+\ \ \ 6.84 \\
\hline
\end{array}
$$

⑪ 5.83 + 3.0   = _____

⑫ 99.01 + 9.09   = _____

⑬ 5.50 + 0.9   = _____

⑭ 324.78 + 1.22 = _____

⑮ 123.45 + 34.56 = _____

⑯ 13.59 + 12.64 = _____

Add these decimals.

⑰ 5 + 7.8 = _____

⑱ 5.9 + 0.78 = _____

⑲ 2.73 + 4.9 = _____

⑳ 7 + 1.23 = _____

㉑ 5.9 + 8.73 = _____

㉒ 5.03 + 2.9 = _____

㉓ 11.67 + 40.9 = _____

㉔ 22.45 + 6.7 = _____

㉕ 52.93 + 109.2 = _____

㉖ 809 + 2.82 = _____

㉗ 141.05 + 26.4 = _____

㉘ 17.42 + 353 = _____

㉙ 0.98 + 3.2 + 12 = _____

㉚ 9 + 61.4 + 45.5 = _____

㉛ 14.07 + 6.67 + 9.91 = _____

㉜ 4.5 + 2.77 + 1.82 = _____

㉝ 5 + 4.23 + 12.6 = _____

㉞ 4.97 + 9.3 + 1.87 + 5 = _____

㉟ 902 + 77.13 + 0.87 = _____

Write these decimals in expanded form.

㊱ 25.87 = _____

㊲ 12.93 = _____

Write the decimals.

㊳ 500 + 70 + 0.8 = _____

㊴ 100 + 8 + 0.6 + 0.04 = _____

15

Add the money. If the sum is larger than the amount in the previous question, write it on the line in ㊼ and add the sums to find Sally's savings.

㊵ $9.32 + $0.95   = _____

㊶ $9.85 + $1.32   = _____

㊷ $5.23 + $6.09   = _____

㊸ $10.93 + $0.21   = _____

㊹ $53.29 + $6.78   = _____

㊺ $70.94 + $0.50   = _____

㊻ $29.84 + $39.99 = _____

㊼   _____

㊽   sum =
     _____

㊾   Sally saves _____ .

Do the following addition. Write + or – in the ◯ to show the relation of P, Q, R, and S.

㊿   5.9 + 12.8 = ⬭P⬭   ⑤   15.2 + 9.4 = ⬭R⬭

㉒   19.4 + 3.9 = ⬭Q⬭   ㉝   7.8 + 9.6   = ⬭S⬭

㉞   Ⓟ ◯ Ⓠ = Ⓡ ◯ Ⓢ

Solve the problems. Show your work.

(55) Casla and Sally go to a movie. The tickets cost $5.50 each. Popcorn costs $3.75 and drinks cost $1.20 each. If they each have a drink and share the popcorn, how much do they pay altogether?

______________________________ = ____________

They pay ____________ altogether.

(56) Ann's allowance in September is $6.75 the first week, $5.90 the second week, $6.50 the third week, and only $5 the fourth week. How much does she get over the 4-week period?

(57) Ron is training for triathlon. He cycles 25.2 miles on Monday, 22.1 miles on Wednesday, 24.8 miles on Friday, and 28.2 miles on Saturday. How far does he cycle during the week?

Bob has 17 coins. They are dimes, nickels, and pennies. Their total value is $0.90. How many of each coin does he have?

Bob has ________ dimes, ________ nickels, and ________ pennies.

Subtracting Decimals

EXAMPLES

1. 29.43 − 17.86 =   ?

$$
\begin{array}{r}
2\,9\overset{3}{.}\overset{13}{\cancel{4}\cancel{3}} \\
-\;1\,7\,.8\,6 \\
\hline
7
\end{array}
\quad\longrightarrow\quad
\begin{array}{r}
2\overset{8}{\cancel{9}}\overset{13}{.}\cancel{4}3 \\
-\;1\,7\,.8\,6 \\
\hline
5\,7
\end{array}
\quad\longrightarrow\quad
\begin{array}{r}
2\overset{8}{\cancel{9}}.4\,3 \\
-\;1\,7\,.8\,6 \\
\hline
1\;5\,7
\end{array}
\quad\longrightarrow\quad
\begin{array}{r}
2\,9\,.4\,3 \\
-\;1\,7\,.8\,6 \\
\hline
1\,1\,.5\,7
\end{array}
$$

2. Jim ran 5.8 miles and Andrea ran 7.25 miles. How much farther did Andrea run?

7.25 − 5.8 = 1.45

$$
\begin{array}{r}
\overset{6}{\cancel{7}}.\overset{12}{\cancel{2}}\,5 \\
-\;\;5\,.8\,0 \\
\hline
1\,.4\,5
\end{array}
$$

Andrea ran 1.45 miles farther.

HINTS:

- Align the decimal points when doing vertical subtraction.
- Write zeros to fill the empty places.
- Subtract decimal numbers the same way we subtract whole numbers.
- Use addition to check your answer.
- Don't forget to put the decimal point in the answer.

Subtract these decimals in tenths.

①
$$
\begin{array}{r}
0.7 \\
-\;0.2 \\
\hline
\end{array}
$$

②
$$
\begin{array}{r}
5\,8.3 \\
-\;1.8 \\
\hline
\end{array}
$$

③
$$
\begin{array}{r}
9.2 \\
-\;2.9 \\
\hline
\end{array}
$$

④
$$
\begin{array}{r}
5.0 \\
-\;3.8 \\
\hline
\end{array}
$$

⑤ 45.3 − 16.9 = _____

⑥ 72.4 − 38.6 = _____

Subtract these decimals in hundredths.

⑦
$$
\begin{array}{r}
1\,7.0\,4 \\
-\;1\,2.0\,0 \\
\hline
\end{array}
$$

⑧
$$
\begin{array}{r}
1.5\,7 \\
-\;0.8\,8 \\
\hline
\end{array}
$$

⑨
$$
\begin{array}{r}
8.0\,4 \\
-\;4.9\,8 \\
\hline
\end{array}
$$

⑩ 704.23 − 125.07 = _____

⑪ 32.16 − 8.45 = _____

Subtract these decimals.

⑫ 2.0 − 0.02 = _____ ⑬ 9.03 − 4 = _____

⑭ 7.9 − 4.13 = _____ ⑮ 10.4 − 2.13 = _____

⑯ 8.1 − 5.08 = _____ ⑰ 15 − 3.62 = _____

⑱ 12.1 − 4.23 = _____ ⑲ 9.5 − 7.68 = _____

⑳ 0.96 − 0.08 = _____ ㉑ 0.72 − 0.5 = _____

㉒ 1.1 − 0.84 = _____ ㉓ 2.3 − 1.49 = _____

㉔ 0.26 − 0.26 = _____ ㉕ 0.36 − 0.3 = _____

㉖ 42.1 − 9.63 = _____ ㉗ 98 − 71.6 = _____

㉘ 206.37 − 55.6 = _____ ㉙ 58.9 − 8.9 = _____

㉚ 42.48 − 22.7 = _____ ㉛ 1,200 − 1,000.6 = _____

Round each of the following differences to the nearest whole number.

㉜ 8.4 − 5.7 = _____ ㉝ 3.1 − 1.7 = _____

㉞ 58.9 − 19.2 = _____ ㉟ 14.2 − 5.4 = _____

㊱ 22.4 − 8.9 = _____ ㊲ 36.4 − 22.8 = _____

Round each of the following differences to the nearest tenth.

㊳ 9.23 − 6.57 = _____ ㊴ 7.63 − 5.87 = _____

㊵ 28.97 − 17.85 = _____ ㊶ 32.04 − 13.68 = _____

㊷ 45 − 10.73 = _____ ㊸ 19.4 − 6.83 = _____

Complete the number sentences, color the boxes containing your answers in the number chart below, and answer the question.

㊹ 9.2 − 7.8 = ____________

㊺ 9.3 − ____________ = 1.3

㊻ 9.23 − 5.87 = ____________

㊼ 8.2 − ____________ = 5.8

㊽ 5.2 + ____________ = 7.1

㊾ 3 − 0.39 = ____________

㊿ 2 + 3 − 0.8 = ____________

(51) 5.2 − 3.97 = ____________

(52) ____________ − 2.3 = 4.7

(53) 5 + ____________ + 2.3 = 7.9

(54) 15 − ____________ = 7.3

(55) 9.37 − 1.99 = ____________

(56) 27.62 − 13.49 = ____________

(57) 12.13 − ____________ = 2.67

(58)

11.4	7.7	7.38	7.0	6.94
17.0	5.8	1.4	10.6	9.17
7.5	0.2	14.13	5.2	3.61
15.1	9.3	4.2	14.0	15.2
14.8	3.63	9.46	41.11	12.3
12.3	22.3	2.61	2.60	11.36
2.63	0.6	8.0	1.23	3.27

(59) What is the letter formed by the colored boxes?

The letter formed by the colored boxes is ____________ .

Solve the problems. Show your work.

⑥⓪ Bill pays $35 for his groceries. How much change does he get if the total is $32.85?

_____ = _____

He gets _____ change.

⑥① Sue weighs 99.7 pounds. Her sister weighs 91.5 pounds. How much heavier is Sue than her sister?

⑥② The CN Tower in Toronto is 0.55 kilometer high. The Calgary Tower is 0.19 kilometer high. How much taller is the CN Tower?

⑥③ At a high school track meet, Ben ran 100 meters in 11.87 seconds and Carl ran the same distance in 12.13 seconds. How much longer did Carl take?

Just for Fun

Fill in the missing numbers in the magic square. All numbers from 1 to 9 must be used.

In a magic square, the sum of the numbers in a row, column, or diagonal is the same.

	9	
3		7
8	1	

More Addition and Subtraction of Decimals

5

EXAMPLES

1. $5.93 + 17.29 - 3.74$ or $5.93 + 17.29 - 3.74$
    $= 23.22 - 3.74$ $= 5.93 - 3.74 + 17.29$ ← order of operations changed
    $= 19.48$ $= 2.19 + 17.29$
                                          $= 19.48$ ← still the same answer

2. $2 - 3.1 + 1.93$
    $= 2 + 1.93 - 3.1$ ← Order of operations is changed because you can't take away 3.1 from 2.
    $= 3.93 - 3.1$
    $= 0.83$

$$\begin{array}{r} 2.00 \\ +\ 1.93 \\ \hline 3.93 \end{array} \qquad \begin{array}{r} 3.93 \\ -\ 3.10 \\ \hline 0.83 \end{array}$$

Find the answers mentally.

① $5.2 - 3.2 + 17.5$ = _____

② $3.75 - 1.25 - 0.5$ = _____

③ $5.99 - 3.99 + 4.99$ = _____

④ $12 - 0.5 + 2.5$ = _____

⑤ $7.55 + 3.45 - 0.50$ = _____

⑥ $3 - 0.75 - 0.75$ = _____

⑦ $1.9 - 0.5 - 1.4$ = _____

⑧ $9.99 + 10.01 - 5.00$ = _____

⑨ $13.25 - 5.5 + 2.25$ = _____

⑩ $26.5 - 2 + 3.5$ = _____

⑪ $45.85 - 70.5 + 25.15$ = _____

⑫ $175.5 - 155.5 - 2.5$ = _____

⑬ $115.50 - 100.00 - 5.50$ = _____

⑭ $125.75 + 25.25 - 51.0$ = _____

HINTS:

- To change the order of operations in multi-step operations, move the number together with the sign immediately in front of it.

    e.g. $5.1 + 3.2 - 4.9$

        $= 5.1 + 4.9 - 3.2$

        $= 10 - 3.2$

        $= 6.8$ ✗

        $5.1 + 3.2 - 4.9$

        $= 5.1 - 4.9 + 3.2$

        $= 0.2 + 3.2$

        $= 3.4$ ✓

- Remember to add zeros for missing decimal places in vertical addition or subtraction.

Find the answers. Show your work.

⑮ $19.2 - 3.75$

= _____

⑯ $7 - 3.72$

= _____

⑰ $22 - 3.5 - 9.7$

= _____

⑱ $7.1 + 3 - 5.09$

= _____

⑲ $1 - 0.09 + 3.78$

= _____

⑳ $7.3 + 2.9 - 5.4$

= _____

㉑ $123.55 - 17.55 + 3.25$

= _____

㉒ $125 - 100.95 - 3.72$

= _____

㉓ $197.8 + 188.7 - 142.9$

= _____

㉔ $1,000 - 1.2 + 5.00$

= _____

㉕ $0.09 + 0.92 - 0.08$

= _____

㉖ $77 + 29.2 - 5.93$

= _____

㉗ $26.94 - 47.86 + 35.48$

= _____

㉘ $6.73 - 28.45 + 32.38$

= _____

Solve the following money problems.

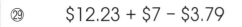

㉙ $12.23 + $7 − $3.79

    = _____

㉚ $100 − $7.55 − $19.35

    = _____

㉛ $59.70 − $32.90 − $2

    = _____

㉜ $100 − $3.50 + $1.50

    = _____

㉝ $10 + $0.79 − $0.55

    = _____

㉞ $15.25 − $6.75 + $3.02

    = _____

Round each answer to the nearest cent.

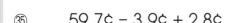

㉟   59.7¢ − 3.9¢ + 2.8¢

    = _____

㊱   39.8¢ − 5.2¢ − 1.3¢

    = _____

㊲   120.1¢ + 9.8¢ − 108.2¢

    = _____

㊳   0.9¢ + 0.7¢ + 5.3¢

    = _____

Fill in the missing numbers in the following number sentences.

㊴   12.3 − ☐ + 1.7 = 5.9

㊵   0.23 + ☐ = 1.90

㊶   25.3 − 19.8 + ☐ = 7.0

㊷   ☐ − 7.8 = 12.2

㊸   ☐ + 15.77 − 8.69 = 7.73

㊹   12.51 − ☐ = 9.07

Solve the problems. Show your work.

㊺ Sam has saved $25 for a trip to town. He spends $4.55 on transportation and $6.99 on lunch. How much does he have left?

_____ = _____

He has _____ left.

㊻ Rebecca earns $35 from a baby-sitting job. She uses the money to buy gifts for Clara and Debbie. Clara's gift costs $5.95 and Debbie's gift costs $17.45. How much does Rebecca have left?

㊼ Adam, Bob, and Colin went to the amusement park together. The fare cost them $6.50 each and a 1-day pass cost $19.95 each. Lunch cost $7.50 each and they each had a discount coupon worth $2. How much did each of them spend?

㊽ Penny, Peter, and Pam contribute $17.50 each to buy a birthday gift for Sue. They decide to buy 2 CDs which cost $20.95 each. The tax for 2 CDs is $2.10. Do they have enough money?

Answer Sally's question.

If you put 1¢ in your piggy bank on Monday, 2¢ on Tuesday, 4¢ on Wednesday, 8¢ on Thursday and so on, how much will you have saved at the end of 1 week?

I will have saved _____ at the end of 1 week.

Multiplying Decimals by Whole Numbers

EXAMPLES

1. 7.3 x 9 = 65.7

    $$\begin{array}{r} \overset{2}{7}.3 \\ \times \quad 9 \\ \hline 65.7 \end{array}$$
      7.3 ← 1 decimal place
      x 9 ← align the numbers
      65.7 ← 1 decimal place in the product

2. Danielle buys 5 books at $5.95 each. How much does she pay altogether?
    $5.95 x 5 = $29.75

    $$\begin{array}{r} \overset{4}{5}.\overset{2}{9}5 \\ \times \quad 5 \\ \hline 29.75 \end{array}$$
    5.95 ← 2 decimal places
    x 5 ← align the numbers
    29.75 ← 2 decimal places in the product

    She pays $29.75 altogether.

3. 0.75 x 10 = 7.5 ← move the decimal point one place to the right

4. 0.75 x 100 = 75. ← move the decimal point two places to the right

HINTS:

- Align all numbers on the right-hand side.

- Multiply the decimals as with whole numbers, from right to left.

- The number of decimal places in the product is the same as that in the question.

- Multiplying a decimal number

  by 10 → move the decimal point one place to the right

  by 100 → move the decimal point two places right

  and so on.

- Check if your answer is reasonable by rounding the decimal to the nearest whole number and estimate the answer.

Find the products mentally.

① 0.2 × 5 = _____

② 3.2 × 10 = _____

③ 0.1 × 7 = _____

④ 0.01 × 8 = _____

⑤ 3.0 × 4 = _____

⑥ 1.1 × 9 = _____

⑦ 4.01 × 6 = _____

⑧ 5.4 × 100 = _____

⑨ 9.15 × 10 = _____

⑩ 0.01 × 10 = _____

⑪ 0.1 × 100 = _____

⑫ 9.3 × 10 = _____

⑬ 100.4 × 2 = _____

⑭ 0.08 × 100 = _____

⑮ 0.62 × 10 = _____

⑯ 0.1 × 10 = _____

⑰ 24.8 × 10 = _____

⑱ 0.01 × 100 = _____

Write the decimal point in each product.

⑲	⑳	㉑
4.7 x 3 ――― 1 4 1	2.69 x 4 ――― 1 0 7 6	10.9 x 5 ――― 5 4 5

㉒ 6.47 x 7 = 4 5 2 9	㉓ 5.55 x 8 = 4 4 4 0

Find the products. Show your work.

㉔ 7.3 x 9	㉕ 4.9 x 7	㉖ 12.2 x 8
㉗ 5.72 x 5	㉘ 9.89 x 6	㉙ 2.7 x 4
㉚ 0.98 x 4	㉛ 4.83 x 7	㉜ 0.18 x 9
㉝ 3.25 x 9	㉞ 1.38 x 7	㉟ 2.9 x 8
㊱ 72.3 x 7	㊲ 9.99 x 3	㊳ 0.76 x 6

Estimate. Then find the exact products.

		Estimate	Exact Product
㊴	5.2 x 7		
㊵	3.7 x 2		
㊶	9.81 x 5		
㊷	8.23 x 6		
㊸	3.75 x 3		
㊹	0.36 x 8		
㊺	0.17 x 9		
㊻	8.44 x 4		

Check each of the answers of the following multiplication. Put a check mark ✓ in the box if the answer is correct; otherwise, write the correct answer in the box.

㊼
$$\begin{array}{r} 2.31 \\ \times \quad 6 \\ \hline 1.386 \end{array}$$ ☐

㊽
$$\begin{array}{r} 0.02 \\ \times \quad 5 \\ \hline 0.10 \end{array}$$ ☐

㊾
$$\begin{array}{r} 1.03 \\ \times \quad 3 \\ \hline 3.9 \end{array}$$ ☐

Fill in the boxes.

㊿ 7.15 x ☐ = 715

(51) 5.1 x ☐ = 15.3

(52) ☐ x 3.2 = 32

(53) ☐ x 0.9 = 90

(54) $\frac{\square}{10} = 15.9$

(55) $\frac{\square}{3} = 10.3$

Solve the problems. Show your work.

56   Sina buys 3 CDs at $23.99 each. How much does she pay altogether?

_____ = _____

She pays _____ altogether.

57   Ron buys 4 trees at $89.50 each. Calculate the total cost.

58   Adam walks 1.4 miles to school each day. How far does he walk in a 5-day week?

59   How much space do 8 textbooks occupy on a bookshelf if each is 1.25 inches thick?

60   Susanne buys 3 T-shirts at $12.95 each and 2 pairs of jeans at $39.99 each. How much does she pay altogether to the nearest dollar?

Just for Fun

Help Bob solve the problem.

How can I add four + signs in the following number sentence to make it true?

4   4   4   4   4   4   4   4   =   500

Dividing Decimals by Whole Numbers

EXAMPLES

1. $5.7 \div 3 = 1.9$

$3\overline{)5.7}$ → $3\overline{)5.7}$ $\frac{3}{2}$
divisor → dividend

→ $\begin{array}{r} 1 \\ 3\overline{)5.7} \\ \underline{3}\downarrow \\ 2\,7 \end{array}$

→ $\begin{array}{r} 1.9 \\ 3\overline{)5.7} \\ \underline{3} \\ 2\,7 \\ \underline{2\,7} \end{array}$ ← quotient

2. $6.2 \div 4 = 1.55$

$\begin{array}{r} 1 \\ 4\overline{)6.2} \\ \underline{4} \end{array}$ → $\begin{array}{r} 1 \\ 4\overline{)6.2} \\ \underline{4}\downarrow \\ 2\,2 \end{array}$ → $\begin{array}{r} 1\ 5 \\ 4\overline{)6.2} \\ \underline{4} \\ 2\,2 \\ \underline{2\,0} \\ 2 \end{array}$ → $\begin{array}{r} 1\ 5 \\ 4\overline{)6.2\,0} \\ \underline{4} \\ 2\,2 \\ \underline{2\,0}\downarrow \\ 2\,0 \end{array}$ → $\begin{array}{r} 1.5\ 5 \\ 4\overline{)6.2\,0} \\ \underline{4} \\ 2\,2 \\ \underline{2\,0} \\ 2\,0 \\ \underline{2\,0} \end{array}$

add extra zero

3. $7.5 \div 10 = 0.7\,5$

move the decimal point one place to the left

4. $7.5 \div 100 = 0.0\,7\,5$

move the decimal point two places to the left

HINTS:

- Divide the decimals as with whole numbers, from left to right.

- If there is a remainder, add zero(s) to the right of the dividend after the decimal point. Continue to divide until the remainder is zero or you have enough decimal places.

- Don't forget to put a decimal point in the quotient above the one in the dividend.

- Always check if your answer makes sense.
  e.g. $6 \div 3 = 2$
  so $5.7 \div 3 = 1.9$ is reasonable.

- Dividing a decimal number
  by 10 → move the decimal point one place to the left
  by 100 → move the decimal point two places to the left
  and so on.

Find the quotients mentally.

① $9.8 \div 10$ = _____

② $0.32 \div 10$ = _____

③ $75.0 \div 100$ = _____

④ $9.2 \div 1,000$ = _____

⑤ $3.28 \div 10$ = _____

⑥ $0.05 \div 100$ = _____

⑦ $0.08 \div 10$ = _____

⑧ $154.93 \div 100$ = _____

⑨ $316.45 \div 100$ = _____

Write the decimal point in each quotient. Add zeros where necessary.

⑩ $52.8 \div 3$ =   1 7 6   ⑪ $0.84 \div 7$ =   1 2

⑫ $14.28 \div 7$ =   2 0 4   ⑬ $2.08 \div 4$ =   5 2

Find the quotients. Show your work.

⑭ $7 \overline{)8.05}$	⑮ $9 \overline{)66.6}$	⑯ $7 \overline{)73.5}$
⑰ $6 \overline{)8.52}$	⑱ $4 \overline{)0.24}$	⑲ $8 \overline{)160.8}$
⑳ $3 \overline{)12.09}$	㉑ $5 \overline{)52.65}$	㉒ $8 \overline{)36.4}$
㉓ $4 \overline{)70.4}$	㉔ $5 \overline{)10.4}$	㉕ $9 \overline{)19.35}$

Divide. Show your work. Match the letters with the numbers in the boxes. What is the message?

26 (I)	27 (A)	28 (T)
$4\overline{)9.2}$	$3\overline{)0.57}$	$2\overline{)5.1}$

29 (E)	30 (T)	31 (L)
$7\overline{)35.84}$	$5\overline{)760.5}$	$5\overline{)35.05}$

32 (R)	33 (S)	34 (P)
$8\overline{)10.4}$	$7\overline{)380.1}$	$4\overline{)503.4}$

35 (T)	36 (L)	37 (S)
$5\overline{)0.45}$	$9\overline{)58.77}$	$6\overline{)502.38}$

38 What does Sally see in the night sky?

7.01	2.3	2.55	152.1	6.53	5.12

54.3	0.09	0.19	1.3	83.73

Solve the problems. Show your work.

㊴ John mails 10 packages, each having the same weight. The total weight is 71.7 pounds. How much does each package weigh?

_____ = _____

Each package weighs _____ .

㊵ On his summer holidays Bob drove 4,570 miles in 100 hours. How far did he travel each hour?

㊶ Sam divides 36.4 yards of phone cable into 8 equal parts. How long is each part?

㊷ 8 students share the cost of a trip. If the total cost of the trip is $394, how much does each student pay?

㊸ An equilateral triangle has all sides equal. If its perimeter is 13.5 centimeters, what is the length of each side?

Look for the pattern. What are the next 3 numbers?

1 , 1 , 2 , 3 , 5 , 8 , 13 , , ,

8 More Multiplying and Dividing of Decimals

EXAMPLES

1. $7.92 \times 5 = 39.60$

$$\begin{array}{r} \overset{4}{}\overset{1}{} \\ 7.9\,2 \\ \times\quad 5 \\ \hline 3\,9.6\,0 \end{array}$$

↑ this zero can be deleted

2. $10.25 \div 5 = 2.05$

put a zero in the quotient

$$\begin{array}{r} 2.5 \\ 5\,\overline{)10.25} \\ 10 \\ \hline 25 \\ 25 \end{array}\ ✗ \qquad \begin{array}{r} 2.05 \\ 5\,\overline{)10.25} \\ 10 \\ \hline 25 \\ 25 \end{array}\ ✓$$

Find the answers mentally.

① 7.34×10 = _____

② $9.23 \div 10$ = _____

③ $123.4 \div 100$ = _____

④ $2.42 \div 2$ = _____

⑤ $36.9 \div 3$ = _____

⑥ 1.2×100 = _____

HINTS:

- The number of decimal places in the product is the same as that in the question, but a zero at the last decimal place can be deleted.

  e.g. $7.92 \times 5 = 39.6$ ←

  only one decimal place in the product because the zero in the hundredths place is deleted

- Remember to put a zero in the quotient when the dividend is smaller than the divisor.

  e.g. $10.25 \div 5 = 2.05$ but not 2.5

  ↑ a zero is put at the tenths place because 2 in the dividend is smaller than the divisor 5

⑦ $0.15 \div 5$ = _____ ⑧ $80.8 \div 8$ = _____

⑨ $342.9 \div 100$ = _____ ⑩ $34.29 \times 1,000$ = _____

⑪ 1.25×100 = _____ ⑫ $0.02 \div 10$ = _____

⑬ 0.4×10 = _____ ⑭ 1.18×10 = _____

⑮ 0.04×100 = _____ ⑯ $1.25 \div 100$ = _____

⑰ 0.02×10 = _____ ⑱ 63.5×10 = _____

Do the calculation. Show your work.

⑲ $4\overline{)94.4}$

⑳ $7\overline{)7.28}$

㉑ $3\overline{)45.09}$

㉒
```
  3.92
X    4
```

㉓
```
  10.3
X    7
```

㉔
```
  5.91
X    6
```

㉕ $6\overline{)7.92}$

㉖ $9\overline{)17.1}$

㉗ $5\overline{)6.2}$

㉘
```
  0.47
X    8
```

㉙
```
  18.2
X    9
```

㉚
```
  36.7
X    2
```

Find the answers.

㉛ 1.25 × 8   = _____

㉜ 1.75 × 4   = _____

㉝ 1.19 ÷ 7   = _____

㉞ 10.4 ÷ 4   = _____

㉟ 3.08 × 9   = _____

㊱ 76.8 ÷ 3   = _____

㊲ 89 × 10 ÷ 10 = _____

㊳ 1.9 × 10 × 10 = _____

Estimate. Then complete only those questions with a product greater than 15.

㊴ $\begin{array}{r} 7.2 \\ \times \quad 2 \\ \hline \end{array}$	㊵ $\begin{array}{r} 7.9 \\ \times \quad 2 \\ \hline \end{array}$	㊶ $\begin{array}{r} 3.8 \\ \times \quad 4 \\ \hline \end{array}$
㊷ $\begin{array}{r} 1.9 \\ \times \quad 9 \\ \hline \end{array}$	㊸ $\begin{array}{r} 3.1 \\ \times \quad 5 \\ \hline \end{array}$	㊹ $\begin{array}{r} 0.25 \\ \times \quad 10 \\ \hline \end{array}$

Estimate. Then complete only those questions with a quotient smaller than 2.

㊺ $9\overline{)12.6}$	㊻ $3\overline{)7.2}$	㊼ $10\overline{)23.4}$
㊽ $3\overline{)5.7}$	㊾ $6\overline{)10.8}$	㊿ $7\overline{)13.3}$

Fill in the blanks.

(51) 12.7 ÷ ________ = 0.127

(52) 3.92 X ________ = 39.2

(53) ________ ÷ 3 = 1.14

(54) 5.8 X ________ = 11.6

(55) 2 X ________ = 12.4

(56) ________ ÷ 7 = 1.3

(57) 0.18 X ________ = 18

(58) 54 ÷ ________ = 5.4

Answer the questions. Show your work.

⑤⑨ The Grade 5 class collects $58.20 to buy gifts for 3 children in a needy family. How much can they spend on each gift if the money is divided evenly?

_____ = _____

They can spend _____ on each gift.

⑥⓪ Mrs. Ling buys plants for her patio. She buys 3 plants at $19.95 each, 2 plants at $12.45 each, and 10 plants at $1.25 each. How much does she pay altogether?

⑥① 5 friends buy 2 pizzas at $12.99 each, 2 cans of juice at $1.29 each, and 2 packets of chips at $1.49 each. They divide the total cost among them. How much must they each pay? Give the answer to the nearest cent.

⑥② Carol is buying food for her dog. She can buy a 6-pound bag for $29.40 or a 10-pound bag for $39.50. Calculate the cost per pound for each bag. Which is the better buy?

What number am I?

I am a decimal number. Multiply me by 35. Divide the product by 7. The result is 2.5.

_____

Calculate. Show your work.

① 3.75 + 4.2 + 11 = _____	② 13.04 − 2.87 + 1.59 = _____
③ 8.4 × 8 = _____	④ 8.4 ÷ 8 = _____
⑤ 3 × 5.42 = _____	⑥ 5.58 ÷ 9 = _____
⑦ 26.13 × 8 = _____	⑧ 9.6 ÷ 3 = _____

Help Sally put the digits and decimal point in the right order to solve the problems.

①⑤⑨④.

⑨   The largest decimal number with one decimal place   _____

⑩   The smallest decimal number with two decimal places   _____

⑪   The sum of the two decimals in ⑨ and ⑩   _____

⑫   The smallest decimal number with one decimal place and 9 at the ones place   _____

⑬   The largest decimal number with two decimal places and 9 at the hundredths place   _____

⑭   The difference of the two decimals in ⑫ and ⑬   _____

Complete the chart.

	Number	Number x 10	Number ÷ 10
⑮	52.0		
⑯	0.7		
⑰	0.12		
⑱		75.0	
⑲		3.0	
⑳			0.8
㉑			15.0

Circle the letter which represents the correct answer to each problem.

㉒ John earns $15 per hour. He works 9 hours a day and 5 days a week. How much does he earn per week?

    A. $135   B. $630   C. $450   D. $675

㉓ If U.S.$1 is worth Canadian$1.18, how much is U.S.$7 worth in Canadian money?

    A. $5.93   B. $0.82   C. $8.26   D. $82.60

㉔ Mrs. Wing earns 1.5 times her regular hourly wage on Sundays. She earns $8 per hour on weekdays. How much is her hourly wage on Sundays?

    A. $6   B. $10   C. $12   D. $16

㉕ John reads 10 pages per hour. How many pages does he read in 2.5 hours?

    A. 20   B. 22.5   C. 25   D. 27.5

㉖ If 1 cm = 0.39 in, how many inches are there in 100 centimeters?

    A. 3.9 in   B. 39 in   C. 390 in   D. 3900 in

㉗ Mandy's mother buys her 2 new T-shirts at $9.50 each, 1 pair of jeans at $29.95, and 1 pair of sandals at $19.95. How much does Mandy's mother pay to the nearest dollar?

A. $60   B. $70   C. $68   D. $69

㉘ In August, Detroit's highest temperature is 35.5°C and the lowest temperature is 16.2°C. What is the difference between these temperatures?

A. 51.7 °C   B. 19.3 °C   C. 26 °C   D. 29 °C

㉙ The product of 1.6 and 2 is _____ .

A. 3.6   B. 0.8   C. 3.2   D. 1.4

㉚ When 1.2 is divided by 4, the quotient is _____ .

A. 0.3   B. 3.0   C. 4.8   D. 5.6

㉛ To calculate the average of 2 numbers is to add them up and then divide the sum by 2. The average of 13 and 10.2 is _____ .

A. 23.2   B. 11.6   C. 1.6   D. 3.2

㉜ When you divide a number by 10, the result is the same as multiplying the number by _____ .

A. 10   B. 0.1   C. 0.01   D. 100

㉝ When you multiply a number by 100, you move the decimal point

A. 3 places to the right.   B. 3 places to the left.

C. 2 places to the right.   D. 2 places to the left.

㉞ Which of the following statements is correct?

A. $5 \div 2 = 0.5 \div 20$ B. $5 \div 2 = 2 \div 5$

C. $5 \div 2 = 50 \div 20$ D. $5 \div 2 = 50 \div 0.2$

Kenneth's dog likes to run around in the backyard. Answer the questions using the measurements given in the diagram.

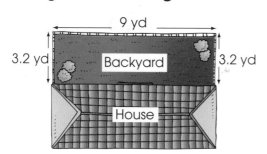

㉟ How much fencing is needed to enclose the backyard on 3 sides?

_____ yards fencing is needed.

㊱ The fencing costs $20 per yard. What is the total cost of the fencing?

㊲ What is the perimeter of the backyard?

㊳ What is the area of the backyard?

㊴ If both the width and the length of the backyard are doubled, what effect would this have on the perimeter and the area of the backyard?

   a. perimeter

   b. area

9 Introducing Fractions

1. Write a fraction for the colored part in each diagram.

   a.  $\dfrac{1}{3}$

   b. $\dfrac{1}{4}$

   c. $\dfrac{3}{6} = \dfrac{1}{2}$

2. Write the fraction in its lowest terms.

   $$\dfrac{10}{15} = \dfrac{10 \div 5}{15 \div 5} = \dfrac{2}{3}$$

3. Label each of the divisions on the number line below. Write the fractions in lowest terms.

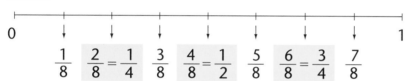

$\dfrac{1}{8}$ $\dfrac{2}{8} = \dfrac{1}{4}$ $\dfrac{3}{8}$ $\dfrac{4}{8} = \dfrac{1}{2}$ $\dfrac{5}{8}$ $\dfrac{6}{8} = \dfrac{3}{4}$ $\dfrac{7}{8}$

HINTS:

- A fraction represents a part of a whole or a part of a set.

  e.g.   3 slices of an 8-slice pizza

  $= \dfrac{3}{8}$ of the pizza

- To represent a fraction in lowest terms (or simplest form), divide both the numerator and denominator by the same number.

- A fraction in lowest terms means the only number that will divide into both the numerator and denominator is 1.

Write the fractions represented on the number line below.

① _____   ② _____

③ _____   ④ _____

Write a fraction for the colored part in each diagram.

⑤  _____   ⑥ _____   ⑦ 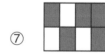 _____

⑧  _____   ⑨ _____   ⑩  _____

Color the diagrams to show each fraction.

⑪ 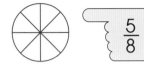 $\dfrac{5}{8}$

⑫ 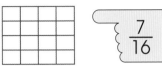 $\dfrac{7}{16}$

⑬ 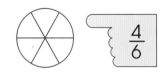 $\dfrac{4}{6}$

⑭ 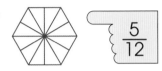 $\dfrac{5}{12}$

⑮ $\dfrac{4}{10}$

⑯ 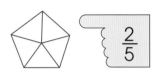 $\dfrac{2}{5}$

Place the following fractions on the number line below.

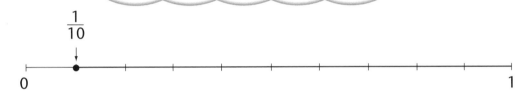

$$\dfrac{1}{10} \qquad \dfrac{2}{5} \qquad \dfrac{1}{2} \qquad \dfrac{9}{10} \qquad \dfrac{1}{20} \qquad \dfrac{4}{5}$$

⑰ $\dfrac{1}{10}$

0 ————————————— 1

Write a fraction for the colored shapes of each set.

⑱

⑲

⑳

_____   _____   _____

Color the correct number of shapes to show each fraction.

㉑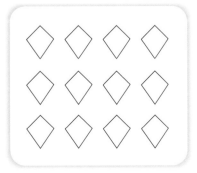

㉒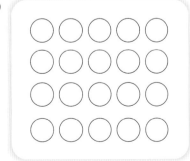

㉓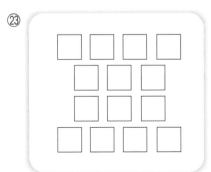

$\dfrac{8}{12}$ $\dfrac{11}{20}$ $\dfrac{9}{14}$

Use the pictures to write the numbers.

㉔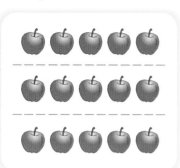

㉕

㉖

$\frac{1}{3}$ of 15 = _____

$\frac{3}{4}$ of 16 = _____

$\frac{2}{6}$ of 18 = _____

Fill in the boxes to express the following fractions in lowest terms.

㉗ $\frac{20}{30} = \frac{\square}{3}$

㉘ $\frac{5}{10} = \frac{1}{\square}$

㉙ $\frac{21}{28} = \frac{3}{\square}$

Write the following fractions in lowest terms.

㉚ $\frac{15}{20}$ = _____

㉛ $\frac{7}{21}$ = _____

㉜ $\frac{9}{18}$ = _____

㉝ $\frac{12}{18}$ = _____

㉞ $\frac{6}{16}$ = _____

㉟ $\frac{12}{15}$ = _____

Answer the following questions.

㊱ List any 3 fractions which lie between 0 and $\frac{1}{2}$. _____

㊲ What fraction of a dollar is represented by

    a. 7 nickels? _____

    b. 6 dimes? _____

㊳ Bill watches TV for 3 hours a day. What fraction of a day does he spend watching TV? _____

㊴ Margaret has 8 pairs of shoes. 6 pairs are black. What fraction of her shoes are not black? _____

㊵ Rick has finished reading 50 pages of a 250-page book. What fraction of the book has he read? _____

㊶ Pam is a rock climber. After she has climbed 30 yards up a 45-yard cliff, what fraction of the cliff must she climb to reach the top? _____

㊷ 5 letters of the 26 letters in the alphabet are vowels. The others are consonants. What fraction of the alphabet do consonants make up? _____

㊸ Tom worked 18 out of the 30 days in September. What fraction of the month did he work? _____

㊹ Carol earns $7 per hour as a waitress. One weekend she worked for 10 hours and got $50 in tips. What fraction of her total earnings that day did her tips make up? _____

㊺ Every day, Suzie sharpens her 16-centimeter-long pencil and it loses 1 centimeter of its length. After 4 days, what fraction of its length remains? _____

㊻ An ant crawls 50 inches along a 100-inch log on the first day. On the second day the ant crawls 25 inches and on the third day it crawls 12 inches.

a. What fraction of the log has it covered in three days? _____

b. What fraction of the log remains to be covered till it reaches the end? _____

Look for the pattern.

① What are the next 3 fractions?

$$\frac{1}{2} \quad \frac{1}{4} \quad \frac{1}{8} \quad \text{_____} \quad \text{_____} \quad \text{_____}$$

② If you continue the pattern, will you get to zero?

_____

10 Equivalent Fractions and Ordering of Fractions

1. Fill in the boxes to find the equivalent fractions of $\frac{2}{3}$.

$$\overset{\times 2}{\underset{\times 2}{\frac{2}{3}}} = \frac{\boxed{4}}{6} \overset{\times 5}{\underset{\times 5}{=}} \frac{\boxed{20}}{30} \overset{\div 2}{\underset{\div 2}{=}} \frac{\boxed{10}}{15}$$

$$\frac{2}{3} = \frac{4}{6}$$

2. Order the following fractions from least to greatest.

$$\frac{2}{3} , \frac{5}{6} , \frac{7}{12} , \frac{1}{2}$$

$$\overset{\times 4}{\underset{\times 4}{\frac{2}{3}}} = \frac{8}{12} \qquad \overset{\times 2}{\underset{\times 2}{\frac{5}{6}}} = \frac{10}{12} \qquad \overset{\times 6}{\underset{\times 6}{\frac{1}{2}}} = \frac{6}{12}$$

$$\therefore \quad \frac{1}{2} < \frac{7}{12} < \frac{2}{3} < \frac{5}{6}$$

HINTS:

- To find an equivalent fraction, multiply or divide the numerator and denominator by the same number.

- To compare the fractions, find their equivalent fractions with common denominator first. Then compare their numerators.

- Equivalent fractions are fractions that are equal in value.

Fill in the boxes to find the equivalent fractions.

① $\frac{1}{2} = \frac{\boxed{}}{50}$

② $\frac{5}{6} = \frac{\boxed{}}{30}$

③ $\frac{5}{7} = \frac{\boxed{}}{21}$

④ $\frac{3}{4} = \frac{\boxed{}}{100}$

⑤ $\frac{\boxed{}}{8} = \frac{14}{56}$

⑥ $\frac{11}{12} = \frac{\boxed{}}{84}$

Write each fraction in lowest terms.

⑦ $\frac{25}{30} = \underline{\hspace{2cm}}$

⑧ $\frac{19}{38} = \underline{\hspace{2cm}}$

⑨ $\frac{22}{121} = \underline{\hspace{2cm}}$

⑩ $\frac{36}{84} = \underline{\hspace{2cm}}$

⑪ $\frac{250}{1,000} = \underline{\hspace{2cm}}$

⑫ $\frac{32}{48} = \underline{\hspace{2cm}}$

Circle the smaller fraction in each pair of fractions.

⑬ $\dfrac{3}{4}$ $\dfrac{7}{8}$ ⑭ $\dfrac{1}{3}$ $\dfrac{1}{2}$ ⑮ $\dfrac{1}{5}$ $\dfrac{1}{6}$

⑯ $\dfrac{5}{6}$ $\dfrac{2}{3}$ ⑰ $\dfrac{3}{7}$ $\dfrac{8}{21}$ ⑱ $\dfrac{4}{5}$ $\dfrac{11}{15}$

Order the fractions from least to greatest using < .

⑲ $\dfrac{3}{5}$ $\dfrac{4}{5}$ $\dfrac{1}{2}$ $\dfrac{1}{5}$ $\dfrac{1}{10}$ $\dfrac{7}{10}$ _____

⑳ $\dfrac{1}{3}$ $\dfrac{1}{4}$ $\dfrac{3}{4}$ $\dfrac{2}{3}$ $\dfrac{2}{4}$ _____

Write True (T) or False (F) for each statement.

㉑ $\dfrac{2}{3} < \dfrac{4}{5}$ (   )   ㉒ $\dfrac{5}{9} < \dfrac{1}{2}$ (   )

㉓ $\dfrac{21}{28} < \dfrac{6}{7}$ (   )   ㉔ $\dfrac{24}{27} < \dfrac{7}{9}$ (   )

Fill in the boxes.

㉕ $\dfrac{9}{15} = \dfrac{\boxed{}}{5} = \dfrac{\boxed{}}{20}$ ㉖ $\dfrac{9}{45} = \dfrac{1}{\boxed{}} = \dfrac{\boxed{}}{10}$

㉗ $\dfrac{14}{35} = \dfrac{\boxed{}}{5} = \dfrac{\boxed{}}{10}$ ㉘ $\dfrac{11}{\boxed{}} = \dfrac{1}{5} = \dfrac{\boxed{}}{20}$

Write 3 equivalent fractions for each of the following fractions.

㉙ $\dfrac{1}{8}$ = _____ = _____ = _____   ㉚ $\dfrac{2}{3}$ = _____ = _____ = _____

㉛ $\dfrac{1}{4}$ = _____ = _____ = _____   ㉜ $\dfrac{5}{7}$ = _____ = _____ = _____

Order each group of fractions from greatest to least using > .

㉝ $\frac{3}{4}$ $\frac{7}{8}$ $\frac{1}{2}$ $\frac{5}{8}$ $\frac{3}{16}$ $\frac{1}{4}$ $\frac{3}{8}$

_____

㉞ $\frac{2}{3}$ $\frac{1}{6}$ $\frac{7}{18}$ $\frac{1}{2}$ $\frac{5}{6}$ $\frac{13}{18}$ $\frac{1}{3}$

_____

Compare each pair of fractions and write >, <, or = between them.

㉟ $\frac{5}{6}$ $\frac{7}{8}$ ㊱ $\frac{14}{18}$ $\frac{7}{9}$ ㊲ $\frac{11}{12}$ $\frac{9}{10}$

㊳ $\frac{2}{3}$ $\frac{11}{15}$ ㊴ $\frac{5}{16}$ $\frac{3}{8}$ ㊵ $\frac{15}{30}$ $\frac{7}{16}$

Write each fraction in lowest terms and order the fractions from least to greatest.

㊶ $\frac{15}{20}$ = _____   ㊷ $\frac{75}{125}$ = _____   ㊸ $\frac{45}{54}$ = _____

㊹ $\frac{200}{450}$ = _____   ㊺ $\frac{14}{18}$ = _____   ㊻ $\frac{150}{175}$ = _____

㊼ _____ < _____ < _____ < _____ < _____ < _____

Find the missing numbers.

㊽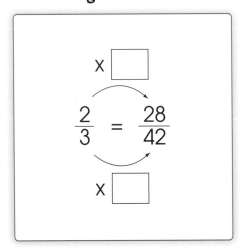

㊾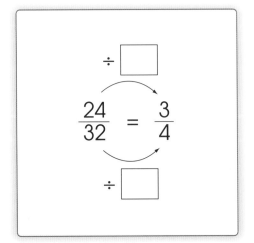

48

Answer the questions.

50 John gets 22 out of 25 on a test. What is his mark out of 100?

$\dfrac{22}{25} = \dfrac{}{100}$

His mark is _____.

51 Nadine gets 9 out of 12 in a quiz. Danielle gets 14 out of 18 in another quiz. Who has the better score?

_____ has the better score.

52 The table below shows the world population in 1994 and the projected value in 2025. (Use your calculator to calculate, if necessary.)

World Population (in millions)		
	1994	2025
Africa	682	1,583
North Africa	373	498
Europe	512	542
World Total	5,421	8,474

a. What is the fraction of the world's population living in Africa in 1994? And in 2025?

In 1994 _____   In 2025 _____

b. Is this fraction increasing or decreasing from 1994 to 2025? _____

c. What is the fraction of the world's population living in Europe in 1994? And in 2025?

In 1994 _____   In 2025 _____

d. Is this fraction increasing or decreasing from 1994 to 2025? _____

Look for the pattern. Write the next 3 terms.

$1 \quad \dfrac{1}{4} \quad \dfrac{1}{9}$ _____ _____ _____

Adding Fractions with Like Denominators

1. $\dfrac{1}{4} + \dfrac{3}{4} = \dfrac{1+3}{4} = \dfrac{4}{4} = \dfrac{4 \div 4}{4 \div 4} = 1$

add the numerators;
keep the denominator

reduce to lowest terms

2. $\dfrac{1}{8} + \dfrac{5}{8} = \dfrac{1+5}{8} = \dfrac{6}{8} = \dfrac{3}{4}$

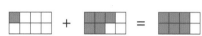

HINTS:

- To add fractions with like denominators, add the numerators and leave the denominator the same.

- Remember to reduce the sums to lowest terms.

- Reduce the fraction to 1 if its numerator and denominator are equal.

Find the sums mentally.

① $\dfrac{2}{3} + \dfrac{1}{3}$ = _____

② $\dfrac{1}{14} + \dfrac{13}{14}$ = _____

③ $\dfrac{1}{3} + \dfrac{1}{3}$ = _____

④ $\dfrac{1}{5} + \dfrac{1}{5}$ = _____

⑤ $\dfrac{1}{9} + \dfrac{4}{9}$ = _____

⑥ $\dfrac{1}{7} + \dfrac{3}{7}$ = _____

⑦ $\dfrac{3}{5} + \dfrac{1}{5}$ = _____

⑧ $\dfrac{1}{10} + \dfrac{9}{10}$ = _____

⑨ $\dfrac{5}{7} + \dfrac{2}{7}$ = _____

⑩ $\dfrac{1}{9} + \dfrac{7}{9}$ = _____

⑪ $\dfrac{1}{13} + \dfrac{10}{13}$ = _____

⑫ $\dfrac{5}{11} + \dfrac{3}{11}$ = _____

⑬ $\dfrac{2}{8} + \dfrac{5}{8}$ = _____

⑭ $\dfrac{6}{20} + \dfrac{7}{20}$ = _____

⑮ $\dfrac{5}{17} + \dfrac{4}{17}$ = _____

⑯ $\dfrac{6}{19} + \dfrac{3}{19}$ = _____

⑰ $\dfrac{4}{25} + \dfrac{17}{25}$ = _____

⑱ $\dfrac{5}{12} + \dfrac{5}{12}$ = _____

⑲ $\dfrac{4}{21} + \dfrac{13}{21}$ = _____

⑳ $\dfrac{7}{15} + \dfrac{1}{15}$ = _____

㉑ $\dfrac{1}{16} + \dfrac{5}{16}$ = _____

㉒ $\dfrac{1}{4} + \dfrac{1}{4}$ = _____

㉓ $\dfrac{5}{18} + \dfrac{7}{18}$ = _____

㉔ $\dfrac{11}{23} + \dfrac{11}{23}$ = _____

㉕ $\dfrac{1}{6} + \dfrac{3}{6}$ = _____

㉖ $\dfrac{14}{27} + \dfrac{11}{27}$ = _____

Add and reduce the answers to lowest terms. Show your work.

㉗ $\dfrac{6}{20} + \dfrac{7}{20}$ = _____

㉘ $\dfrac{4}{15} + \dfrac{8}{15}$ = _____

㉙ $\dfrac{2}{9} + \dfrac{1}{9}$ = _____

㉚ $\dfrac{11}{14} + \dfrac{1}{14}$ = _____

㉛ $\dfrac{5}{8} + \dfrac{1}{8}$ = _____

㉜ $\dfrac{3}{10} + \dfrac{3}{10}$ = _____

㉝ $\dfrac{3}{16} + \dfrac{5}{16}$ = _____

㉞ $\dfrac{1}{12} + \dfrac{5}{12}$ = _____

㉟ $\dfrac{1}{20} + \dfrac{3}{20}$ = _____

㊱ $\dfrac{1}{6} + \dfrac{1}{6}$ = _____

㊲ $\dfrac{3}{7} + \dfrac{1}{7}$ = _____

㊳ $\dfrac{1}{18} + \dfrac{2}{18}$ = _____

㊴ $\dfrac{1}{24} + \dfrac{5}{24}$ = _____

㊵ $\dfrac{5}{32} + \dfrac{3}{32}$ = _____

㊶ $\dfrac{2}{7} + \dfrac{3}{7} + \dfrac{2}{7}$ = _____

㊷ $\dfrac{2}{11} + \dfrac{2}{11} + \dfrac{3}{11} + \dfrac{4}{11}$ = _____

Complete each equation with a diagram. Then write each addition sentence using fractions. Give the sums in lowest terms.

(43) + ⊘ =

$$\dfrac{3}{8} + \dfrac{1}{8} =$$

(44) + =

(45) + =

(46) + =

(47) + =

(48) + =

Fill in the boxes.

(49) $\dfrac{3}{7} + \boxed{} = \dfrac{5}{7}$

(50) $\dfrac{4}{11} + \boxed{} = \dfrac{5}{11}$

(51) $\dfrac{1}{6} + \boxed{} = 1$

(52) $\dfrac{1}{8} + \boxed{} = 1$

(53) $\dfrac{1}{4} + \boxed{} = \dfrac{1}{2}$

(54) $\dfrac{3}{8} + \boxed{} = \dfrac{1}{2}$

(55) $\dfrac{8}{15} + \boxed{} = \dfrac{3}{5}$

(56) $\dfrac{1}{10} + \boxed{} = \dfrac{1}{5}$

(57) $\boxed{} + \dfrac{7}{20} = \dfrac{9}{10}$

(58) $\boxed{} + \dfrac{7}{12} = 1$

(59) $\boxed{} + \dfrac{9}{25} = \dfrac{4}{5}$

(60) $\boxed{} + \dfrac{4}{9} = \dfrac{2}{3}$

Answer the questions. Show your work.

(61) Suzie has 3 dogs. They each eat $\frac{1}{4}$ of a tin of dog food each day. How much dog food do they eat in all each day?

They eat ________ tin of dog food.

(62) Bob, Carrie, and Dan go out for pizza. They order 1 pizza. Bob and Carrie each eat $\frac{2}{6}$ of the pizza and Dan eats $\frac{1}{6}$ of the pizza.

a. How much of the pizza do they eat in all?

b. Is there any pizza left?

(63) Janet needs 2 pieces of ribbon, one of $\frac{5}{8}$ foot and the other of $\frac{1}{8}$ foot.

a. How much ribbon does she need altogether?

b. If she buys 1 foot of ribbon, will she have enough?

(64) Brenda spends $\frac{3}{10}$ of her weekly allowance on Monday and $\frac{1}{10}$ of it on Tuesday.

a. What fraction of her allowance has she spent?

b. What fraction of her allowance does she have left?

Find the missing fractions in the given magic square. The sum of each row, column, and diagonal is the same.

$\frac{8}{15}$	$\frac{1}{15}$	$\frac{6}{15}$
	$\frac{5}{15}$	

Improper Fractions and Mixed Numbers

1. Change $\frac{13}{6}$ to a mixed number.

   $\frac{13}{6} = 2\frac{1}{6}$ ← quotient ← remainder ← original denominator

   $$6\overline{)13} \quad \begin{array}{r} 2 \text{ R } 1 \\ \underline{12} \\ 1 \end{array}$$

2. Change $5\frac{3}{4}$ to an improper fraction.

   $5 \times 4 = 20$

   $5\frac{3}{4} = \frac{20}{4} + \frac{3}{4} = \frac{23}{4}$

3. Use a diagram to show that $3\frac{1}{4} = \frac{13}{4}$.

   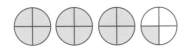 ← Divide each circle into 4 equal parts. Color 13 quarters.

4. Put $\frac{9}{2}$, $\frac{15}{4}$, $\frac{17}{5}$ in order from least to greatest.

   $\frac{9}{2} = 4\frac{1}{2}$ $\frac{15}{4} = 3\frac{3}{4}$ $\frac{17}{5} = 3\frac{2}{5}$

   $\quad = 4\frac{10}{20}$ $\quad = 3\frac{15}{20}$ $\quad = 3\frac{8}{20}$

   $\therefore \frac{17}{5} < \frac{15}{4} < \frac{9}{2}$

HINTS:

- Proper fraction: the numerator is smaller than the denominator
  e.g. $\frac{3}{7}$

- Improper fraction: the numerator is greater than or equal to the denominator
  e.g. $\frac{10}{7}$, $\frac{7}{7}$

- Mixed number: formed by a whole number and a proper fraction
  e.g. $1\frac{3}{7}$

- To convert an improper fraction to a mixed number, divide the numerator by the denominator. The quotient is the whole number part of the mixed number. The remainder is the new numerator. The denominator is unchanged.

- To convert a mixed number to an improper fraction, the denominator is unchanged. The new numerator is the sum of the old numerator and the product of the whole number and the denominator.

Complete the table.

	Improper Fraction	Mixed Number
①	$\frac{15}{7}$	
②		$3\frac{3}{8}$
③	$\frac{11}{3}$	
④		$11\frac{1}{4}$
⑤	$\frac{7}{5}$	

Write the fractions or mixed numbers on the right screens.

$3\frac{3}{10}$ $\frac{9}{9}$ $\frac{4}{7}$ $\frac{5}{20}$ $\frac{25}{20}$ $\frac{7}{9}$ $3\frac{1}{2}$ $1\frac{5}{20}$ $\frac{15}{8}$ $\frac{11}{12}$ $\frac{16}{7}$ $1\frac{2}{5}$

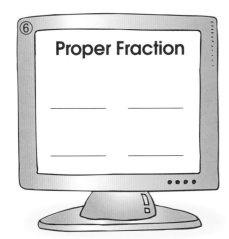

⑥ Proper Fraction

_____ _____

_____ _____

⑦ Improper Fraction

_____ _____

_____ _____

⑧ Mixed Number

_____ _____

_____ _____

Write the mixed number represented by each of the following groups of diagrams. Then convert each to an improper fraction.

⑨

mixed number _____

improper fraction _____

⑩

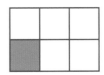

mixed number _____

improper fraction _____

Place the improper fractions on the number line below.

$\frac{3}{2}$ $\frac{15}{4}$ $\frac{17}{5}$ $\frac{5}{2}$ $\frac{7}{3}$ $\frac{6}{5}$ $\frac{23}{5}$

⑪

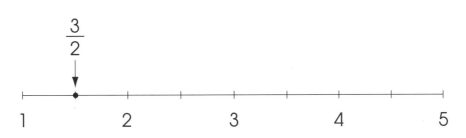

$\frac{3}{2}$

1   2   3   4   5

Write an improper fraction and a mixed number to represent each number on the number line below.

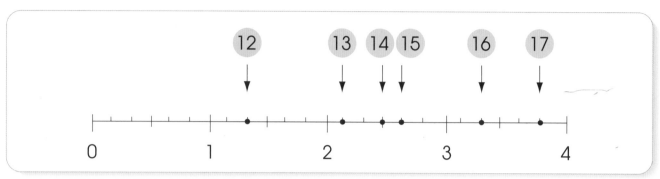

⑫ _____ ⑬ _____ ⑭ _____

⑮ _____ ⑯ _____ ⑰ _____

Order the fractions from greatest to least using > .

⑱ $\dfrac{5}{3}$ $\dfrac{7}{2}$ $\dfrac{9}{4}$ $\dfrac{7}{3}$ $\dfrac{15}{4}$ _____

⑲ $\dfrac{17}{2}$ $\dfrac{17}{5}$ $\dfrac{17}{6}$ $\dfrac{17}{3}$ $\dfrac{17}{4}$ _____

Circle the right numbers in each group.

⑳ The numbers between 3 and 4

$\dfrac{22}{3}$ $\dfrac{15}{7}$ $\dfrac{23}{6}$ $\dfrac{19}{6}$ $\dfrac{17}{4}$ $\dfrac{7}{2}$

㉑ The numbers between 8 and 9

$\dfrac{27}{4}$ $\dfrac{60}{7}$ $\dfrac{49}{6}$ $\dfrac{15}{2}$ $\dfrac{37}{5}$ $\dfrac{25}{3}$

Match the fractions and the mixed numbers.

㉒

$1\dfrac{1}{2}$ $4\dfrac{1}{2}$ $\dfrac{2}{3}$ $\dfrac{12}{9}$ $1\dfrac{3}{8}$ $1\dfrac{2}{5}$ $\dfrac{36}{5}$

$\dfrac{9}{2}$ $\dfrac{12}{18}$ $\dfrac{36}{24}$ $\dfrac{7}{5}$ $7\dfrac{1}{5}$ $1\dfrac{1}{3}$ $\dfrac{11}{8}$

Answer the questions. Show your work. Drawing diagrams may be helpful.

㉓ 5 friends each drink $\frac{1}{2}$ quart of juice. How much juice do they drink in all? Write your answer

    a.   as an improper fraction.   _____ quarts

    b.   as a mixed number.   _____ quarts

㉔ Joanne has $2\frac{1}{4}$ dollars in her pocket. The coins are all quarters. How many quarters does she have?

                                              _____ quarters

㉕ Each worker paves $\frac{1}{5}$ of a driveway per day. How many driveways do 8 workers pave per day?

                                              _____ driveways

㉖ A group of students eat $4\frac{1}{2}$ pizzas altogether. If they eat $\frac{1}{2}$ pizza each, how many students are there?

                                              _____ students

㉗ Candy says that $\frac{15}{4}$ is greater than $\frac{13}{3}$ since $15 > 13$ and $4 > 3$. Is this statement true or false? Explain.

How many sixteenths are there in three and a half?

There are _____ sixteenths.

13 Adding Improper Fractions and Mixed Numbers

1. $\dfrac{13}{7} + \dfrac{1}{7} = \dfrac{13+1}{7}$ ← add the numerators; keep the denominator

$= \dfrac{14}{7}$

$= 2$ ← reduce to lowest terms

2. $1\dfrac{1}{4} + 2\dfrac{1}{4} = \dfrac{5}{4} + \dfrac{9}{4}$ ← change mixed numbers to improper fractions

$= \dfrac{14}{4}$

$= 3\dfrac{1}{2}$ ← change back to a mixed number

3. $1\dfrac{1}{4} + 2\dfrac{1}{4} = 1 + \dfrac{1}{4} + 2 + \dfrac{1}{4}$ ← split the mixed numbers into whole numbers and fractions

$= 3 + \dfrac{1+1}{4}$ ← add the whole numbers and fractions separately

$= 3\dfrac{2}{4}$

$= 3\dfrac{1}{2}$ ← reduce to lowest terms

HINTS:

- Adding mixed numbers:
  Change the mixed numbers to improper fractions and add the fractions
  or
  add the whole numbers and fractions separately.

- Remember to reduce the sums to lowest terms.

- If the sum is an improper fraction, change back to a mixed number.

Find the sums mentally. All the answers are whole numbers.

① $1\dfrac{1}{2} + \dfrac{1}{2} =$ _____

② $2\dfrac{1}{3} + \dfrac{2}{3} =$ _____

③ $4\dfrac{1}{4} + \dfrac{3}{4} =$ _____

④ $\dfrac{8}{3} + \dfrac{1}{3} =$ _____

⑤ $\dfrac{11}{2} + \dfrac{3}{2} =$ _____

⑥ $\dfrac{11}{5} + \dfrac{4}{5} =$ _____

⑦ $5\dfrac{3}{5} + \dfrac{2}{5} =$ _____

⑧ $\dfrac{17}{3} + \dfrac{4}{3} =$ _____

⑨ $\dfrac{2}{9} + 2\dfrac{7}{9} =$ _____

⑩ $\dfrac{11}{6} + \dfrac{1}{6} =$ _____

⑪ $1\dfrac{2}{7} + \dfrac{5}{7} =$ _____

⑫ $\dfrac{5}{8} + 2\dfrac{3}{8} =$ _____

⑬ $\dfrac{3}{10} + 3\dfrac{7}{10} =$ _____

⑭ $\dfrac{13}{11} + \dfrac{9}{11} =$ _____

Find the sums. Show your work. Write the answers in lowest terms.

⑮ $2\frac{1}{8} + \frac{1}{8}$ = _____

⑯ $4\frac{2}{5} + 2\frac{1}{5}$ = _____

⑰ $3\frac{1}{5} + \frac{1}{5}$ = _____

⑱ $5\frac{1}{4} + \frac{1}{4}$ = _____

⑲ $\frac{11}{5} + \frac{6}{5}$ = _____

⑳ $1\frac{3}{4} + 1\frac{3}{4}$ = _____

㉑ $\frac{3}{8} + \frac{9}{8}$ = _____

㉒ $2\frac{2}{3} + 1\frac{2}{3}$ = _____

㉓ $\frac{3}{10} + \frac{13}{10}$ = _____

㉔ $2\frac{7}{16} + \frac{7}{16}$ = _____

㉕ $2\frac{7}{8} + \frac{3}{8}$ = _____

㉖ $\frac{3}{10} + \frac{17}{10}$ = _____

㉗ $1\frac{3}{8} + 3\frac{3}{8}$ = _____

㉘ $\frac{13}{6} + \frac{1}{6}$ = _____

㉙ $4\frac{1}{5} + 3\frac{2}{5} + 1\frac{4}{5}$ = _____

㉚ $\frac{5}{6} + 1\frac{1}{6} + 4$ = _____

Fill in the boxes.

(31) $1\frac{1}{4} + \boxed{} = 2$

(32) $3\frac{3}{8} + \boxed{} = 4$

(33) $\boxed{} + 1\frac{1}{5} = 3$

(34) $\boxed{} + 3\frac{1}{2} = 5$

(35) $\frac{3}{2} + \boxed{} = 2$

(36) $\frac{7}{5} + \boxed{} = 2$

(37) $5\frac{1}{3} + \boxed{} = 6$

(38) $\frac{11}{6} + \boxed{} = 3$

(39) $\boxed{} + \frac{4}{5} = 4$

(40) $\boxed{} + 4\frac{1}{4} = 5$

Write True (T) or False (F) for each of the following statements.

(41) $\frac{2}{3} + \frac{2}{3} > 1$ (   )

(42) $1\frac{3}{4} + \frac{1}{2} > 2$ (   )

(43) $\frac{1}{3} + \frac{1}{3} > \frac{5}{6}$ (   )

(44) $2\frac{1}{2} < 2\frac{4}{7}$ (   )

(45) $1\frac{3}{8} + \frac{3}{4} > 2$ (   )

(46) $1\frac{1}{3} > 1\frac{4}{11}$ (   )

(47) $1\frac{2}{5} = \frac{7}{5}$ (   )

(48) $3\frac{1}{3} > 3\frac{1}{2}$ (   )

Answer only the questions that have a sum greater than 3.

(49) $2\frac{2}{3} + \frac{2}{3} = \underline{}$

(50) $2\frac{1}{3} + \frac{1}{3} = \underline{}$

(51) $\frac{15}{7} + \frac{5}{7} = \underline{}$

(52) $1\frac{5}{8} + 1\frac{7}{8} = \underline{}$

(53) $\frac{9}{4} + \frac{5}{4} = \underline{}$

(54) $\frac{4}{5} + \frac{12}{5} = \underline{}$

(55) $\frac{5}{6} + 1\frac{5}{6} = \underline{}$

(56) $1\frac{7}{9} + 1\frac{7}{9} = \underline{}$

Answer the questions. Show your work.

㊄⑦ Ann has 3 cats. Shadow eats $1\frac{1}{4}$ cans of food per week. Rocky eats $2\frac{1}{4}$ cans and Peppy eats $1\frac{3}{4}$ cans. How many cans of food do they eat altogether per week?

㊄⑧ Shares in Riverview International were sold for $45\frac{3}{8}$ ¢ per share. They increase in value by $2\frac{1}{8}$ ¢ per share. What is the new selling price?

㊄⑨ Janet is sewing 2 dresses. One needs $3\frac{1}{8}$ yards of fabric and the other needs $4\frac{3}{4}$ yards.

a.   How much fabric must she buy?

b.   Would 8 yards be enough?

㊌⓪ Peggy keeps a record of her weekly TV watching in the chart below.

Day	Sun	Mon	Tue	Wed	Thu	Fri	Sat
Time (hour)	$1\frac{1}{4}$	$1\frac{1}{4}$	$\frac{3}{4}$	$1\frac{1}{4}$	2	$1\frac{3}{4}$	$2\frac{3}{4}$

How much TV did she watch during the week?

Look for the pattern. Fill in the missing number.

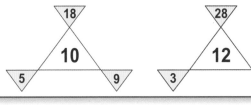
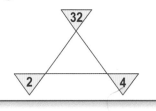

61

Subtracting Fractions with Like Denominators

1. $\dfrac{3}{8} - \dfrac{1}{8} = \dfrac{3-1}{8}$ ←——— subtract the numerators; keep the denominator

   $= \dfrac{2}{8}$

   $= \dfrac{1}{4}$ ←——— reduce to lowest terms

HINTS:

- To subtract fractions with like denominators, subtract the numerators and leave the denominator the same.

- Remember to reduce the difference to lowest terms.

- If the difference is an improper fraction, change back to a mixed number.

2. $\dfrac{6}{10} - \dfrac{1}{10} = \dfrac{6-1}{10} = \dfrac{5}{10} = \dfrac{1}{2}$

Find the differences mentally.

① $\dfrac{3}{7} - \dfrac{1}{7} =$ _____

② $\dfrac{11}{12} - \dfrac{10}{12} =$ _____

③ $\dfrac{8}{9} - \dfrac{1}{9} =$ _____

④ $\dfrac{9}{11} - \dfrac{7}{11} =$ _____

⑤ $\dfrac{3}{7} - \dfrac{1}{7} =$ _____

⑥ $\dfrac{5}{10} - \dfrac{4}{10} =$ _____

⑦ $\dfrac{16}{17} - \dfrac{13}{17} =$ _____

⑧ $\dfrac{5}{12} - \dfrac{5}{12} =$ _____

⑨ $\dfrac{8}{15} - \dfrac{7}{15} =$ _____

⑩ $\dfrac{5}{8} - \dfrac{3}{8} =$ _____

⑪ $\dfrac{11}{13} - \dfrac{9}{13} =$ _____

⑫ $\dfrac{13}{14} - \dfrac{9}{14} =$ _____

Complete each equation with a diagram.

⑬

⑭

⑮

⑯

Subtract and reduce the answers to lowest terms. Show your work.

⑰ $\dfrac{9}{10} - \dfrac{4}{10} = \underline{\hspace{1.5cm}}$

⑱ $\dfrac{5}{8} - \dfrac{1}{8} = \underline{\hspace{1.5cm}}$

⑲ $\dfrac{4}{9} - \dfrac{1}{9} = \underline{\hspace{1.5cm}}$

⑳ $\dfrac{7}{12} - \dfrac{4}{12} = \underline{\hspace{1.5cm}}$

㉑ $\dfrac{5}{6} - \dfrac{1}{6} = \underline{\hspace{1.5cm}}$

㉒ $\dfrac{13}{16} - \dfrac{1}{16} = \underline{\hspace{1.5cm}}$

㉓ $\dfrac{3}{4} - \dfrac{1}{4} = \underline{\hspace{1.5cm}}$

㉔ $\dfrac{10}{14} - \dfrac{2}{14} = \underline{\hspace{1.5cm}}$

㉕ $\dfrac{7}{9} - \dfrac{1}{9} = \underline{\hspace{1.5cm}}$

㉖ $\dfrac{3}{8} - \dfrac{1}{8} = \underline{\hspace{1.5cm}}$

㉗ $\dfrac{17}{20} - \dfrac{2}{20} = \underline{\hspace{1.5cm}}$

㉘ $\dfrac{42}{50} - \dfrac{12}{50} = \underline{\hspace{1.5cm}}$

㉙ $\dfrac{16}{24} - \dfrac{8}{24} = \underline{\hspace{1.5cm}}$

㉚ $\dfrac{13}{25} - \dfrac{3}{25} = \underline{\hspace{1.5cm}}$

㉛ $\dfrac{19}{26} - \dfrac{6}{26} = \underline{\hspace{1.5cm}}$

㉜ $\dfrac{6}{12} - \dfrac{1}{12} - \dfrac{2}{12} = \underline{\hspace{1.5cm}}$

Fill in the missing number in each box.

33. $\dfrac{1}{4} + \boxed{} = 1$

34. $\boxed{} + \dfrac{4}{7} = \dfrac{5}{7}$

35. $\dfrac{5}{7} - \boxed{} = \dfrac{1}{7}$

36. $\dfrac{3}{4} - \boxed{} = \dfrac{1}{4}$

37. $\boxed{} + \dfrac{1}{2} = \dfrac{3}{4}$

38. $\boxed{} - \dfrac{1}{9} = \dfrac{7}{9}$

39. $\boxed{} + \dfrac{4}{5} = 1$

40. $\dfrac{5}{9} + \boxed{} = 1$

41. $\dfrac{5}{6} - \boxed{} = \dfrac{2}{3}$

42. $\boxed{} - \dfrac{1}{4} = \dfrac{1}{2}$

43. $\dfrac{1}{9} + \boxed{} = \dfrac{7}{9}$

44. $\dfrac{3}{9} + \boxed{} = \dfrac{5}{9}$

45. $\boxed{} - \dfrac{1}{3} = \dfrac{1}{3}$

46. $\dfrac{1}{5} + \boxed{} = \dfrac{3}{5}$

47. $\boxed{} - \dfrac{1}{10} = \dfrac{1}{5}$

48. $\dfrac{3}{11} + \boxed{} = \dfrac{8}{11}$

49. $\dfrac{3}{10} + \dfrac{1}{10} = \boxed{}$

50. $\dfrac{5}{8} - \boxed{} = \dfrac{1}{2}$

Find the answers.

51. $\dfrac{1}{7} + \dfrac{5}{7} - \dfrac{4}{7} = \dfrac{1 + 5 - 4}{7} = \underline{\hspace{2cm}}$

52. $\dfrac{4}{12} + \dfrac{7}{12} - \dfrac{5}{12} = \underline{\hspace{2cm}} = \underline{\hspace{2cm}}$

53. $\dfrac{11}{18} - \dfrac{7}{18} + \dfrac{1}{18} = \underline{\hspace{2cm}} = \underline{\hspace{2cm}}$

Answer the questions. Show your work.

54. Ron read $\frac{5}{8}$ of his book on Monday and $\frac{3}{8}$ on Tuesday. How much more did he read on Monday than on Tuesday?

He read _____ more of his book on Monday.

55. It takes Ben $\frac{3}{4}$ hour to do his math homework but it only takes Carla $\frac{1}{4}$ hour. How much longer does it take Ben to do the homework?

56. It takes Carol $\frac{5}{6}$ hour to walk to school. It takes Dave $\frac{1}{6}$ hour for the same walk. How much less time does it take Dave to walk to school?

57. It takes Paula 40 minutes to wash her car.

   a. What fraction of the job will she have done after 10 minutes?

   b. What fraction of the job still remains?

58. Bob buys 10 plants for his garden. 2 are violet and 4 are red.

   a. What fraction of the plants are violet? What fraction are red?

   b. What fraction of the plants are neither red nor violet?

Fill in the missing numbers.

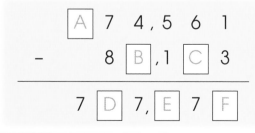

 # Subtracting Improper Fractions and Mixed Numbers

1. $1 - \dfrac{3}{5} = \dfrac{5}{5} - \dfrac{3}{5}$ ← $\dfrac{5}{5} = 1$

   $= \dfrac{2}{5}$

2. $2\dfrac{4}{5} - 1\dfrac{3}{5} = \dfrac{14}{5} - \dfrac{8}{5}$ ← change mixed numbers to improper fractions

   $= \dfrac{14 - 8}{5}$ ← subtract the numerators; keep the denominator

   $= \dfrac{6}{5}$

   $= 1\dfrac{1}{5}$ ← change back to a mixed number

   or

3. $2\dfrac{4}{5} - 1\dfrac{3}{5} = 2 + \dfrac{4}{5} - 1 - \dfrac{3}{5}$ ← split the mixed numbers

   $= 2 - 1 + \dfrac{4 - 3}{5}$ ← subtract the whole numbers and fractions separately

   $= 1\dfrac{1}{5}$

 **HINTS:**

- Subtracting mixed numbers:
  Change mixed numbers to improper fractions and subtract the fractions
  or
  subtract the whole numbers and fractions separately.

- Remember to reduce the difference to lowest terms.

- If the difference is an improper fraction, change back to a mixed number.

Find the differences mentally.

① $2\dfrac{4}{7} - \dfrac{3}{7}$ = _____

② $2\dfrac{3}{5} - \dfrac{1}{5}$ = _____ ③ $\dfrac{11}{9} - \dfrac{4}{9}$ = _____ ④ $1\dfrac{7}{8} - 1\dfrac{6}{8}$ = _____

⑤ $\dfrac{21}{4} - \dfrac{18}{4}$ = _____ ⑥ $5\dfrac{3}{4} - 5$ = _____ ⑦ $\dfrac{3}{2} - \dfrac{3}{2}$ = _____

⑧ $12\dfrac{3}{9} - 12\dfrac{1}{9}$ = _____ ⑨ $5\dfrac{1}{3} - 2\dfrac{1}{3}$ = _____ ⑩ $1\dfrac{4}{9} - 1\dfrac{3}{9}$ = _____

⑪ $8\dfrac{7}{13} - 8\dfrac{4}{13}$ = _____ ⑫ $\dfrac{13}{10} - \dfrac{3}{10}$ = _____ ⑬ $10\dfrac{7}{8} - 10$ = _____

⑭ $\dfrac{10}{3} - \dfrac{8}{3}$ = _____ ⑮ $3\dfrac{5}{6} - 3\dfrac{1}{6}$ = _____ ⑯ $9\dfrac{7}{8} - 4\dfrac{7}{8}$ = _____

Find the differences. Show your work. Write the answers in lowest terms.

⑰ $1\frac{1}{2} - \frac{3}{2}$ = _____

⑱ $2\frac{3}{4} - \frac{1}{4}$ = _____

⑲ $\frac{6}{5} - \frac{1}{5}$ = _____

⑳ $\frac{9}{4} - \frac{3}{4}$ = _____

㉑ $5\frac{1}{4} - 4\frac{3}{4}$ = _____

㉒ $3\frac{1}{8} - 2\frac{7}{8}$ = _____

㉓ $\frac{11}{4} - \frac{3}{4}$ = _____

㉔ $\frac{12}{10} - \frac{8}{10}$ = _____

㉕ $2\frac{1}{6} - 1\frac{5}{6}$ = _____

㉖ $\frac{20}{9} - \frac{11}{9}$ = _____

㉗ $2\frac{3}{8} - \frac{9}{8}$ = _____

㉘ $1\frac{1}{11} - \frac{12}{11}$ = _____

㉙ $\frac{21}{10} - 1\frac{1}{10}$ = _____

㉚ $\frac{21}{3} - 5\frac{1}{3}$ = _____

㉛ $5\frac{3}{4} - 2\frac{1}{4} - \frac{2}{4}$ = _____

㉜ $9 - 6\frac{1}{5} - 1\frac{3}{5}$ = _____

Fill in the missing number in each box.

㉝ $1\frac{1}{4} - \frac{3}{4} = \square$

㉞ $\frac{13}{5} - \square = \frac{9}{5}$

㉟ $\frac{5}{3} + \square = 2$

㊱ $\square - 1\frac{3}{4} = 3\frac{1}{4}$

㊲ $\square - \frac{1}{4} = 1\frac{1}{4}$

㊳ $\square + 2\frac{1}{4} = 3$

㊴ $\square - 3\frac{3}{8} = \frac{5}{8}$

㊵ $\frac{5}{3} - \square = 0$

㊶ $\frac{5}{4} + \square = 2$

㊷ $\square + \frac{4}{7} = 3$

㊸ $\frac{7}{5} - \square = 1$

㊹ $\frac{1}{2} + \square = 4$

㊺ $2 - \square = 1\frac{1}{3}$

㊻ $\square - \frac{1}{9} = \frac{8}{9}$

㊼ $\square + \frac{3}{4} = 1\frac{1}{4}$

㊽ $\square + \frac{6}{5} = 2$

Find the answers.

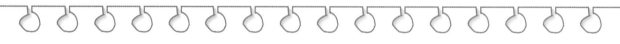

㊾ $3\frac{4}{6} + 4\frac{1}{6} - 2\frac{2}{6} = 3 + 4 - 2 + \frac{4 + 1 - 2}{6} =$ __________

㊿ $9 + 1\frac{2}{8} - 3\frac{1}{8} =$ ____________________ = __________

(51) $4\frac{1}{6} + 1\frac{4}{6} - 3\frac{3}{6} =$ ____________________ = __________

(52) $3\frac{2}{7} + 2\frac{4}{7} - 1\frac{5}{7} =$ ____________________ = __________

Answer the questions. Show your work. Write the fractions in lowest terms.

(53) On Monday, Jonathan watched TV for $2\frac{3}{4}$ hours and Pat watched TV for $3\frac{1}{4}$ hours. How much longer did Pat spend watching TV?

(54) On Monday, Ron ran $8\frac{3}{8}$ miles and on Wednesday he ran $6\frac{5}{8}$ miles. How much farther did he run on Monday?

(55) ABC shares sell for $3\frac{1}{5}$ dollars each and BFI shares sell for $2\frac{4}{5}$ dollars each. What is the difference between the share prices?

(56) The perimeter of the triangle is 1 meter. What is the length of the third side?

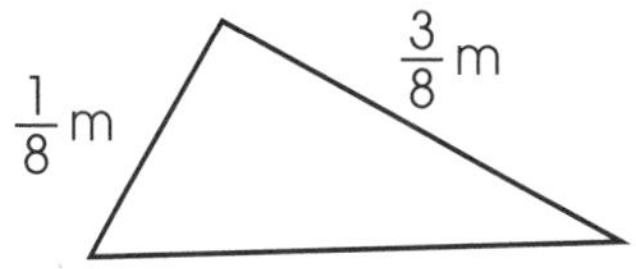

(57) The dimensions of a framed picture are $15\frac{1}{4}$ inches by $10\frac{1}{2}$ inches. The frame is $1\frac{1}{2}$ inches wide. What are the dimensions of the unframed part of the picture?

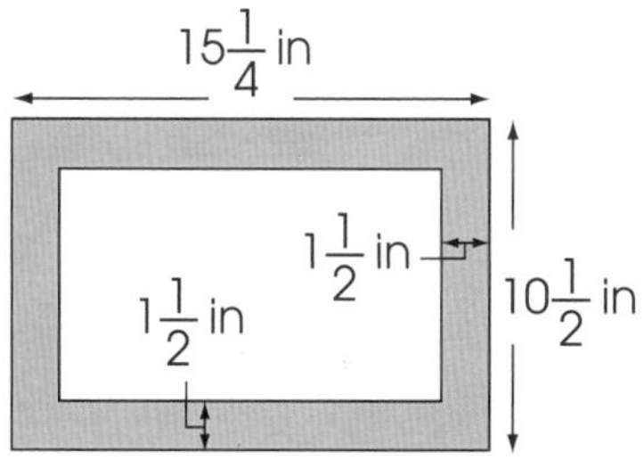

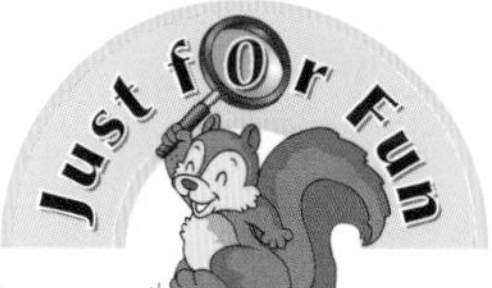

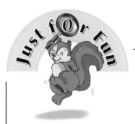

7 people eat $\frac{1}{4}$ of a pizza each. If they buy 2 pizzas, what fraction of a pizza is left?

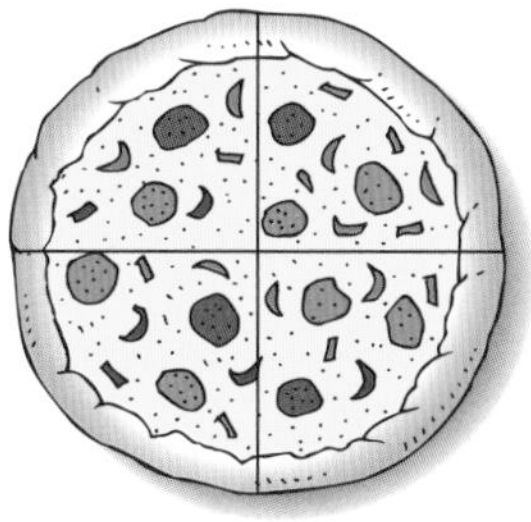

__________ of a pizza is left.

16 Relating Decimals and Fractions

1. Convert 0.7 and 0.55 to fractions.

   $0.7 = \dfrac{7}{10}$ ← put 1 zero in the denominator since 0.7 has 1 decimal place

   $0.55 = \dfrac{55}{100} = \dfrac{11}{20}$ ← reduce the fraction to lowest terms

   ↑

   put 2 zeros in the denominator since 0.55 has 2 decimal places

2. Convert $\dfrac{1}{4}$ and $2\dfrac{1}{5}$ to decimals.

   $\dfrac{1}{4} = 0.25$

   $\begin{array}{r} 0.25 \\ 4\overline{)1.0} \\ 8 \\ \hline 20 \\ 20 \end{array}$ ← divide the numerator by the denominator and continue dividing until the remainder is zero

   $2\dfrac{1}{5} = 2 + \dfrac{1}{5} = 2 + 0.2 = 2.2$

   $\begin{array}{r} 0.2 \\ 5\overline{)1\,0} \\ 1\,0 \end{array}$

   ↑

   change the fraction part to decimal

Change the following fractions to decimals.

Fraction	Decimal
① $\dfrac{1}{10}$	_____
② $\dfrac{7}{10}$	_____
③ $\dfrac{3}{100}$	_____
④ $\dfrac{49}{100}$	_____
⑤ $\dfrac{9}{100}$	_____
⑥ $\dfrac{73}{100}$	_____

HINTS:

- Change decimals to fractions:

  Write the decimal part as numerator with a denominator of 10, 100, 1,000, etc.,

  e.g. $0.07 = \dfrac{7}{100}$ ← number of zeros in the denominator equals the number of decimal places

  Remember to reduce the fractions to lowest terms.

- Change fractions to decimals:

  Find the equivalent fraction with a denominator of 10, 100, 1,000, etc., and then write the fraction as a decimal number,

  e.g. $\dfrac{1}{4} = \dfrac{1 \times 25}{4 \times 25} = \dfrac{25}{100} = 0.25$ or

  divide the numerator by the denominator; continue dividing until the remainder is zero or there are enough decimal places.

  e.g. $\dfrac{2}{3} = 0.67$ ← round to the nearest hundredth

Change the following decimals to fractions.

Decimal	Fraction		Decimal	Fraction
⑦ 0.3	_____		⑧ 0.7	_____
⑨ 0.9	_____		⑩ 0.01	_____
⑪ 0.09	_____		⑫ 0.07	_____
⑬ 0.31	_____		⑭ 0.19	_____
⑮ 0.47	_____		⑯ 0.03	_____

Use division to convert each of the following fractions to decimals.

Fraction	Decimal		Fraction	Decimal
⑰ $\frac{1}{2}$	_____		⑱ $\frac{1}{5}$	_____
⑲ $\frac{3}{4}$	_____		⑳ $\frac{3}{5}$	_____
㉑ $\frac{1}{8}$	_____		㉒ $\frac{5}{8}$	_____
㉓ $\frac{3}{8}$	_____		㉔ $\frac{4}{5}$	_____

Convert the following fractions to decimals. Round the answers to the nearest hundredth if necessary.

㉕ $1\frac{5}{8}$ = _____   ㉖ $3\frac{4}{7}$ = _____   ㉗ $12\frac{4}{5}$ = _____

㉘ $2\frac{3}{8}$ = _____   ㉙ $3\frac{5}{6}$ = _____   ㉚ $5\frac{4}{9}$ = _____

㉛ $1\frac{2}{3}$ = _____   ㉜ $2\frac{3}{5}$ = _____   ㉝ $4\frac{1}{4}$ = _____

㉞ $10\frac{2}{5}$ = _____   ㉟ $8\frac{6}{7}$ = _____   ㊱ $6\frac{7}{10}$ = _____

Change the decimals to fractions. Give your answers in lowest terms.

③⑦ 0.65 = $\frac{65}{100}$ = _____   ③⑧ 0.75 = _____ = _____

③⑨ 0.05 = _____ = _____   ④⓪ 0.12 = _____ = _____

④① 0.45 = _____ = _____   ④② 0.36 = _____ = _____

④③ 1.45 = _____ = _____   ④④ 6.55 = _____ = _____

④⑤ 2.8 = _____ = _____   ④⑥ 2.25 = _____ = _____

How many cents are there in each of the following fractions of a dollar?

④⑦ $\$\frac{1}{4}$ = _____ ¢   ④⑧ $\$\frac{3}{4}$ = _____ ¢

④⑨ $\$\frac{2}{5}$ = _____ ¢   ⑤⓪ $\$\frac{3}{5}$ = _____ ¢

⑤① $\$\frac{7}{10}$ = _____ ¢   ⑤② $\$\frac{9}{10}$ = _____ ¢

Circle the larger number in each pair.

⑤③ 0.65 $\frac{1}{2}$ ⑤④ $\frac{4}{5}$ 0.9   ⑤⑤ 1.3 $1\frac{2}{5}$

⑤⑥ $\frac{2}{3}$ 0.62   ⑤⑦ 4.26 $4\frac{1}{4}$ ⑤⑧ 0.57 $\frac{8}{15}$

⑤⑨ 3.69 $3\frac{3}{5}$ ⑥⓪ 8.38 $8\frac{1}{3}$ ⑥① $6\frac{3}{8}$ 6.37

Arrange the following numbers in order from least to greatest.

⑥② $1\frac{7}{8}$ 1.54 $1\frac{8}{9}$ _____ < _____ < _____

⑥③ 2.68 $2\frac{3}{5}$ $2\frac{4}{7}$ _____ < _____ < _____

⑥④ $5\frac{9}{10}$ $5\frac{4}{5}$ 5.83   _____ < _____ < _____

Complete the table. Then list the fractions in order from least to greatest.

65

Fraction	$\frac{1}{8}$	$\frac{1}{4}$	$\frac{3}{4}$	$\frac{3}{8}$	$\frac{7}{8}$	$\frac{1}{5}$	$\frac{7}{10}$
Decimal							

66 _____ < _____ < _____ < _____ < _____ < _____ < _____

Answer the questions.

67 Canada produces about 0.24 of the world's supply of nickel ore. Express this as a fraction in lowest terms. _____

68 Paul climbs 100 steps up a 160-step tower.

    a.   What fraction of the tower has he climbed? _____

    b.   Express your answer as a decimal. _____

69 $\frac{1}{5}$ of the cost of a gallon of gas is tax.

    a.   Express this fraction as a decimal. _____

    b.   If gas costs $3 a gallon, how much is the tax? _____

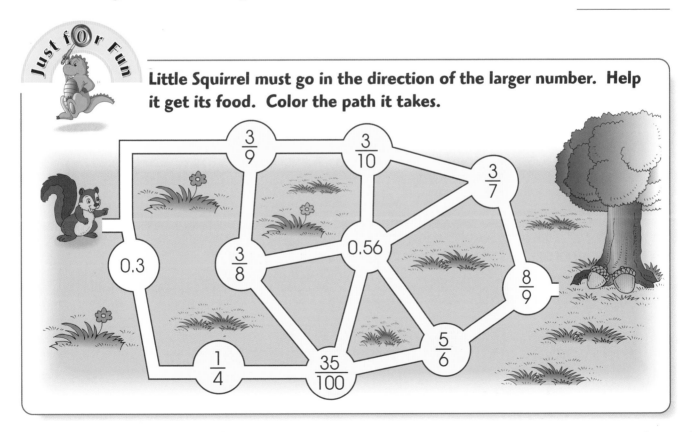

Just for Fun

Little Squirrel must go in the direction of the larger number. Help it get its food. Color the path it takes.

73

Circle the letter which represents the correct answer in each problem.

① A fraction equivalent to $\frac{3}{4}$ is _____ .

   A. $\frac{5}{6}$ B. $\frac{6}{8}$ C. $\frac{35}{45}$ D. $\frac{9}{16}$

② The fraction $\frac{36}{92}$ expressed in lowest terms is _____ .

   A. $\frac{1}{2}$ B. $\frac{18}{46}$ C. $\frac{9}{23}$ D. $\frac{2}{5}$

③ The fraction $\frac{1}{8}$ expressed as a decimal is _____ .

   A. 0.12   B. 0.2   C. 0.1   D. 0.125

④ The decimal 0.95 expressed as a fraction in lowest terms is _____ .

   A. $\frac{19}{20}$ B. $\frac{9}{10}$ C. $\frac{9.5}{10}$ D. $\frac{9}{100}$

⑤ The mixed number $3\frac{1}{3}$ expressed as an improper fraction is _____ .

   A. $\frac{1}{2}$ B. $\frac{10}{3}$ C. $\frac{31}{3}$ D. $\frac{10}{9}$

⑥ The improper fraction $\frac{27}{7}$ expressed as a mixed number is _____ .

   A. $3\frac{1}{7}$ B. $27\frac{1}{7}$ C. $4\frac{6}{7}$ D. $3\frac{6}{7}$

⑦ The sum of $\frac{3}{11}$ and $\frac{7}{11}$ is _____ .

   A. $\frac{10}{11}$ B. $\frac{10}{22}$ C. $\frac{21}{121}$ D. $\frac{21}{11}$

⑧ The difference between $\frac{7}{9}$ and $\frac{2}{9}$ is _____ .

   A. $\frac{1}{7}$ B. 5   C. $\frac{5}{9}$ D. $\frac{14}{81}$

⑨ The improper fraction $\frac{24}{5}$ expressed as a decimal is _____ .

   A. 2.8   B. 4.8   C. 24.2   D. 5.2

Represent each diagram as a fraction in lowest terms and also as a decimal.

⑩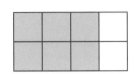

Fraction _____

Decimal _____

⑪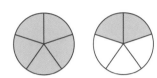

Fraction _____

Decimal _____

⑫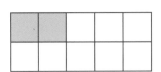

Fraction _____

Decimal _____

Write the numbers labeled A - E on the number line below as fractions and decimals.

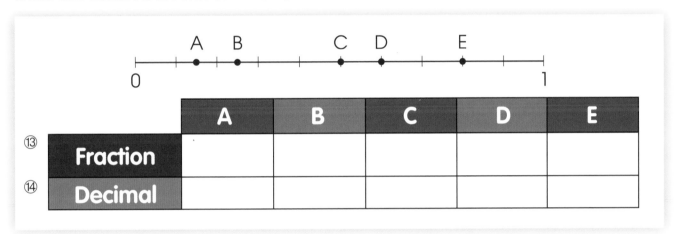

	A	B	C	D	E
⑬ **Fraction**					
⑭ **Decimal**					

Change the fractions to mixed numbers. Place the fractions on the number line below.

⑮ $\dfrac{15}{4}$ = _____

⑯ $\dfrac{3}{2}$ = _____

⑰ $\dfrac{17}{5}$ = _____

⑱ $\dfrac{19}{9}$ = _____

⑲ $\dfrac{4}{3}$ = _____

⑳ $\dfrac{7}{2}$ = _____

㉑ $\dfrac{14}{3}$ = _____

㉒ $\dfrac{25}{6}$ = _____

㉓ $\dfrac{35}{8}$ = _____

㉔ $\dfrac{7}{4}$ = _____

㉕ $\dfrac{13}{5}$ = _____

㉖ $\dfrac{24}{5}$ = _____

㉗ $\dfrac{3}{2}$

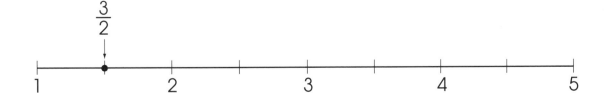

Add or subtract. Write your answers in lowest terms.

㉘ $\dfrac{10}{3} - \dfrac{10}{3} =$ _____

㉙ $\dfrac{9}{2} - \dfrac{5}{2} =$ _____

㉚ $7\dfrac{1}{4} - 3\dfrac{1}{4} =$ _____

㉛ $6\dfrac{3}{8} - 5\dfrac{1}{8} =$ _____

㉜ $\dfrac{16}{5} + \dfrac{6}{5} =$ _____

㉝ $5\dfrac{1}{4} + 3\dfrac{3}{4} =$ _____

㉞ $5\dfrac{1}{4} - 4\dfrac{3}{4} =$ _____

㉟ $3\dfrac{1}{5} - 2\dfrac{3}{5} =$ _____

The chart shows the minimum hourly wage in a number of states in the United States. Read the chart and answer the questions. Write the number sentences where necessary.

State	Vermont	Texas	Hawaii	Alaska	California	Washington
Wage ($)	7.25	5.15	7.25	7.15	8.00	7.95

㊱ What is the difference between the highest and lowest wages?

_____ = _____

㊲ How much would a student working for 5 hours at minimum wage earn in

   a. California? _____ = _____

   b. Texas? _____ = _____

㊳ What is the difference between the two amounts in ㊲ ?

_____ = _____

㊴ Write the minimum wage in Vermont as

   a. a mixed number.   _____

   b. an improper fraction.   _____

㊵ Brenda lives in Hawaii and earns $\$\dfrac{1}{2}$ per hour more than the minimum wage. How much does she earn per hour?

_____ = _____

Solve the problems. Show your work.

④ In 1990, the population of the United States was 248.8 million and in 2000, it was 281.4 million.

    a.   Express each of these numbers as a mixed number in lowest terms.

    b.   What was the increase in the population of the United States between 1990 and 2000? Express your answer as a decimal and also as a mixed number.

    c.   If this trend continues, what will the population of the United States be in 2010?

④ Dan is training for a Marathon race. His monthly goal is 100 miles. He ran 35 miles during the first week of the month.

    a.   What fraction of his monthly goal has he run? Express your answer as a proper fraction in lowest terms and as a decimal.

    b.   What distance does he still have to run during the month to achieve his goal?

    c.   What fraction of the total distance does he still have to run? Express your answer as a fraction and as a decimal.

    d.   What is the difference between the fraction of the total distance run in the first week and the fraction run during the rest of the month?

㊸ Mr. King drinks an average of $2\frac{1}{4}$ cups of tea each day. Mrs. King drinks an average of $3\frac{3}{4}$ cups per day.

a. How many cups of tea do they drink in all each day?

b. What is the difference between the amounts they drink per day?

c. Change the amount Mr. King drinks to a decimal. How much tea does Mr. King drink per week?

d. Change the amount Mrs. King drinks to a decimal. How much tea does Mrs. King drink per week?

㊹ Peter watches TV for $8\frac{1}{5}$ hours per week. David watches $9\frac{3}{5}$ hours and Ruth watches $7\frac{1}{5}$ hours.

a. How much TV do they watch in all in a week?

b. How much longer does David watch TV than Peter?

c. How much longer does David watch TV than Ruth?

d. Ruth's mother says that Ruth must cut down watching TV by $1\frac{3}{5}$ hours. How much TV can she watch now?

Section II

Overview

In Section I, fraction and decimal skills were practiced. In this section, these skills are expanded to include percents, reducing fractions to simplest form, and multiplying decimals by decimals.

Students also practice solving simple equations, analyzing line graphs, and dealing with inverse proportion. New arithmetic skills include rounding large numbers, identifying prime and composite numbers, and finding GCF (greatest common factor) and LCM (least common multiple).

In learning measurements, students practice how to find the area of triangles and parallelograms. They also practice the calculation of volume and surface area of rectangular prisms.

In learning geometry, students carry out transformations of points as well as shapes. Time applications include the calculation of the duration of an event. Money applications involve finding change and calculating sale prices.

Large Numbers

Rounding - expressing a number to the nearest ten, hundred, thousand, or other value

Help Dave write the price of each house in standard form.

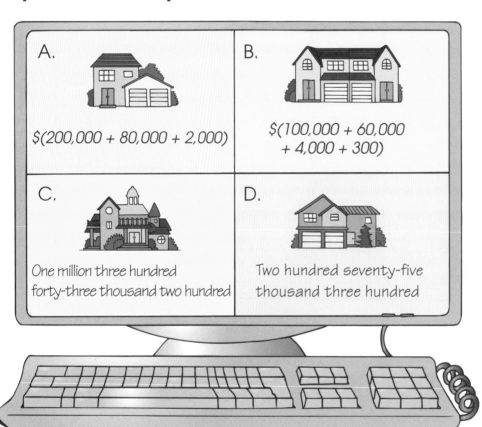

A.

$(200,000 + 80,000 + 2,000)$

B.

$(100,000 + 60,000 + 4,000 + 300)$

C.

One million three hundred forty-three thousand two hundred

D.

Two hundred seventy-five thousand three hundred

Hi! My name is Dave. My dad and I are looking for a house through my computer.

Millions			Thousands			Hundreds	Tens	Ones
H	T	O	H	T	O			
4	9	7	5	2	3	6	1	8

① House A : $_____

② House B : $_____

③ House C : $_____

④ House D : $_____

Write the meaning of each underlined digit.

⑤ 465,200,623 _____

⑥ 1,620,973 _____

⑦ 126,305,704 _____

⑧ 248,273,046 _____

Read what Dave says. Then help him round the prices of the houses.

Round 123,205 to the nearest ten thousand.

1st Mark in multiples of 10,000 on a number line; look at the thousands digit.

123,205

110,000   120,000   130,000

2nd 123,205 is between 120,000 and 130,000 but closer to 120,000.

123,205 rounds to 120,000.

Price of the house	Rounded to the nearest		
	hundred	thousand	ten thousand
⑨ 123,205			120,000
⑩ 174,158		174,000	
⑪ 246,523	246,500		
⑫ 477,099		477,000	
⑬ 1,205,103			1,210,000
⑭ 985,804		986,000	

Round up if a number is halfway between 2 multiples.

 A C T I V I T Y

Which of these numbers have been rounded? Check ✔ the right boxes.

A **CITY NEWS**

About 2,500,000 people live in Toronto

B **GAZETTE**

42,436 cases of flu reported

C **SUN WEEKLY**

Exactly $140,000 stolen in bank robbery

D **THE SYSTEM**

Over 20,000 people go south for vacation

Prime and Composite Numbers

WORDS TO LEARN

Composite number - any number that has more than 2 factors

Prime number - any number with only 1 and itself as factors

Find the number of stickers in each group and write composite or prime.

 $6 = 2 \times 3$; 6 can form a rectangle.

6 is a <u>composite</u> number.

① 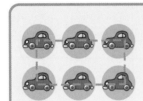 _____ = 2 × 4;

8 is a _____ number.

If any number of things can form a rectangle, then it is a composite number.

②

_____ = 1 × 7 ; 7 is a _____ number.

③

_____ = 1 × 5 ; 5 is a _____ number.

④  _____ = 2 × 2 ;

4 is a _____ number.

Write prime or composite for the following numbers.

⑤ 12 _____   ⑥ 11 _____   ⑦ 18 _____

⑧ 36 _____   ⑨ 41 _____   ⑩ 47 _____

Follow the directions to find all the prime numbers within 100. Color the 100-chart and fill in the blanks.

⑪ Color 1 orange.

⑫ Color all the multiples of 2 (except 2) red.

⑬ Color all the uncolored multiples of 3, 5, and 7 (except 3, 5, and 7) yellow.

⑭ There are _____ uncolored numbers. All of them are _____ numbers.

1	2	3	4	5	6	7	8	9	10
11	12	13	14	15	16	17	18	19	20
21	22	23	24	25	26	27	28	29	30
31	32	33	34	35	36	37	38	39	40
41	42	43	44	45	46	47	48	49	50
51	52	53	54	55	56	57	58	59	60
61	62	63	64	65	66	67	68	69	70
71	72	73	74	75	76	77	78	79	80
81	82	83	84	85	86	87	88	89	90
91	92	93	94	95	96	97	98	99	100

⑮ All the colored numbers (except 1) are _____ numbers.

Write True or False for each statement.

⑯ All prime numbers except 2 are odd numbers.   _____

⑰ 5 is the only prime number ending in 5.   _____

⑱ From 1 to 100, there are 24 prime numbers.   _____

 A C T I V I T Y

Read what Dave says. Then try out what he says on the following numbers.

1. 20 = _____ + _____

2. 24 = _____ + _____

3. 32 = _____ + _____

4. 98 = _____ + _____

Mathematicians believe that all even numbers except 2 can be made by adding 2 prime numbers together.

Examples

$10 = 7 + 3$ $8 = 5 + 3$

Fractions

Proper fraction - a fraction with the numerator smaller than the denominator   e.g. $\dfrac{2}{5}$

Improper fraction - a fraction with the numerator greater than or equal to the denominator   e.g. $\dfrac{11}{7}$

Mixed number - a number formed by a whole number and a proper fraction   e.g. $2\dfrac{3}{5}$

Reciprocal - the reciprocal of a fraction is the fraction with the numerator and denominator switched

e.g. $\dfrac{1}{2}$ is the reciprocal of 2. $\dfrac{4}{3}$ is the reciprocal of $\dfrac{3}{4}$.

See how much food the children ate. Write the answers in simplest form.

① Dave and 3 friends each ate $\dfrac{2}{3}$ of a pizza. How many pizzas did they eat in all?

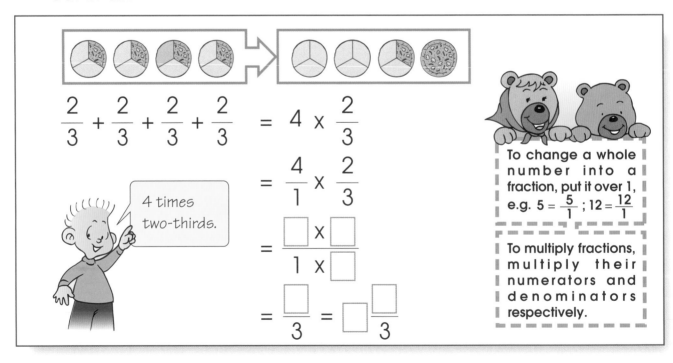

$\dfrac{2}{3} + \dfrac{2}{3} + \dfrac{2}{3} + \dfrac{2}{3} \quad = 4 \times \dfrac{2}{3}$

$= \dfrac{4}{1} \times \dfrac{2}{3}$

4 times two-thirds.

$= \dfrac{\square \times \square}{1 \times \square}$

$= \dfrac{\square}{3} = \square\dfrac{\square}{3}$

To change a whole number into a fraction, put it over 1, e.g. $5 = \dfrac{5}{1}$; $12 = \dfrac{12}{1}$

To multiply fractions, multiply their numerators and denominators respectively.

They ate _____ pizzas in all.

② Dave ate $\frac{1}{2}$ of $1\frac{1}{2}$ cakes. What fraction of a cake did he eat?

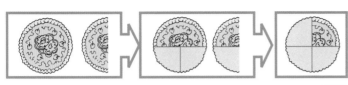

$$\frac{1}{2} \text{ of } 1\frac{1}{2} = \frac{1}{2} \times 1\frac{1}{2} = \frac{1}{2} \times \frac{\square}{2}$$

$$= \frac{1 \times \square}{\square \times \square}$$

$$= \frac{\square}{\square}$$

To multiply a mixed number, change it to an improper fraction first.

Dave ate _____ of a cake.

Try these. Write the answers in simplest form.

③ $2 \times \dfrac{3}{5}$ = _____

④ $3 \times \dfrac{3}{7}$ = _____

⑤ $\dfrac{1}{4} \times \dfrac{2}{3}$ = _____

⑥ $\dfrac{2}{9} \times \dfrac{2}{3}$ = _____

⑦ $3 \times 2\dfrac{5}{6}$ = _____

⑧ $1\dfrac{1}{3} \times \dfrac{3}{8}$ = _____

⑨ $\dfrac{5}{9} \times \dfrac{3}{10}$ = _____

⑩ $\dfrac{6}{7} \times 1\dfrac{2}{3}$ = _____

⑪ There are 28 students in a class. $\dfrac{4}{7}$ of them

are boys. How many boys are there? _____ boys

⑫ There were $\dfrac{5}{6}$ of a cake. Steve ate $\dfrac{3}{5}$ of it.

What fraction of the cake did he eat? _____ cake

See how Steve divided his pizza. Follow his method to do the division and write the answers in simplest form.

 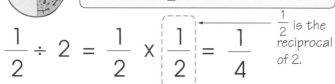 

I shared $\frac{1}{2}$ of a pizza with Dave.

$$\frac{1}{2} \div 2 = \frac{1}{2} \times \frac{1}{2} = \frac{1}{4}$$

$\frac{1}{2}$ is the reciprocal of 2.

Dave and Steve each got $\frac{1}{4}$ of a pizza.

To divide by a fraction is to multiply by its reciprocal, e.g. $5 \div n = 5 \times \frac{1}{n}$

⑬ $\dfrac{1}{3} \div 5 =$ _____

⑭ $\dfrac{4}{7} \div 2 =$ _____

⑮ $\dfrac{5}{9} \div 10 =$ _____

⑯ $\dfrac{3}{4} \div 9 =$ _____

⑰ $\dfrac{4}{3} \div 2 =$ _____

⑱ $\dfrac{8}{5} \div 4 =$ _____

See how Dave cut the cakes. Follow his method to solve the problems and write the answers in simplest form.

Each piece is $\frac{1}{4}$ of a cake.

How many pieces are there in 2 cakes?

$$2 \div \frac{1}{4} = 2 \times \frac{4}{1}$$
$$= 8$$

Multiply 2 by the reciprocal of $\frac{1}{4}$.

There are 8 pieces in 2 cakes.

Dividing by $\frac{1}{n}$ is the same as multiplying by n.

⑲ $3 \div \dfrac{3}{4} =$ _____

⑳ $5 \div \dfrac{5}{6} =$ _____

㉑ $9 \div \dfrac{3}{4}$ = _____

㉒ $6 \div \dfrac{3}{10}$ = _____

㉓ $3 \div \dfrac{2}{5}$ = _____

㉔ $4 \div \dfrac{8}{9}$ = _____

㉕ Dave eats $\dfrac{2}{5}$ of a box of cereal every day. In how many days will he finish 4 boxes of cereal? _____ days

Follow Dave's method to do the division and write the answers in simplest form.

I had $\dfrac{2}{3}$ of a pizza. Each person ate $\dfrac{1}{9}$ of the pizza. How many people were there?

$\dfrac{2}{3} \div \dfrac{1}{9} = \dfrac{2}{3} \boxed{\times \dfrac{9}{1}} = 6$

There were 6 people.   Multiply $\dfrac{2}{3}$ by the reciprocal of $\dfrac{1}{9}$.

㉖ $\dfrac{3}{7} \div \dfrac{1}{2}$ = _____

㉗ $\dfrac{3}{4} \div \dfrac{1}{8}$ = _____

㉘ $\dfrac{7}{8} \div \dfrac{1}{4}$ = _____

㉙ $\dfrac{5}{9} \div \dfrac{2}{3}$ = _____

ACTIVITY

Put +, −, X, or ÷ in the ☐ .

1. $\dfrac{1}{2} \;\boxed{}\; \dfrac{1}{3} = \dfrac{5}{6}$

2. $4 \;\boxed{}\; \dfrac{1}{12} = \dfrac{1}{3}$

3. $\dfrac{2}{3} \;\boxed{}\; \dfrac{1}{6} = 4$

4. $\dfrac{5}{7} \;\boxed{}\; \dfrac{1}{14} = \dfrac{9}{14}$

Distributive Property of Multiplication

WORDS TO LEARN

Distributive property of multiplication	- for any three numbers a, b, and c, it is true that: a x (b + c) = a x b + a x c

Find the perimeter of the picture for Dave and Steve. Circle Yes or No.

5 in

3 in

① Perimeter = 2 x 5 + 2 x 3

= _____ + _____

= _____ in

② Perimeter = 2 x (5 + 3)

= _____ x _____

= _____ in

③ Is 2 x (5 + 3) the same as 2 x 5 + 2 x 3?   Yes   No

Try these.

④ 7 x (3 + 5)

= 7 x _____ + 7 x _____

= _____ + _____

= _____

> Distributive property
> of multiplication
> $a \times (b + c) = a \times b + a \times c$

⑤ 4 x (18 – 7)

= 4 x _____ – 4 x _____

= _____ – _____

= _____

⑥ 5 x 12 – 5 x 7

= 5 x (_____ – _____)

= 5 x _____

= _____

Follow Dave and Steve's method to solve the problems.

4 x 82 = 4 x (80 + 2)

82 = 80 + 2

      = 4 x 80 + 4 x 2

      = 320 + 8

      = 328

5 x 99 = 5 x (100 − 1)

99 = 100 − 1

      = 5 x 100 − 5 x 1

      = 500 − 5

      = 495

⑦   5 x 73

= 5 x (_____ + _____)

= 5 x _____ + 5 x _____

= _____ + _____

= _____

⑧   6 x 98

= 6 x (_____ − _____)

= 6 x _____ − 6 x _____

= _____ − _____

= _____

⑨   7 x 102 = _____

⑩   9 x 49 = _____

⑪   6 x 93 = _____

⑫   4 x 83 = _____

⑬   9 x 62 = _____

⑭   5 x 79 = _____

ACTIVITY

Use the distributive property of multiplication to find the answers.

1. $10 \times 5\frac{1}{5}$

= 10 x (5 + ☐)

= 10 x ☐ + 10 x ☐

= ☐ + ☐

= ☐

2. $6 \times 54\frac{1}{5}$

= 6 x (50 + 4 + ☐)

= 6 x ☐ + 6 x ☐ + 6 x ☐

= ☐ + ☐ + ☐

= ☐

 **Simple Equations**

Equation - a mathematical sentence with an equal sign

e.g. $2 \times 5 = 10$ $y - 5 = 12$

Read what Uncle Ray says and help Dave check ✔ the right equations.

① 5 more than a number y is 12.

☐ $5 - y = 12$ ☐ $5 + y = 12$

② 6 less than a number n is 8.

☐ $n \div 6 = 8$ ☐ $6 - n = 8$ ☐ $n - 6 = 8$

③ 3 times a number m is 12.

☐ $3 \times m = 12$ ☐ $m = 12 \times 3$ ☐ $m \div 3 = 12$

④ A number k divided by 5 is 2.

☐ $5 \div k = 2$ ☐ $k = 5 \div 2$ ☐ $k \div 5 = 2$

Use the balance below to find the weight of Dave's toy cars and check the answers.

⑤

To solve this addition equation, subtract 20 from both sides to undo the addition.

 $+ 20 = 50 + $ _____

 $+ 20 - 20 = $ _____ $- $ _____

 $= $ _____   **Check:** _____ $+ 20 = 60$

The weight of is _____ grams.

⑥

To solve this multiplication equation, divide both sides by 2 to undo the multiplication.

 x 2 = _____ + _____

 x 2 ÷ 2 = _____ ÷ 2

 = _____

Check: _____ x 2 = 70

The weight of is _____ grams.

Solve these equations and check the answers.

⑦ $x + 3 = 12$

$x + 3 -$ _____ $= 12 -$ _____

$x =$ _____

Check : _____ + 3 = 12

Substitute the answer for the letter. If two sides of the equation are equal, the answer is correct.

⑧ $7 × n = 28$

$7 × n ÷$ _____ $= 28 ÷$ _____

$n =$ _____

Check : 7 x _____ = _____

⑨ $m ÷ 2 = 9$

$m ÷ 2 ×$ _____ $= 9 ×$ _____

$m =$ _____

Check : _____ ÷ 2 = _____

⑩ $p - 9 = 26$

$p - 9 +$ _____ $= 26 +$ _____

$p =$ _____

Check : _____ − 9 = _____

⑪ $q × 5 = 35$

$q × 5 ÷$ _____ $= 35 ÷$ _____

$q =$ _____

Check : _____ x 5 = _____

See how Dave set up the equations. Then use his equations to complete the tables.

In my birthday party, I have 2 sandwiches for each guest.

Number of guests

Equation : $(n) \times 2$ = Total number of sandwiches

Number of sandwiches	Equation	Number of guests (n)
6	$n \times 2 = 6$	(3)
⑫ 10		
⑬ 14		
⑭ 18		
⑮ 36		

You can use this equation to find the number of guests in my party.

$n \times 2 = 6$

$n \times 2 \div 2 = 6 \div 2$

$(n = 3)$

Each box holds 6 cupcakes.

Total number of cupcakes

Equation : $(m) \div 6$ = Number of boxes

Number of boxes	Equation	Number of cupcakes (m)
3	$m \div 6 = 3$	(18)
⑯ 4		
⑰ 6		
⑱ 8		
⑲ 9		

You can use this equation to find the number of cupcakes I have.

$m \div 6 = 3$

$m \div 6 \times 6 = 3 \times 6$

$(m = 18)$

Complete the equation for each problem. Then solve the equations and check the answers.

⑳ There were m guests at Dave's party. For a game, he divided his guests into 3 groups, with 5 guests in each group. How many guests were there?

$$m \div \underline{\hspace{1cm}} = \underline{\hspace{1cm}}$$

$$m \div \underline{\hspace{1cm}} \times \underline{\hspace{1cm}} = \underline{\hspace{1cm}} \times \underline{\hspace{1cm}}$$

$$m = \underline{\hspace{1cm}}$$

Check : $\underline{\hspace{1cm}} \div \underline{\hspace{1cm}} = \underline{\hspace{1cm}}$

There were _____ guests.

㉑ There was p quart of juice in the bottle. Dave drank 0.5 quart leaving 0.125 quart behind. How much juice was in the bottle at the beginning?

$$p - \underline{\hspace{1cm}} = \underline{\hspace{1cm}}$$

$$p - \underline{\hspace{1cm}} + \underline{\hspace{1cm}} = \underline{\hspace{1cm}} + \underline{\hspace{1cm}}$$

$$p = \underline{\hspace{1cm}}$$

Check : $\underline{\hspace{1cm}} - \underline{\hspace{1cm}} = \underline{\hspace{1cm}}$

There was _____ quart of juice.

ACTIVITY

Check ✔ the children who wrote the equivalent equations.

A
| $x + 5 = 14$ |
| $5 + x = 14$ |

B
| $p \div 6 = 4$ |
| $6 \div p = 4$ |

C
| $y - 10 = 5$ |
| $10 - y = 5$ |

D
| $q \times 2 = 8$ |
| $2 \times q = 8$ |

Time

WORD TO LEARN

Duration - how long an event lasts

e.g. $\frac{1}{2}$ hour or 30 minutes

Complete Dave's schedule.

Dave's schedule			Duration		
Breakfast	SAT	①	$\frac{1}{2}$ h	=	___ min
	SUN	②	20 min	=	___ h
Swimming	SAT	③	$1\frac{1}{2}$ h	=	___ min
	SUN	④	95 min	=	___ h ___ min
Lunch	SAT	⑤	1 h 40 min	=	___ min
	SUN	⑥	105 min	=	___ h ___ min
Baseball	SAT	⑦	1 h 50 min	=	___ min
	SUN	⑧	135 min	=	___ h ___ min
Dinner	SAT	⑨	1 h 5 min	=	___ min
	SUN	⑩	85 min	=	___ h ___ min

$\frac{1}{4}$ h = $\frac{1}{4}$ × 60 min

= 15 min

65 min = 60 min + 5 min

= 1 h 5 min

Convert hours to minutes
Multiply each hour by 60.

Convert minutes to hours
Divide the minutes by 60; leave the remainder as minutes.

Follow Dave's method to solve the problems.

Addition	**Subtraction**
1st Add the minutes.	**1st** Subtract the minutes.
2nd Trade every 60 minutes (1 hour) to the hours.	**2nd** If you can't take away the minutes, trade 1 hour (60 minutes) to the minutes.
3rd Add the hours.	**3rd** Subtract the hours.

Addition:
```
   1
  4 h 25 min
+ 2 h 55 min
-----------
  7 h 20 min
```

Subtraction:
```
   3   8 5
  4 h 25 min
- 2 h 55 min
-----------
  1 h 30 min
```

⑪ 3 h 40 min
+   30 min
_____
    h   min
	⑫ 8 h 12 min
	− 5 h 49 min
	_____
	    h min
		⑬ 4 h 30 min
		− 3 h 50 min
		_____
		    h min

⑭ 2 h 53 min after 6:17 a.m.   _____ a.m.

⑮ 9 h 13 min before 12:00 noon   _____ a.m.

⑯ 4 h 44 min after 2:16 p.m.   _____ p.m.

Read what Uncle Ray says and answer the questions.

⑰

> The ball game lasted 1 hour 5 minutes. It ended at 5:00 p.m. What time did it start?

_____ = _____

It started at _____ p.m.

⑱

> My favorite TV program starts at 7:30 p.m. and ends at 9:15 p.m. How long does it last?

_____ = _____

Uncle Ray's favorite program lasts _____ hour (s)

_____minutes.

 𝒜𝒞𝒯ℐ𝒱ℐ𝒯𝒴

Help Dave write the times.

		Start	End	Duration
1.	Swimming Class	9:35 a.m.	10:10 a.m.	
2.	Hockey Class	12:05 p.m.		45 min
3.	Baseball Class		4:55 p.m.	1 h 10 min

7 Area

Area - the number of square units of a surface

e.g.

1 in

1 in ☐ ← Area = 1 in²

1 m

1 m ☐ ← Area = 1 m²

Height - the shortest distance from top to bottom of an object or a shape

Base - the length of the bottom edge

Count the squares for each shape to complete the table.

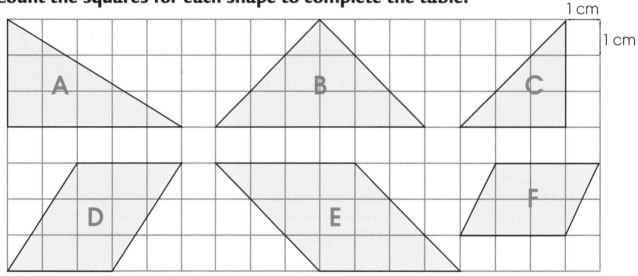

1 cm

1 cm

	Height (cm)	Base (cm)	Area (cm²)
① Triangle A	3		
② Triangle B		6	
③ Triangle C			
④ Parallelogram D	3		
⑤ Parallelogram E		4	
⑥ Parallelogram F			

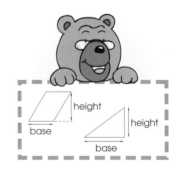

Count the fully covered squares first. Then combine the partly covered squares to make whole squares.

Read what Dave says. Then help him find the base, height, and area of each parallelogram.

I can make a rectangle from a parallelogram by cutting out a triangle and put it on the other side.

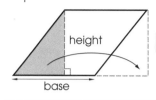

Area of a parallelogram = Area of a rectangle
= base X height

---

⑦
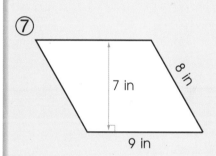
7 in
8 in
9 in

Base = _____ in

Height = _____ in

Area = _____ in²

⑧
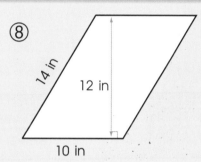
14 in
12 in
10 in

Base = _____ in

Height = _____ in

Area = _____ in²

b = base, h = height

⑨
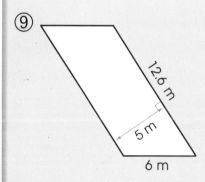
12.6 m
5 m
6 m

Base = _____ m

Height = _____ m

Area = _____ m²

⑩
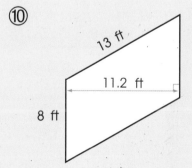
13 ft
11.2 ft
8 ft

Base = _____ ft

Height = _____ ft

Area = _____ ft²

⑪
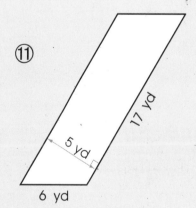
17 yd
5 yd
6 yd

Base = _____ yd

Height = _____ yd

Area = _____ yd²

Follow Steve's method to find the base, height, and area of each triangle.

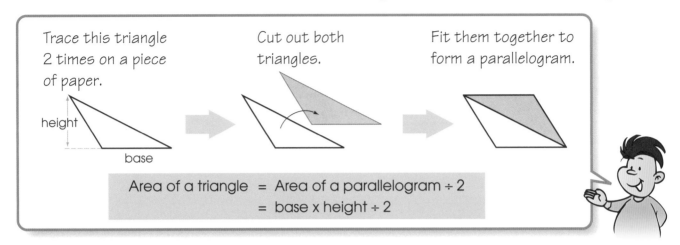

Trace this triangle 2 times on a piece of paper.

height

base

Cut out both triangles.

Fit them together to form a parallelogram.

Area of a triangle = Area of a parallelogram ÷ 2
= base x height ÷ 2

⑫

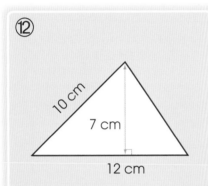

10 cm

7 cm

12 cm

Base   = _____ cm

Height = _____ cm

Area   = _____ cm²

⑬

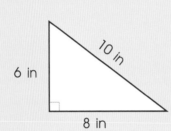

10 in

6 in

8 in

Base   = _____ in

Height = _____ in

Area   = _____ in²

b = base, h = height

⑭

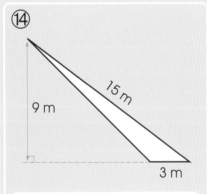

9 m

15 m

3 m

Base   = _____ m

Height = _____ m

Area   = _____ m²

⑮

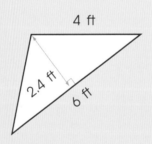

4 ft

2.4 ft

6 ft

Base   = _____ ft

Height = _____ ft

Area   = _____ ft²

⑯

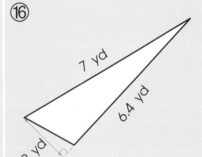

7 yd

6.4 yd

2 yd

Base   = _____ yd

Height = _____ yd

Area   = _____ yd²

Find the area of the shapes.

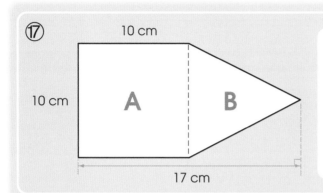

⑰

10 cm

10 cm

A   **B**

17 cm

Area of A   = _____ cm²

Area of B   = _____ cm²

Area of (A + B) = _____ cm²

⑱

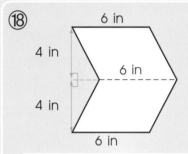

6 in

4 in

6 in

4 in

6 in

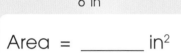

Area = _____ in²

⑲

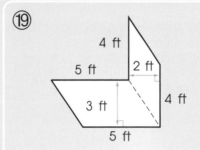

4 ft

5 ft   2 ft

3 ft   4 ft

5 ft

Area = _____ ft²

Cut the shapes into squares, triangles, parallelograms, etc. Then add up the areas.

⑳

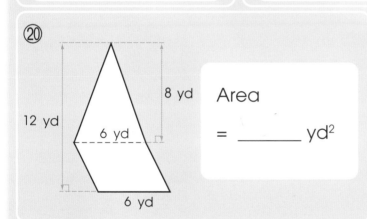

8 yd

12 yd

6 yd

6 yd

Area

= _____ yd²

㉑

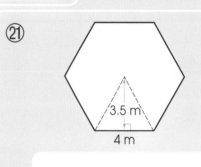

3.5 m

4 m

Area = _____ m²

ACTIVITY

Find the area of the colored parts. Each ☐ = 1 cm².

1.

Area

= _____ cm²

2.

Area

= _____ cm²

Directions

Direction - a point toward which a person or thing looks or faces

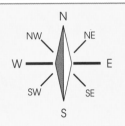

Look at the map and write north, east, south, or west.

Steve's house 		Bank	School

N

Albert Street

| Dave's house  | Hospital  | Restaurant | Church  |

1st Street   2nd Street   3rd Street   4th Street

Victoria Street

Playground   Cinema   Shopping Mall

My house is to the north of the playground.

① Dave's house is to the _____ of Steve's house.

② The hospital is to the _____ of the restaurant.

③ The bank is to the _____ of the shopping mall.

④ The cinema is to the _____ of the playground.

⑤ If Dave wants to go to school from his house, he needs to go 1 block

north and 2 blocks _____ .

⑥ If Dave wants to go to the cinema from the bank, he needs to go

2 blocks _____ and 1 block _____ .

Look at the map on p.100 again and use Uncle Ray's direction board to answer the questions.

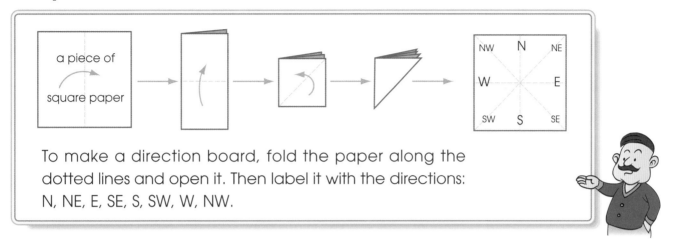

To make a direction board, fold the paper along the dotted lines and open it. Then label it with the directions: N, NE, E, SE, S, SW, W, NW.

⑦ The church is to the _____ of the shopping mall.

⑧ The cinema is to the _____ of Dave's house.

⑨ The restaurant is to the _____ of the school.

⑩ Steve's house is to the _____ of the hospital.

⑪ The playground is to the _____ of the bank.

⑫ The hospital is to the _____ of the shopping mall.

NE : north-east
NW : north-west
SE : south-east
SW : south-west

ACTIVITY

Follow Dave's instruction to draw this shape ⊠ without taking your pencil off the paper.

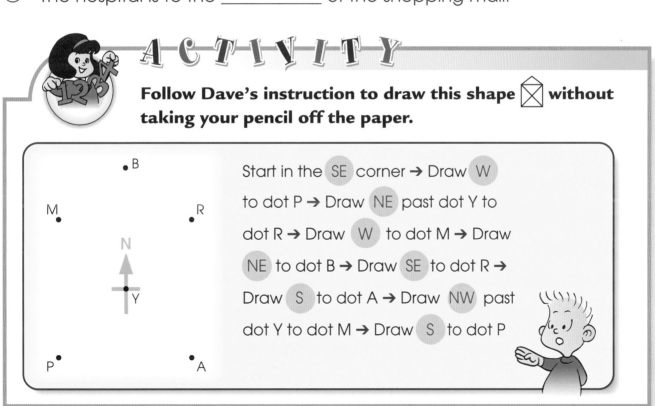

Start in the SE corner → Draw W to dot P → Draw NE past dot Y to dot R → Draw W to dot M → Draw NE to dot B → Draw SE to dot R → Draw S to dot A → Draw NW past dot Y to dot M → Draw S to dot P

Graphs

Bar graph -	a graph using bars to show information
Line graph -	a graph using points and lines to show information

The table shows the profits of ABC Center last week. Complete the table and use the rounded figures to complete the bar graph.

①	SUN	MON	TUE	WED	THU	FRI	SAT
Profit ($)	4,372	2,139	1,426	2,547	2,982	3,759	5,236
Rounded to the nearest thousand	4,000						

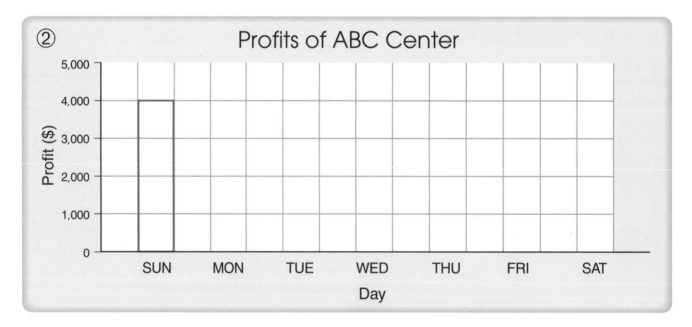

② Profits of ABC Center

Read the bar graph and answer the questions.

③ On which day did ABC Center have the highest profit? _____

④ On which day did ABC Center have the lowest profit? _____

⑤ About how many times more profit was there on

Sunday than on Monday? _____ times

Study the line graph and answer the questions.

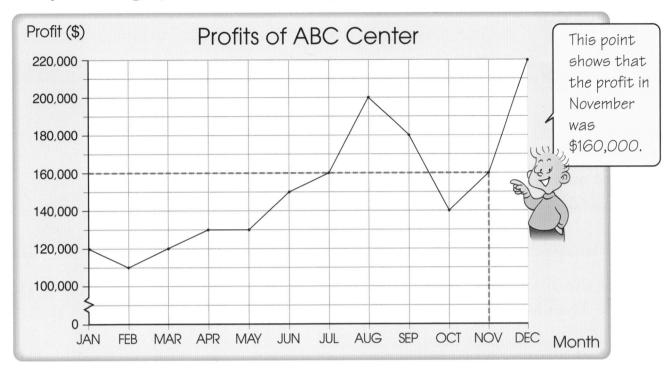

Profit ($) — Profits of ABC Center

This point shows that the profit in November was $160,000.

⑥ In which month did the profit reach $200,000? _____

⑦ In how many months was the profit over $170,000? _____

⑧ What was the difference in profits between July

and March? $ _____

⑨ About how many times more profit was there in

December than in February? _____ times

ACTIVITY

Read the table and help Dave complete the vertical and horizontal scales of the line graph.

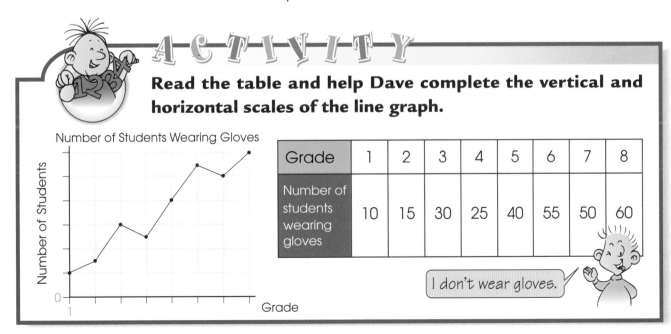

Number of Students Wearing Gloves

Grade	1	2	3	4	5	6	7	8
Number of students wearing gloves	10	15	30	25	40	55	50	60

I don't wear gloves.

 **Factorization**

WORDS TO LEARN

Factor	-	a number that can divide a larger number exactly
Composite number	-	any number that has more than 2 factors
Prime number	-	any number with only 1 and itself as factors
Prime factor	-	a factor that is a prime number

Look at the 10-column board. Put a cross (x) on every multiple of 2, 3, 5, 7, 11, and 13. Then answer the question.

①

101	1̶0̶2̶	103	1̶0̶4̶	1̶0̶5̶	1̶0̶6̶	107	1̶0̶8̶	109	1̶1̶0̶
1̶1̶1̶	1̶1̶2̶	113	114	115	116	117	118	119	120
121	122	123	124	125	126	127	128	129	130
131	132	133	134	135	136	137	138	139	140
141	142	143	144	145	146	147	148	149	150
151	152	153	154	155	156	157	158	159	160
161	162	163	164	165	166	167	168	169	170
171	172	173	174	175	176	177	178	179	180
181	182	183	184	185	186	187	188	189	190
191	192	193	194	195	196	197	198	199	200

All multiples of 2 end in 2, 4, 6, 8, or 0.
All multiples of 5 end in 5 or 0.

All multiples of 3 have digits that add to a multiple of 3.

② Which is the largest prime number up to 200? _____

Write prime or composite for each number.

③ 67 _____   ④ 85 _____   ⑤ 71 _____

⑥ 326 _____   ⑦ 213 _____   ⑧ 367 _____

Follow Dave's method to write each number as a product of prime factors.

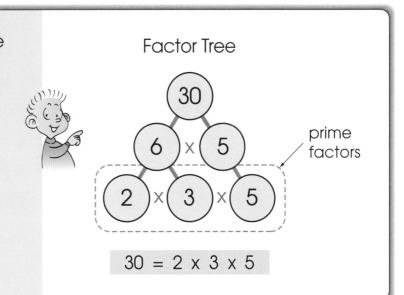

1st Write the number as the product of two factors.

2nd Continue to factorize each composite number until all factors are prime numbers.

3rd Write the number as a product of prime numbers.

Factor Tree

prime factors

$30 = 2 \times 3 \times 5$

⑨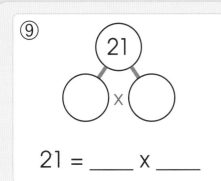

21 = ____ X ____

⑩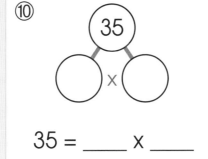

35 = ____ X ____

The number 1 is not used in factor trees.

⑪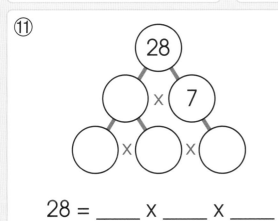

28 = ____ X ____ X ____

⑫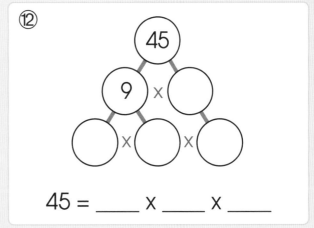

45 = ____ X ____ X ____

Write each number as a product of prime factors.

⑬ 36 = _____

⑭ 54 = _____

⑮ 64 = _____

⑯ 72 = _____

Follow Dave's method to find the GCF of the following numbers.

Find the GCF of 16 and 20.

16 = 2 x 2 x 2 x 2

20 = 2 x 2 x 5

Common prime factors : 2 , 2

GCF = 2 x 2 = 4

Steps to find GCF:

1st Write each number as a product of prime factors.

2nd Multiply all prime factors common to both numbers.

⑰ 26 = ___ X ___

39 = ___ X ___

Common prime factor : _____

GCF = ___

⑱ 30 = ___ X ___ X ___

45 = ___ X ___ X ___

Common prime factors : ___ , ___

GCF = ___ X ___ = ___

⑲ 28 = ___ X ___ X ___

42 = ___ X ___ X ___

Common prime factors : ___ , ___

GCF = ___ X ___ = ___

⑳ 50 = ___ X ___ X ___

75 = ___ X ___ X ___

Common prime factors : ___ , ___

GCF = ___ X ___ = ___

Find the GCF.

㉑ 12 and 20 _____

㉒ 18 and 30 _____

㉓ 80 and 100 _____

㉔ 56 and 64 _____

Follow Steve's method to find the LCM of the following numbers.

Find the LCM of 16 and 20.

16 = 2 x 2 x 2 x 2

20 = 2 x 2   x 5

LCM = 2 x 2 x 2 x 2 x 5

= 80

Steps to find LCM:

1st Write each number as a product of prime factors.

2nd Sort out the prime factors common to both numbers and multiply them by all other factors on the list.

㉕ 12 = ____ X ____ X ____

18 = ____ X ____ X ____

LCM

= ____ X ____ X ____ X ____

= ____

㉖ 15 = ____ X ____

21 = ____ X ____

LCM

= ____ X ____ X ____

= ____

Find the LCM.

㉗ 10 and 15 _____

㉘ 9 and 24 _____

㉙ 16 and 24 _____

㉚ 8 and 20 _____

Solve the riddles.

1. It is a 3-digit prime number under 200. The 2nd and 3rd digits are the same and greater than 4. What number is it?

2. It is a 3-digit prime number under 200. The difference between the 2nd digit and the 3rd digit is 9. What number is it?

Write the numbers in words. (4 marks)

① 20,681 _____

② 433,000 _____

Write the numbers in order from greatest to least. (4 marks)

③ 387,425 ; 378,425 ; 387,245 ; 378,245

_____

④ 941,756 ; 914,576 ; 941,576 ; 914,756

_____

Write the meaning of each underlined digit. (4 marks)

⑤ 4,5̲86,042 _____ ⑥ 1̲,732,469 _____

Check ✔ the right equations. (3 marks)

⑦ 6 more than a number n is 15.

☐ $6 \times n = 15$ ☐ $n - 6 = 15$ ☐ $n + 6 = 15$

⑧ 3 times a number m is 18.

☐ $m = 18 \times 3$ ☐ $3 \times m = 18$ ☐ $18 \times m = 3$

⑨ 5 less than a number k is 9.

☐ $5 - k = 9$ ☐ $k - 5 = 9$ ☐ $k = 9 - 5$

Solve the equations. (4 marks)

⑩ $y + 2 = 21$

$y = $ ____

⑪ $m - 6 = 5$

$m = $ ____

⑫ $4 \times n = 24$

$n = $ ____

⑬ $p \div 9 = 3$

$p = $ ____

Complete the table and use the rounded figures to complete the bar graph. (8 marks)

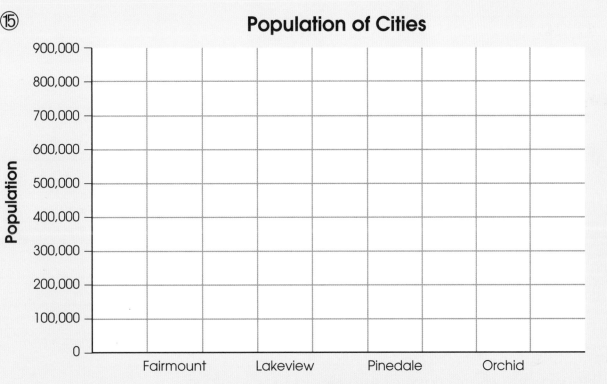

⑭

City	Fairmount	Lakeview	Pinedale	Orchid
Population	680,462	886,217	275,176	239,421
Rounded to the nearest hundred thousand				

⑮

Population of Cities

Population

900,000
800,000
700,000
600,000
500,000
400,000
300,000
200,000
100,000
0

Fairmount   Lakeview   Pinedale   Orchid

City

Read the graph and answer the questions. (10 marks)

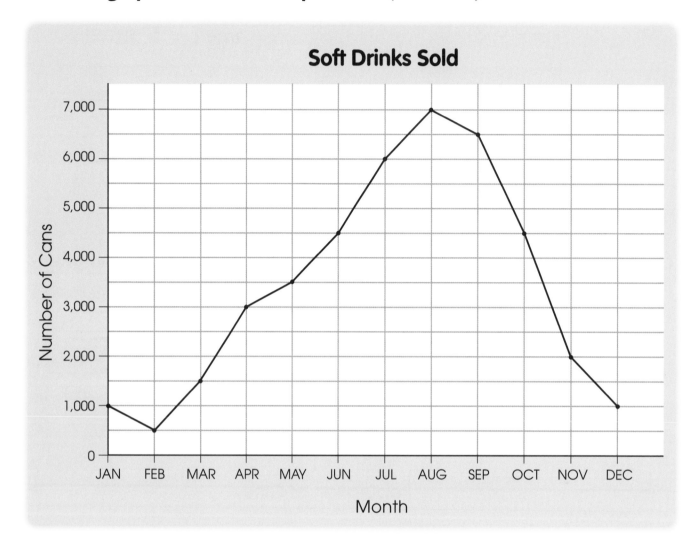

⑯ How many cans of soft drinks were sold in March? _____ cans

⑰ In which month were 7,000 cans sold? _____

⑱ How many cans of soft drinks were sold in February and September? _____ cans

⑲ How many cans of soft drinks were sold in May and December? _____ cans

⑳ How many more cans of soft drinks were sold in October than April? _____ cans

Find the area of each shape. (12 marks)

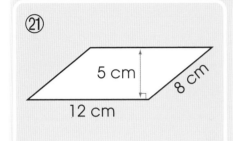

㉑

Area = _____ cm²

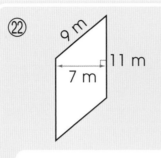

㉒

Area = _____ m²

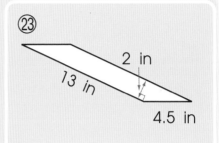

㉓

Area = _____ in²

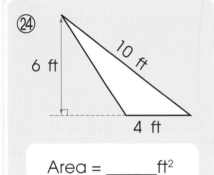

㉔

Area = _____ ft²

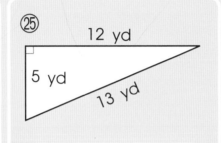

㉕

Area = _____ yd²

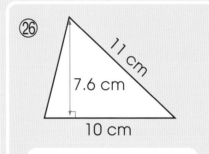

㉖

Area = _____ cm²

Write the answers in simplest form. (20 marks)

㉗ $8 \times \dfrac{2}{3} =$ _____

㉘ $\dfrac{1}{2} \times \dfrac{4}{7} =$ _____

㉙ $7 \div \dfrac{1}{2} =$ _____

㉚ $\dfrac{2}{3} \div \dfrac{1}{6} =$ _____

㉛ $6 \times \dfrac{1}{4} =$ _____

㉜ $\dfrac{3}{5} \times 1\dfrac{2}{3} =$ _____

㉝ $\dfrac{8}{9} \times \dfrac{3}{4} =$ _____

㉞ $\dfrac{5}{8} \div 10 =$ _____

㉟ $1\dfrac{1}{3} \times \dfrac{3}{8} =$ _____

㊱ $\dfrac{6}{7} \div 1\dfrac{5}{7} =$ _____

Write each number as a product of prime factors. Then find the GCF of each pair of numbers. (12 marks)

㊲ 42 = _____

72 = _____

GCF = _____

㊳ 16 = _____

24 = _____

GCF = _____

㊴ 15 = _____

45 = _____

GCF = _____

㊵ 20 = _____

32 = _____

GCF = _____

Write each number as a product of prime factors. Then find the LCM of each pair of numbers. (12 marks)

㊶ 28 = _____

35 = _____

LCM = _____

㊷ 18 = _____

20 = _____

LCM = _____

㊸ 24 = _____

36 = _____

LCM = _____

㊹ 30 = _____

40 = _____

LCM = _____

Read Dave's map. Then fill in the blanks and answer the questions. (7 marks)

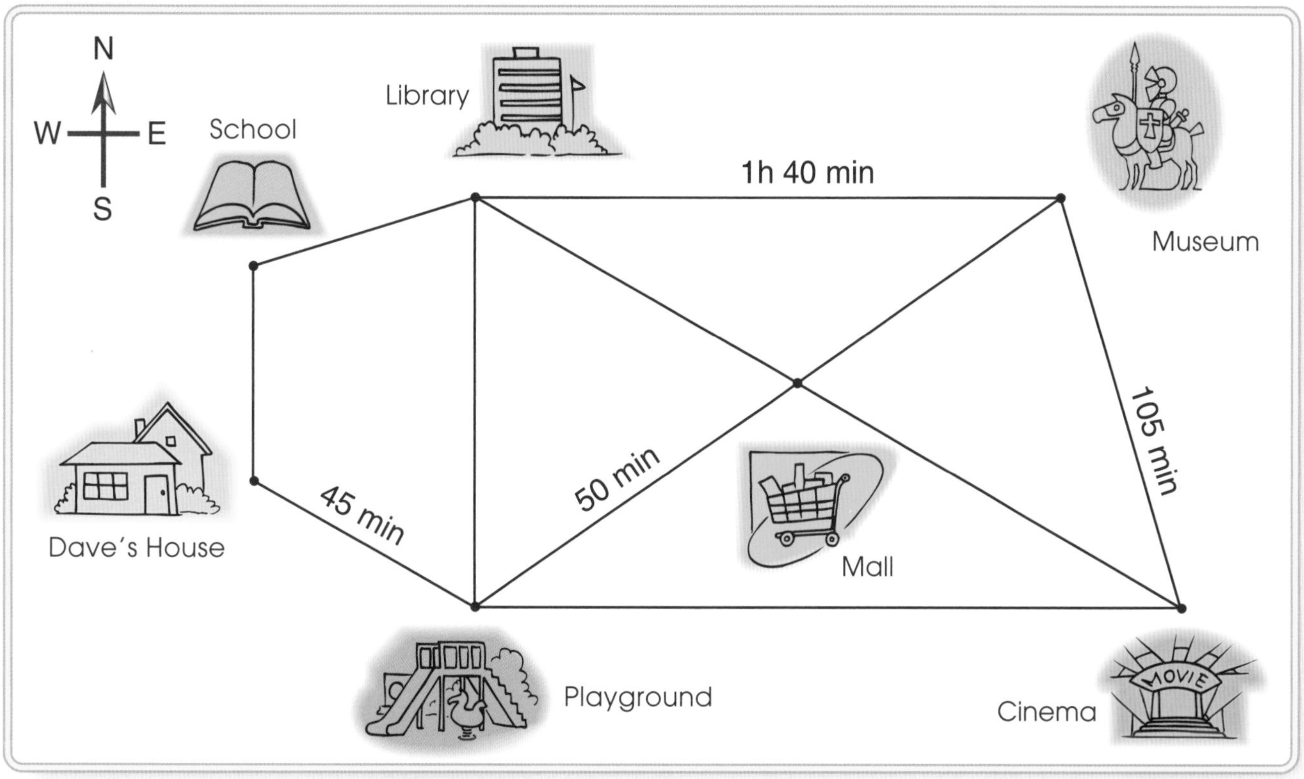
N
W
E
S
Library
School
1h 40 min
Museum
Dave's House
45 min
50 min
105 min
Mall
Playground
Cinema
MOVIE

㊺ The museum is to the ____________ of the mall.

㊻ The playground is to the ____________ of the library.

㊼ The playground is to the ____________ of the mall.

㊽ Where would Dave be if he traveled NW from the mall? ____________

㊾ How many minutes did it take Dave to travel from the library to the museum? _____ minutes

㊿ How long did it take Dave to travel from home to the mall passing the playground? _____ hour (s) _____ minutes

(51) If Dave left the museum at 9:25 a.m., when did he reach the cinema? __________ a.m.

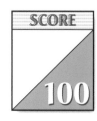

SCORE

100

Inverse Proportion

Increase	-	becoming greater in size, number, or degree
Decrease	-	becoming smaller in size, number, or degree
Inverse proportion	-	the relation of two variables with one increasing and the other decreasing

Today is my birthday. I've got some candies for my friends. If only 2 of my friends come, I can give each of them 12 candies. But if 4 of my friends come, how many candies can each one get?

1st ▶ Find the number of candies that Dave has.

12 x 2 = 24

Dave has 24 candies.

2nd ▶ Divide the number of candies by the number of friends.

24 ÷ 4 = 6

Each friend gets 6 candies.

Help Dave solve the problems. Complete the table.

	No. of friends coming	Total no. of candies	No. of candies each friend can get
①	2		24 ÷ 2 =
②	3		=
③	4	12 x 2 = 24	=
④	6		=
⑤	8		=
⑥	12		=

The more friends that come to my party, the fewer candies each one will get. This is inverse proportion.

My friends will come to help me make the sandwiches. 3 people will take 60 minutes to finish the work.

Help Dave find the answers.

⑦ How long will it take 6 people to finish the work?

_____ X _____ ÷ _____ = _____

It will take them _____ minutes.

⑧ How long will it take 9 people to finish the work?

_____ X _____ ÷ _____ = _____

It will take them _____ minutes.

First, find the time needed for 1 person to finish the work.

48 of my friends have come to my party. I want to group them with the same number of people in each group.

How does Dave group his friends? Fill in the table.

⑨

No. of groups	2	3	4			
No. of people in each group				8	6	4

ACTIVITY

Write the number of glasses or mugs needed.

I want to pour this jar of juice into different kinds of mugs or glasses.

3 L

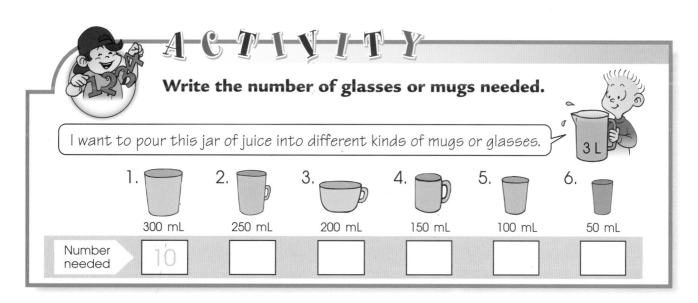

	1.	2.	3.	4.	5.	6.
	300 mL	250 mL	200 mL	150 mL	100 mL	50 mL
Number needed	10					

Decimals and Fractions

Place value of decimal numbers –

Thousands Hundreds Tens Ones Tenths Hundredths Thousandths

1,2 3 4 . 5 6 7

Decimal point

Equivalent Fractions – fractions that have the same value

e.g. $\frac{1}{2}$ and $\frac{2}{4}$ are equivalent fractions.

Numerator – the top number in a fraction   e.g. $\frac{4}{5}$ — numerator, denominator

Denominator – the bottom number in a fraction

My brother, Tony, is a marathon runner.

Read how far Tony runs. Write the answers as decimal numbers.

① 16 and 25 hundredths of a kilometer | kilometers

② 14 and 62 thousandths of a kilometer | kilometers

③ 15 and 2 tenths of a kilometer | kilometers

④ 13 and 424 thousandths of a kilometer | kilometers

⑤ 17 and 7 hundredths of a kilometer | kilometers

Write the meaning of each underlined digit.

⑥ 14.3<u>3</u>4

⑦ 1.37<u>5</u>

⑧ 16.01<u>6</u>

⑨ <u>1</u>1.52

There is another way to write my records.

$$15.2 = 15\frac{2}{10}$$
$$= 15\frac{2 \div 2}{10 \div 2}$$
$$= 15\frac{1}{5}$$

$$15.2 \text{ km} = 15\frac{1}{5} \text{ km}$$

$$16.25 = 16\frac{25}{100}$$
$$= 16\frac{25 \div 25}{100 \div 25}$$
$$= 16\frac{1}{4}$$

$$16.25 \text{ km} = 16\frac{1}{4} \text{ km}$$

$$13.424 = 13\frac{424}{1,000}$$
$$= 13\frac{424 \div 8}{1,000 \div 8}$$
$$= 13\frac{53}{125}$$

$$13.424 \text{ km} = 13\frac{53}{125} \text{ km}$$

Change the decimals to fractions in simplest form.

⑩ 16.3 = ☐

⑪ 18.2 = ☐

⑫ 19.4 = ☐

⑬ 13.16 = ☐

⑭ 13.75 = ☐

⑮ 18.02 = ☐

⑯ 18.025 = ☐

⑰ 14.866 = ☐

⑱ 9.105 = ☐

Tony has run $\frac{3}{4}$ kilometer. It is equal to 0.75 kilometer.

1st ▶ Find a fraction equivalent to $\frac{3}{4}$ with a denominator of 10, 100, or 1,000, e.g.

$$\frac{3}{4} = \frac{3 \times 25}{4 \times 25} = \frac{75}{100}$$

2nd ▶ Write as a decimal number.

$$\frac{75}{100} = 0.75$$

Find an equivalent fraction with denominator of 10, 100, or 1,000. Then write as a decimal number.

⑲ $\frac{1}{4}$ = $\frac{}{100}$ = ☐

⑳ $\frac{6}{50}$ = $\frac{}{100}$ = ☐

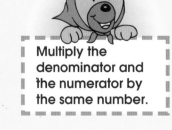

Multiply the denominator and the numerator by the same number.

117

㉑ $\dfrac{5}{8}$ = ☐

㉒ $\dfrac{7}{20}$ = ☐

㉓ $\dfrac{9}{25}$ = ☐

㉔ $1\dfrac{1}{5}$ = ☐

㉕ $2\dfrac{6}{40}$ = ☐

㉖ $12\dfrac{24}{125}$ = ☐

Change fractions into decimals:
Divide the numerator by the denominator;
add zeros to the dividend when necessary.

Example $\dfrac{3}{7}$ = 0.43 (rounded to the nearest hundredth)

$$\begin{array}{r} 0.4\,2\,8 \\ 7\,\overline{)\,3.0\,0\,0} \\ 2\,8 \\ \hline 2\,0 \\ 1\,4 \\ \hline 6\,0 \\ 5\,6 \\ \hline 4 \end{array}$$

round up
0.42 0.43
0.428

Change all the signs on Tony's running course into decimals. Round to the nearest hundredth.

㉗
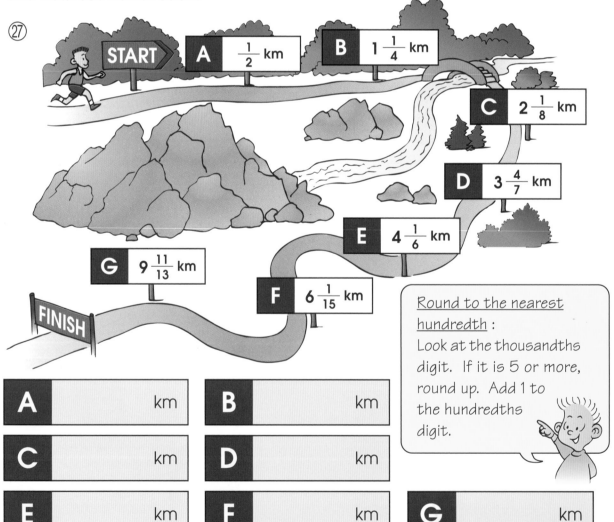

START

A $\dfrac{1}{2}$ km

B $1\dfrac{1}{4}$ km

C $2\dfrac{1}{8}$ km

D $3\dfrac{4}{7}$ km

E $4\dfrac{1}{6}$ km

G $9\dfrac{11}{13}$ km

F $6\dfrac{1}{15}$ km

FINISH

Round to the nearest hundredth :
Look at the thousandths digit. If it is 5 or more, round up. Add 1 to the hundredths digit.

A ☐ km

B ☐ km

C ☐ km

D ☐ km

E ☐ km

F ☐ km

G ☐ km

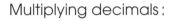

Multiplying decimals :

Example   0.25 x 0.5 = 0.125

$$
\begin{array}{r}
0.2\,5 \\
\times \qquad 0.5 \\
\hline
0.1\,2\,5
\end{array}
$$

0.25 — 2 decimal places

0.5 — 1 decimal place

0.125 — 2 + 1 = 3 3 decimal places

1st Align the right-hand digits.

2nd Multiply as with whole numbers.

3rd Count the number of decimal places in the question.

4th Place the decimal point in the product.

Put the decimal points in the products correctly.

㉘	㉙	㉚	㉛
1.6	2.1	0.9 3	1.5 0
x 1.3	x 3.0	x 1.2	x 0.8 1
2 0 8	6 3 0	1 1 1 6	1 2 1 5 0

Find the answers.

㉜	㉝	㉞
1 . 3	3 . 0 6	0 . 0 6
x 1 . 9	x 1 . 4	x 0.1 2

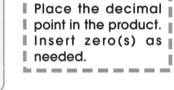

Place the decimal point in the product. Insert zero(s) as needed.

㉟   0.62 x 1.40 = _____

㊱   4.8 x 0.31 = _____

㊲   2.5 x 0.3 = _____

㊳   1.62 x 1.30 = _____

㊴   1.2 x 1.03 = _____

㊵   1.45 x 0.42 = _____

119

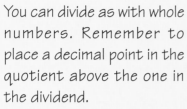

You can divide as with whole numbers. Remember to place a decimal point in the quotient above the one in the dividend.

To divide 2.85 by 5, follow these steps:

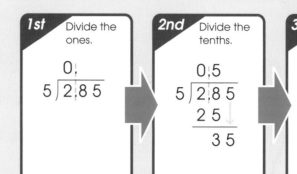

Try these.

㊶
$$6 \overline{)8.82}$$
8
2
_____

㊷
$$18 \overline{)1.998}$$
9
8
_____

㊸
$$7 \overline{)14.91}$$
9
1
_____

㊹
$$12 \overline{)5.52}$$

㊺
$$8 \overline{)27.76}$$

㊻
$$9 \overline{)32.85}$$

㊼ $38.57 \div 7 =$ _____

㊽ $17.08 \div 14 =$ _____

㊾ $4.95 \div 11 =$ _____

㊿ $24.48 \div 18 =$ _____

(51) 2.55 ÷ 3 = ________

(52) 16.45 ÷ 5 = ________

(53) 10.92 ÷ 4 = ________

(54) 74.64 ÷ 6 = ________

(55) 50.24 ÷ 16 = ________

Don't forget to put a decimal point in the quotient above the one in the dividend.

Find the answers.

(56) Tony bought 7 sandwiches for $18.13. How much did each sandwich cost?

18.13 ÷ 7 = ______ Each sandwich cost $ ______ .

(57) If candy bars are 6 for $3.78, how much is one candy bar?

______ ÷ ______ = ______ One candy bar is $ ______ .

(58) Tony shared $8.62 with Dave. How much did each person get?

______ ÷ ______ = ______ Each person got $ ______ .

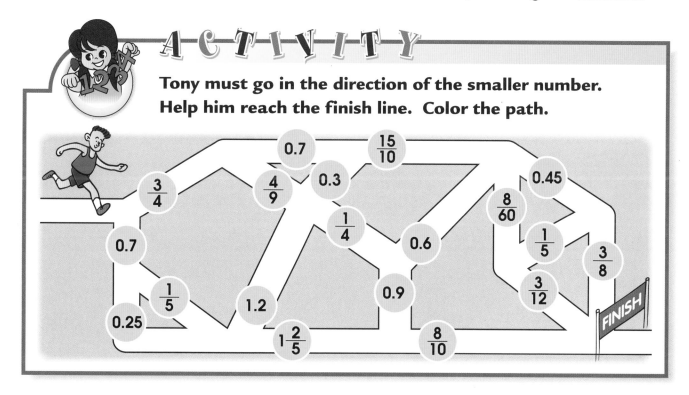

ACTIVITY

Tony must go in the direction of the smaller number. Help him reach the finish line. Color the path.

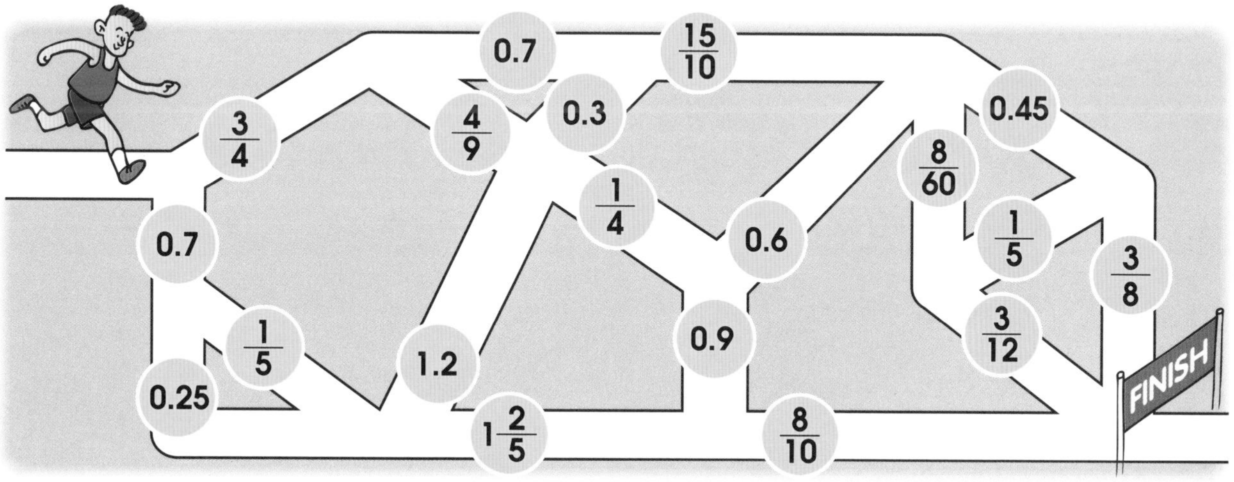

More about Simple Equations

Equation - a mathematical sentence with an equal sign

e.g. $9 + 7 = 16$ $2y + 5 = 12$

Read what Dave says. Then help him solve the equations.

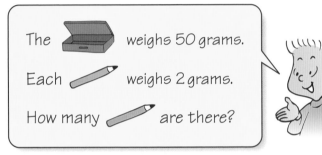

The ▭ weighs 50 grams.

Each ✏ weighs 2 grams.

How many ✏ are there?

① $50 + 2 \times k = 90$

k = number of

$50 + 2 \times k - \underline{} = 90 - \underline{}$

$2 \times k = \underline{}$

$2 \times k \div \underline{} = \underline{} \div \underline{}$

$k = \underline{}$

There are $\underline{}$ ✏ in the box.

To solve an equation, undo addition or subtraction first.

Try these.

② $3 \times p + 12 = 48$

$3 \times p + 12 - \underline{} = 48 - \underline{}$

$3 \times p = \underline{}$

$3 \times p \div \underline{} = \underline{} \div \underline{}$

$p = \underline{}$

③ $9 \times q - 16 = 29$

$9 \times q - 16 + \underline{} = 29 + \underline{}$

$9 \times q = \underline{}$

$9 \times q \div \underline{} = \underline{} \div \underline{}$

$q = \underline{}$

④ $m \div 4 + 13 = 19$

$m \div 4 + 13 - \underline{\quad} = 19 - \underline{\quad}$

$m \div 4 = \underline{\quad}$

$m \div 4 \times \underline{\quad} = \underline{\quad} \times \underline{\quad}$

$m = \underline{\quad}$

⑤ $n \div 5 - 12 = 8$

$n \div 5 - 12 + \underline{\quad} = 8 + \underline{\quad}$

$n \div 5 = \underline{\quad}$

$n \div 5 \times \underline{\quad} = \underline{\quad} \times \underline{\quad}$

$n = \underline{\quad}$

Write and solve the equations.

⑥

The difference between $2y$ and 9 is 3.

$2y - \boxed{} = \boxed{}$ $\qquad y = \boxed{}$

⑦

$4m$ divided by 2 is 6.

$\underline{\quad} \div \boxed{} = \boxed{}$ $\qquad m = \boxed{}$

⑧

The sum of $2p$ and 5 is 7.

$\underline{\quad} + \boxed{} = \boxed{}$ $\qquad p = \boxed{}$

ACTIVITY

Help Dave find the weights of his toys.

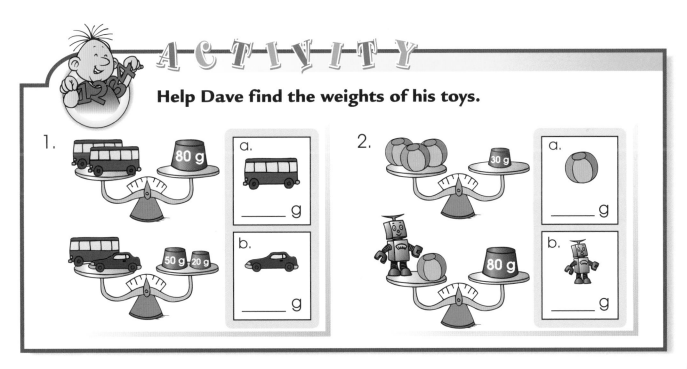

1.
a. _____ g
b. _____ g

2.
a. _____ g
b. _____ g

 **Percents**

Percent (%) - means a part of 100 or "out of 100"

e.g. Dave got 86 out of 100 on his test. That means he got 86% on his test.

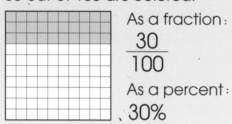

1 = 100%
30 out of 100 are colored.

As a fraction :
$$\frac{30}{100}$$

As a percent :
30%

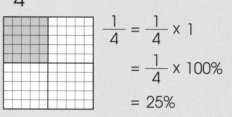

$\frac{1}{4}$ is colored.

$$\frac{1}{4} = \frac{1}{4} \times 1$$

$$= \frac{1}{4} \times 100\%$$

$$= 25\%$$

As a decimal : 0.25

Write the colored part of each 100-square as a fraction, a decimal, and a percent.

①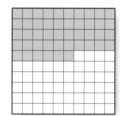

Fraction : _____

Decimal : _____

Percent : _____%

②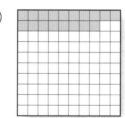

Fraction : _____

Decimal : _____

Percent : _____%

Rewrite as percents.

③ $\frac{13}{100}$ = _____ _____

④ $\frac{9}{100}$ = _____ _____

⑤ $\frac{8}{10}$ = _____ _____

⑥ $\frac{7}{20}$ = _____ _____

⑦ $\frac{3}{4}$ = _____ _____

⑧ $\frac{8}{25}$ = _____ _____

⑨ $\frac{1}{2}$ = _____ _____

Change the denominator to 100 first,
e.g. $\frac{1}{4} = \frac{1 \times 25}{4 \times 25} = \frac{25}{100} = 25\%$

Write as fractions in simplest form.

⑩ 38% = $\dfrac{}{}$ ⑪ 60% = $\dfrac{}{}$ ⑫ 8% = $\dfrac{}{}$

⑬ 4% = $\dfrac{}{}$ ⑭ 135% = $\dfrac{}{}$ ⑮ 285% = $\dfrac{}{}$

Steve got 8 out of 10 questions correct on his math test.
The grade he got is

$$\frac{8}{10} = \frac{80}{100} = 80\%$$

Math Test
Student: Steve $\dfrac{8}{10}$
1. ✔   6. ✔
2. ✔   7. ✔
3. ✔   8. ✔
4. ✘   9. ✔
5. ✔   10. ✘

Change to fractions with 100 as the denominator first.

Follow Dave's method to grade the children's tests.

⑯ **Science Test**
Student: Steve $\dfrac{20}{25}$

$$\frac{20}{25} = \frac{}{100}$$
$$= \boxed{}\ \%$$

⑰ **History Test**
Student: Helen $\dfrac{38}{50}$

$$\frac{38}{50} = \frac{}{}$$
$$= \boxed{}\ \%$$

⑱ **Geography Test**
Student: Elaine $\dfrac{14}{20}$

$$\frac{14}{20} = \frac{}{}$$
$$= \boxed{}\ \%$$

Check ✔ the correct answers and give a grade to Dave's math test.

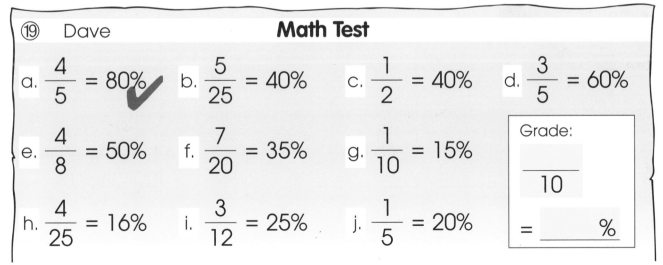

⑲ Dave   **Math Test**

a. $\dfrac{4}{5} = 80\%$ ✔   b. $\dfrac{5}{25} = 40\%$ c. $\dfrac{1}{2} = 40\%$ d. $\dfrac{3}{5} = 60\%$

e. $\dfrac{4}{8} = 50\%$ f. $\dfrac{7}{20} = 35\%$ g. $\dfrac{1}{10} = 15\%$

h. $\dfrac{4}{25} = 16\%$ i. $\dfrac{3}{12} = 25\%$ j. $\dfrac{1}{5} = 20\%$

Grade: $\dfrac{}{10}$ = %

Use the box graph to fill in the blanks.

GRADE 5 MATH CONTEST

Fractions of Students by Scores

| Over 80 marks |
| Between 60 and 80 marks |
| Under 60 marks |

⑳ _____ % of the students got marks between 60 and 80.

㉑ _____ % of the students got more than 80 marks.

㉒ _____ % of the students got less than 60 marks.

㉓ There were 100 students.

_____ students got more than 80 marks.

㉔ _____ students got marks between 60 and 80.

㉕ _____ students got less than 60 marks.

Decimals can be changed to percents.

Examples

$$0.5 = \frac{5}{10} = \frac{50}{100} = 50\%$$

$$1.25 = 1\frac{25}{100} = \frac{125}{100} = 125\%$$

1 equals 100%.

Complete the table.

㉖

Decimal	0.16			1.2	
Percent		45%			134%
Fraction (in simplest form)			$\frac{1}{4}$		

126

Solve the problems.

㉗ 60% of the students in Steve's class are boys. What % are girls?

1 – _____ %

= _____ % – _____ %

= _____ %

_____ % are girls.

1 = 100%

㉘ In Steve's class, 30% of the students have blonde hair, 25% black hair, and the rest brown hair. What % have brown hair?

_____

= _____

= _____

_____ % have brown hair.

A C T I V I T Y

Study the bar graph and answer the questions.

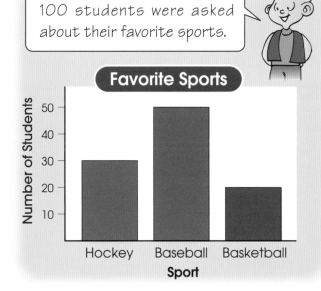

100 students were asked about their favorite sports.

Favorite Sports

Number of Students

50
40
30
20
10

Hockey   Baseball   Basketball

Sport

1. What kind of sport was the most popular?

   _____

2. What percent of students preferred:

   a. hockey? _____ %

   b. baseball? _____ %

   c. basketball? _____ %

127

15 More about Time

Twelve-hour clock   - using a.m. for time between midnight and 12 noon, and p.m. for time between 12 noon and midnight

Twenty-four-hour clock - using 01 - 24 to show hours of a day

Read what Steve says. Then write the times using the 24-hour clock.

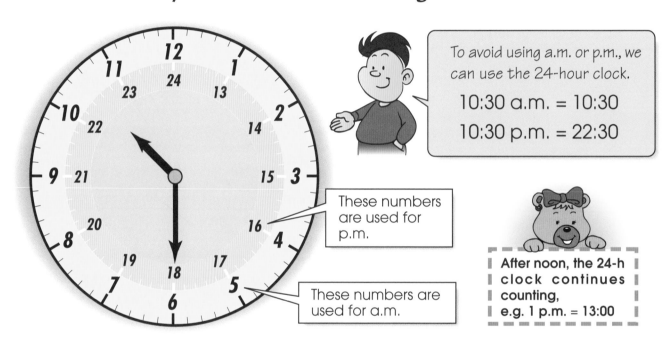

To avoid using a.m. or p.m., we can use the 24-hour clock.

10:30 a.m. = 10:30

10:30 p.m. = 22:30

These numbers are used for p.m.

These numbers are used for a.m.

After noon, the 24-h clock continues counting, e.g. 1 p.m. = 13:00

① 4:30 a.m. _____ ② 11:45 p.m. _____

③ 6:15 p.m. _____ ④ 9:20 p.m. _____

Write these times using a.m. or p.m.

⑤ 15:35 _____ ⑥ 09:28 _____

⑦ 21:19 _____ ⑧ 13:06 _____

⑨ 06:55 _____ ⑩ 2 h before 14:05 _____

⑪ 1 h after 19:25 _____ ⑬ 10 min before 09:07 _____

⑬ 3 h before 16:40 _____ ⑭ 45 min after 07:15 _____

Dave noted down the times he reached some spots along the trail. Read what he says and answer his questions.

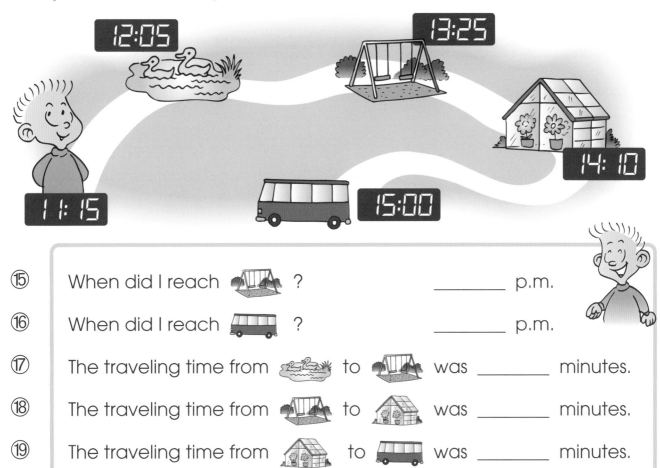

⑮ When did I reach ? _____ p.m.

⑯ When did I reach ? _____ p.m.

⑰ The traveling time from to was _____ minutes.

⑱ The traveling time from to was _____ minutes.

⑲ The traveling time from to was _____ minutes.

ACTIVITY

Put the pictures in order from A to E to show what Dave did after school.

Circles

Circumference - the distance around a circle

Center - the middle point of a circle

Diameter - a line segment joining two points on a circle and passing through the center

Radius - a line segment joining the center of a circle to a point on the circle

radius ─── diameter

center

─── circumference

Write center, circumference, diameter, or radius.

①

a. Line AOB : _____

b. Line OC : _____

c. Y : _____

d. O : _____

Measure and write the answers.

② Line AOB = ☐ cm

③ Line OC = ☐ cm

④ Line OD = ☐ cm

⑤ Line EF = ☐ cm

⑥ Line AOB = Line OC x ☐

⑦ Line ☐ is the diameter.

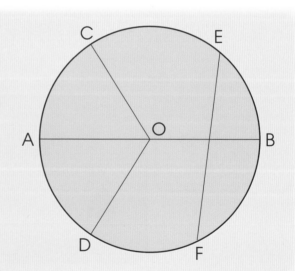

130

I can find the diameter of a quarter in this way.

1st Draw a circle around a quarter on a piece of paper.

2nd Use a ruler to find the longest distance from side to side of the circle. That is the diameter.

I can find the circumference in this way.

1st Make a roll of quarters for easy rolling.

2nd Make a mark on the quarter and roll one full turn on a tape or ruler.

Circumference

Follow Dave's methods to find the circumference and the diameter of a quarter. Check ✔ the right boxes.

⑧ The approximate diameter is ☐ 1 inch ☐ 2 inches ☐ 3 inches.

⑨ The approximate circumference is ☐ 3 inches ☐ 6 inches ☐ 9 inches.

⑩ The circumference is approximately ☐ 2 ☐ 3 ☐ 4 times bigger than the diameter.

ACTIVITY

Draw and think.

1. Try the following methods to draw circles.

   A pair of compasses

   Thumb pin   String

2. Think and check ✔ the right answers.

   a. How many diameters can you draw in a circle?

   ☐ 1   ☐ 2   ☐ many

   b. When the radius is longer, how will the circle be?

   ☐ the same   ☐ bigger   ☐ smaller

Volume and Surface Area

Volume - the amount of space an object takes up

Cubic inch (in^3), cubic foot (ft^3), and cubic yard (yd^3) are customary units for measuring volume.

Cubic centimeter (cm^3) and cubic meter (m^3) are metric units for measuring volume.

e.g.

1cm ← a centimeter cube
1cm
1cm
volume = 1 cm^3

1 in
1 in
1 in
volume = 1 in^3

Surface area - the sum of areas of the faces of a three-dimensional object

Find the volume of each block built by Dave with cubes of volume 1 cubic inch each.

① 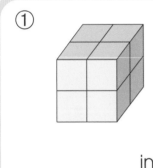 _____ in^3

② 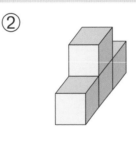 _____ in^3

③ _____ in^3

④ _____ in^3

⑤ 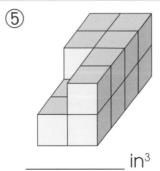 _____ in^3

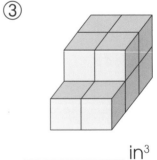

Remember to count the hidden cubes.

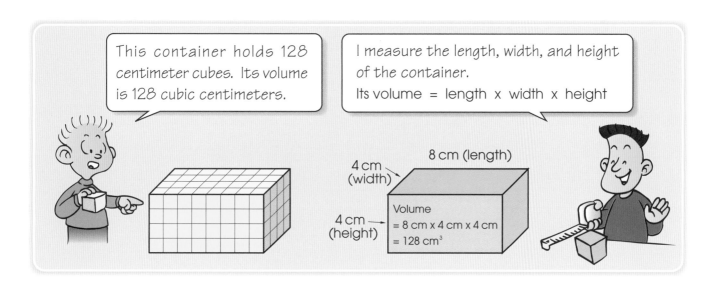

Follow Tony's method to find the volume of each wood block.

⑥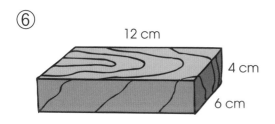

a. Length   = _____ cm

b. Width   = _____ cm

c. Height   = _____ cm

d. Volume = _____ X _____ X _____ cm³

= _____ cm³

⑦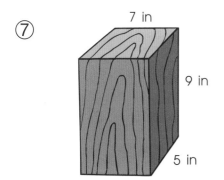

a. Length   = _____ in

b. Width   = _____ in

c. Height   = _____ in

d. Volume = _____ X _____ X _____ in³

= _____ in³

Help Dave find the volumes.

⑧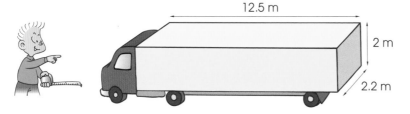

We use cubic yards (yd³) or cubic meters (m³) as the units for large volumes.

The volume of the container

= _____ X _____ X _____ m³ = _____ m³

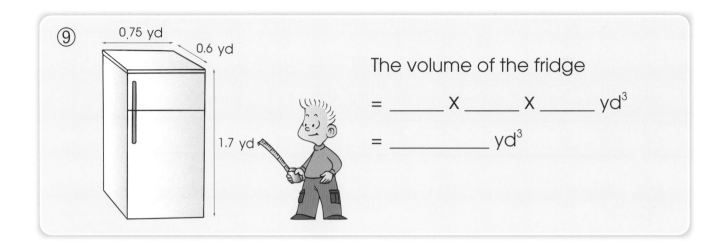

⑨

0.75 yd
0.6 yd
1.7 yd

The volume of the fridge

= _____ X _____ X _____ yd³

= _____ yd³

I can find the volume of an irregular object, e.g. a stone.

1st Pour water into the container to a depth of 4 inches.

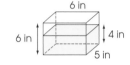

6 in
6 in
4 in
5 in

2nd Put the stone into the container and mark the new water level. (e.g. 5 inches)

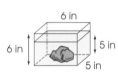

6 in
6 in
5 in
5 in

3rd The volume of the stone = volume of water displaced

$= \dfrac{\text{rise in water}}{\text{level}} \times \dfrac{\text{base area of}}{\text{the container}}$

= (5 – 4) x 6 x 5 in³

= 30 in³

Help Dave find the volume of his toys. The base area of the large container is 50 square inches.

⑩

5 in
4
3
2
1

base area
= 12 in² →

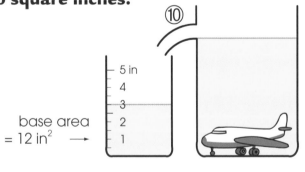

⑪

5 in   2nd water level
4 - - - - - 1st water level
3
2
1

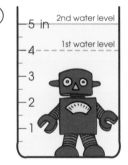

⑫

5 in
4
3 - - - - - 2nd water level
              1st water level
2
1

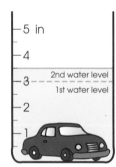

volume of
water displaced →

| in³ | | in³ | | in³ |

volume of
the toy →

| in³ | | in³ | | in³ |

Help Dave find the surface area of his trunks and solve the problem.

⑬

60 cm
40 cm
20 cm

← The trunk has 6 faces.

Surface area = (40 x 60 + 40 x 20 + 20 x 60) x 2 cm²

2 faces have the same area.

= (_____ + _____ + _____) x 2 cm²

= _____ x 2 cm²

= _____ cm²

⑭

20 ft
30 ft
15 ft

Surface area = (_____ x _____ + _____ x _____ + _____ x _____) x 2 ft²

= (_____ + _____ + _____) x 2 ft²

= _____ x 2 ft²

= _____ ft²

⑮ What is the surface area of the block?

_____ in²

= _____ in²

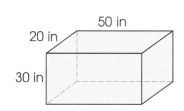

50 in
20 in
30 in

𝔸ℂ𝕋𝕀𝕍𝕀𝕋𝕐

Find the volumes of the blocks.

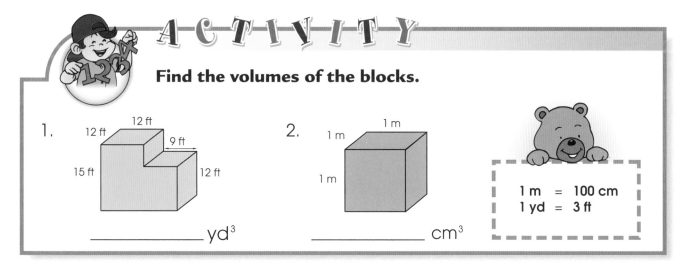

1.
12 ft
12 ft
9 ft
15 ft
12 ft

_____ yd³

2.
1 m
1 m
1 m

_____ cm³

1 m = 100 cm
1 yd = 3 ft

135

Line Graphs

Line Graph - a graph using points and lines to show information
Trend - a pattern of behavior

Look at the line graph which shows Dave's savings. Answer the questions.

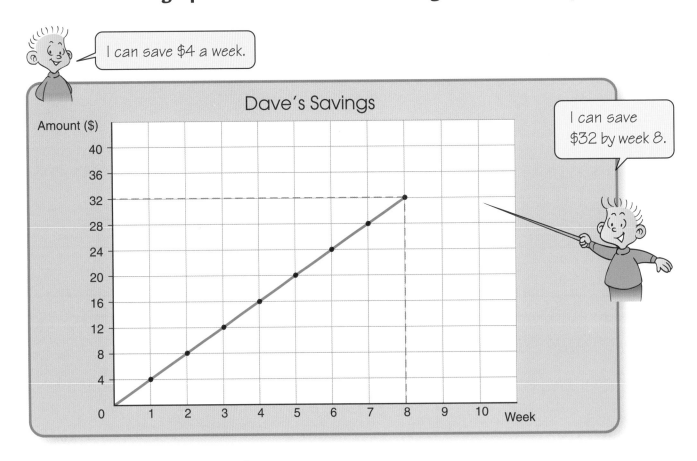

I can save $4 a week.

Dave's Savings

I can save $32 by week 8.

① By which week can Dave save $12?   Week _____

② By which week can Dave save $24?   Week _____

③ How much can he save by week 5? $ _____

④ How much can he save by week 7? $ _____

⑤ Follow the trend to find how much
he can save by week 10. $ _____

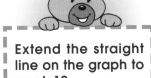

Extend the straight
line on the graph to
week 10.

136

Tony has saved $50. He will spend $5 a week. Finish the table and draw a line graph to show how he spends his savings. Then answer the questions.

⑥

Week	1	2	3	4	5	6	7
Money left ($)	45			30			

⑦

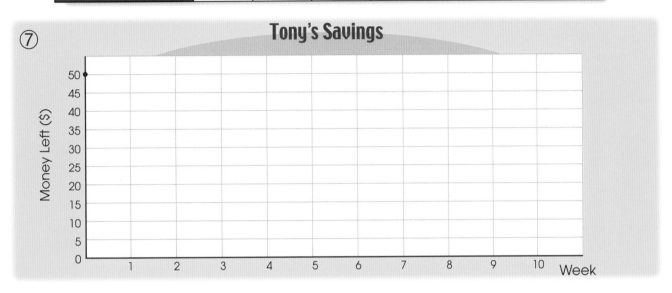

⑧ By which week will Tony have $40 left?   Week _____

⑨ By which week will Tony have $25 left?   Week _____

⑩ How much money will he have by week 3? $ _____

⑪ Follow the trend to find by which week he would
spend all his savings.   Week _____

ACTIVITY

Look at the graph and answer the questions.

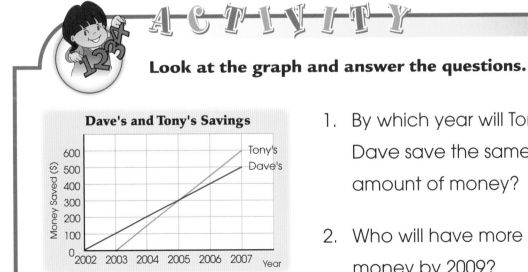

1. By which year will Tony and
Dave save the same
amount of money?

2. Who will have more
money by 2009?

137

Transformations and Coordinates

Transformation — mapping of an object onto its image by translation, rotation, or reflection

Translation — sliding each point of a shape in the same direction and distance

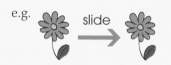

e.g. slide

Rotation — turning the points of a shape about a fixed point

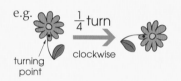

e.g. $\frac{1}{4}$ turn clockwise

turning point

Reflection — flipping the points of a shape over a line

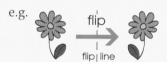

e.g. flip

flip line

Coordinates — an ordered pair of numbers used to locate a point on the grid

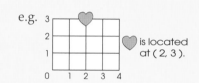

e.g. ♥ is located at (2, 3).

What transformation is shown in each set of pictures? Write translation, reflection, or rotation.

① Before   After

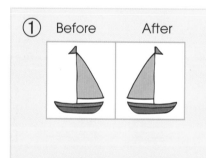

② Before   After

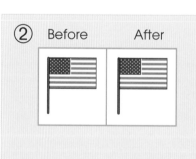

③ Before   After

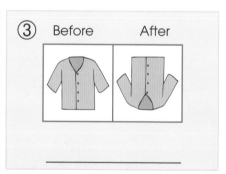

④ Before   After

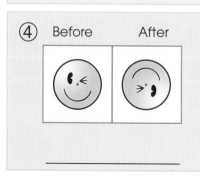

⑤ Before   After

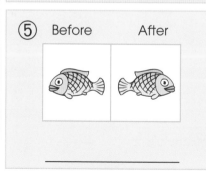

⑥ Before   After

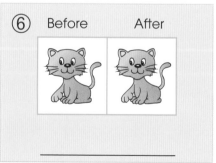

**Follow Dave's method to draw the translation, reflection, or rotation images.
Then write the ordered pairs of the transformed letters.**

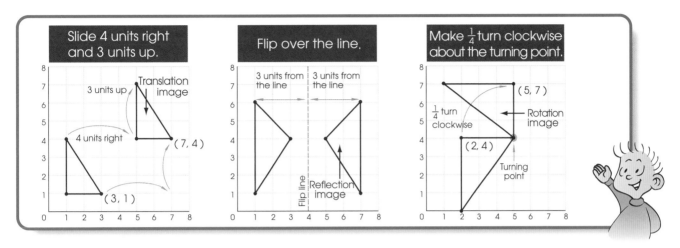

⑦ Slide 4 units left and 2 units down.

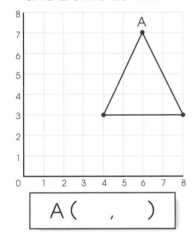

A (,   )

⑧ Flip over the line.

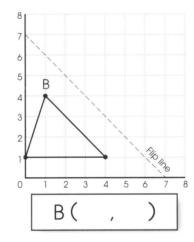

B (,   )

⑨ Make ¼ turn clockwise about the turning point.

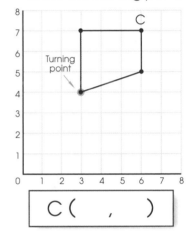

C (,   )

Find the ordered pairs.

1. The translation image of (1, 1) is at _____ .

2. The reflection image of (1, 1) is at _____ .

3. The rotation image of (1, 1) after $\frac{1}{2}$ turn is at _____ .

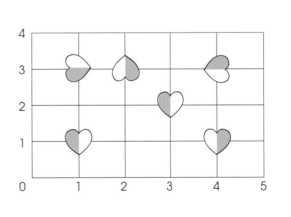

139

Money

Change - the difference between the price and the amount given in payment

Write the missing numbers on the sales receipts.

① SAM'S TOY SHOP

| MONOPOLY | 12.39 |
| CLUE | 27.65 |

TOTAL ▶ ☐

CASH 45.00

CHANGE ▶ ☐

THANK YOU

I paid $45.

Sam's Toy Shop

NO TAX

Monopoly **$12.39**   Puzzle **$15.97**

Scrabble **$32.49**   CLUE? **$27.65**

② SAM'S TOY SHOP

| MONOPOLY | 12.39 |
| SCRABBLE | 32.49 |

TOTAL ▶ ☐

CASH 50.00

CHANGE ▶ ☐

THANK YOU

③ SAM'S TOY SHOP

CLUE	27.65
PUZZLE	15.97
SCRABBLE	32.49

TOTAL ▶ ☐

CASH ☐

CHANGE ▶ 13.89

THANK YOU

④ SAM'S TOY SHOP

MONOPOLY	12.39
PUZZLE	15.97
CLUE	27.65

TOTAL ▶ ☐

CASH ☐

CHANGE ▶ 13.99

THANK YOU

Solve the problems.

⑤ How much do 5 boxes of Monopoly cost? $_____

⑥ How much do 2 boxes of Puzzle and 4 boxes

of Clue cost? $_____

The children are playing Monopoly. See how much toy money they have. Write the amounts and circle the right child.

⑦ $ _____

⑧ $ _____

⑨ $ _____

⑩ Circle the child who has the most toy money.

Write the number of each bill or coin needed to trade the bills on the left.

⑪	10			
⑫				

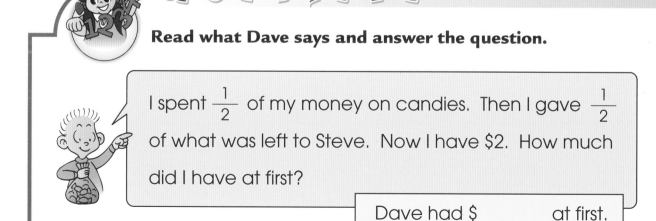

ＡＣＴＩＶＩＴＹ

Read what Dave says and answer the question.

I spent $\frac{1}{2}$ of my money on candies. Then I gave $\frac{1}{2}$ of what was left to Steve. Now I have $2. How much did I have at first?

Dave had $ _____ at first.

Probability

Probability - the chance that something will happen

Outcome - the result of an experiment

Help Dave answer Uncle Ray's questions. Check ✔ the right boxes.

① On which color is the spinner most likely to stop?

☐ Blue ☐ Yellow ☐ Red

② On which color is the spinner least likely to stop?

☐ Blue ☐ Yellow ☐ Red

③ Does red have a better chance than blue?

☐ Yes ☐ No

④ How best can you describe the chance of the spinner stopping on yellow?

☐ Unlikely ☐ Likely ☐ Certain

⑤ If the spinner is spun 100 times, on which color will the spinner most often stop?

☐ Blue ☐ Yellow ☐ Red

⑥ If the spinner is spun 1,000 times, on which color will the spinner least often stop?

☐ Blue ☐ Yellow ☐ Red

Help Dave write the fraction of the times each outcome occurs.

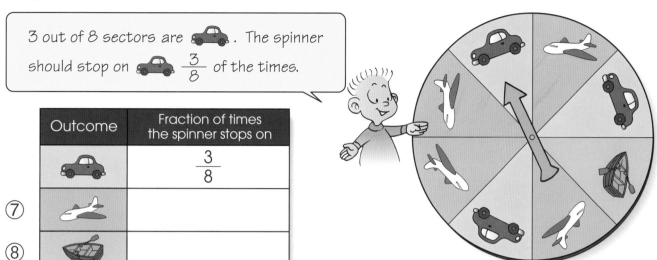

3 out of 8 sectors are 🚗 . The spinner should stop on 🚗 $\frac{3}{8}$ of the times.

Outcome	Fraction of times the spinner stops on
🚗	$\frac{3}{8}$
⑦ ✈	
⑧ 🚣	

Look at the above spinner and circle the right answers.

⑨ Which of the outcomes is most likely?

⑩ Which of the outcomes is least likely?

⑪ What is the chance of getting 🚗 or ✈ ?  $\frac{3}{8}$ $\frac{4}{8}$ $\frac{7}{8}$

⑫ What is the chance of getting 🚣 or ✈ ? 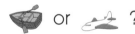 $\frac{5}{8}$ $\frac{4}{8}$ $\frac{1}{8}$

ACTIVITY

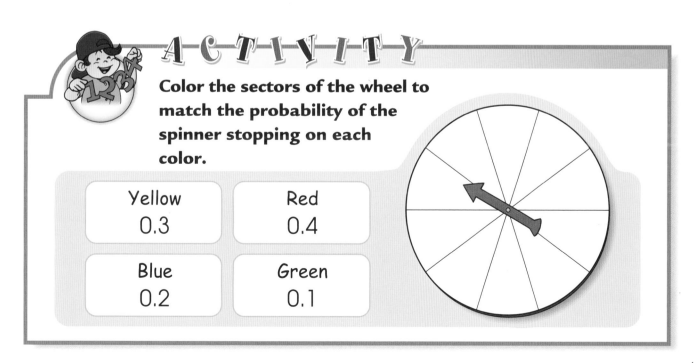

Color the sectors of the wheel to match the probability of the spinner stopping on each color.

Yellow	Red
0.3	0.4

Blue	Green
0.2	0.1

Complete the tables. (8 marks)

① 2 children divide a box of candies with each getting 12. How many candies will each one get if the number of children changes?

Number of children	2	3	4	6	8
Number of candies	12				

② Uncle Ray works 4 hours a day to finish his project in 12 days. How many days are needed if he works for a different number of hours a day?

Number of hours	2	3	4		
Number of days			12	6	4

Write as decimal numbers. (4 marks)

③ 14 and 267 thousandths

④ 5 and 42 hundredths

⑤ 10 and 25 thousandths

⑥ 2 thousandths

Write as decimal numbers and round to the nearest hundredth if necessary.
(4 marks)

⑦ $\dfrac{6}{7}$

⑧ $1\dfrac{2}{5}$

⑨ $3\dfrac{5}{6}$

⑩ $2\dfrac{5}{9}$

Find the answers. (18 marks)

⑪
$$\begin{array}{r} 1.6 \\ \times\ \ 2.3 \\ \hline \end{array}$$

⑫
$$\begin{array}{r} 3.1\ 9 \\ \times\ \ \ 0.4\ 5 \\ \hline \end{array}$$

⑬
$$\begin{array}{r} 0.6\ 2 \\ \times\ \ \ 0.0\ 3 \\ \hline \end{array}$$

⑭ 1.42 × 0.3 = _____

⑮ 3.59 × 0.04 = _____

⑯ 12.36 ÷ 0.06 = _____

⑰ 4.23 ÷ 0.3 = _____

⑱ 5.64 ÷ 0.12 = _____

⑲ 13.5 ÷ 0.15 = _____

Solve the equations. (12 marks)

⑳ 2 × q + 6 = 10

q = _____

㉑ 5 × k − 2 = 18

k = _____

㉒ 3 × p + 1 = 10

p = _____

㉓ m ÷ 4 + 3 = 5

m = _____

Fill in the blanks with center, circumference, diameter, or radius. (4 marks)

㉔ Line POQ : _____

㉕ O : _____

㉖ Line OS : _____

㉗ Y : _____

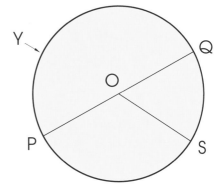

Measure and complete the table. (4 marks)

A

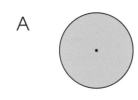

B

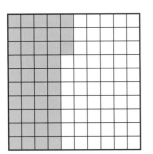

Circle		Radius (cm)	Diameter (cm)
㉘	A		
㉙	B		

Write the colored part of each 100-square as a fraction, a decimal, and a percent. (6 marks)

㉚

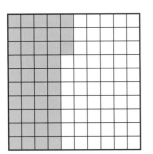

Fraction : _____

Decimal : _____

Percent : _____

㉛

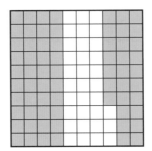

Fraction : _____

Decimal : _____

Percent : _____

Look at the spinner and answer the questions. (3 marks)

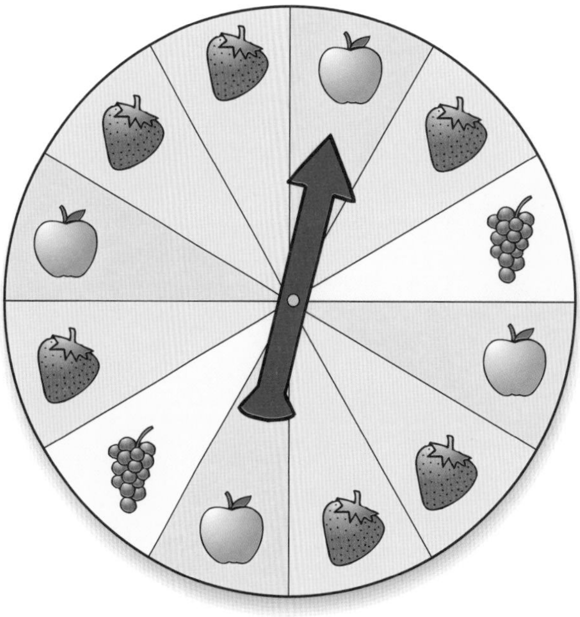

(32) What fraction of the spinner is 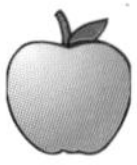 ?

(33) What fraction of the spinner is 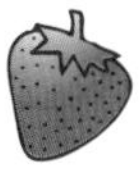 ?

(34) What fraction of the spinner is 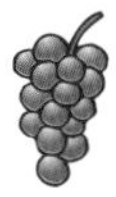 ?

Study the box graph and fill in the blanks. (5 marks)

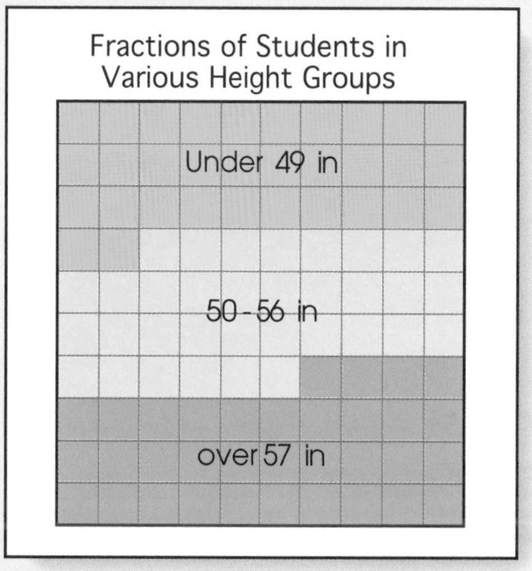
Fractions of Students in Various Height Groups
Under 49 in
50 - 56 in
over 57 in

(35) ______ % of the students are under 49 inches in height.

(36) ______ % of the students are between 50 and 56 inches in height.

(37) ______ % of the students are over 57 inches in height.

(38) If there were 100 students, ______ students would be under 49 inches in height.

(39) If there were 200 students, ______ students would be over 57 inches in height.

Write the show times in a.m. or p.m. and answer the questions. (6 marks)

㊵ When is the first show of Monster Dance?

_____

MEGA Theater	
Movie	Time
Monster Dance	10 : 30
Paper Moon	11 : 45
Rumble	14 : 35
Paper Moon	16 : 40
Monster Dance	18 : 30
The Journey	20 : 35
The Journey	22 : 35

㊶ When is the second show of Paper Moon?

_____

㊷ Which movie is shown at 8:35 p.m.?

_____

㊸ Which movie is shown at 2:35 p.m.?

_____

㊹ Rumble lasts 1 hour and 32 minutes. When does it end?

_____

㊺ The Journey ends at 22:03. How long does it last?

_____ minutes

Tickets	
Adult	$7.25 each
Children	$3.95 each

Solve the problems. (4 marks)

㊻ Dave pays $50 to buy 1 adult and 2 children's tickets.

How much is the change? $_____

㊼ Steve had $49.69. He bought 2 adult and 1 children's

tickets. How much does he have now? $_____

Look at the line graph. Answer the questions. (4 marks)

(48) How much do 10 special tickets cost? $ ______

(49) How much do 40 special tickets cost? $ ______

(50) How much does each special ticket cost? $ ______

(51) How many special tickets can be bought for $125? ______

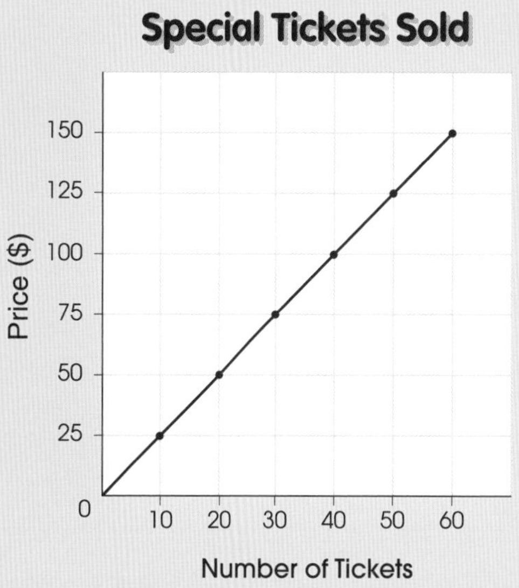

Special Tickets Sold
Price ($)
150
125
100
75
50
25
0
10
20
30
40
50
60
Number of Tickets

Find the volumes of the blocks. The volume of each cube is 1 cubic centimeter. (2 marks)

(52)

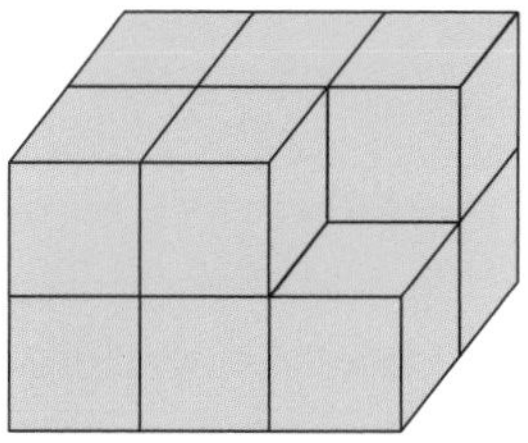

Volume = ________ cm^3

(53)

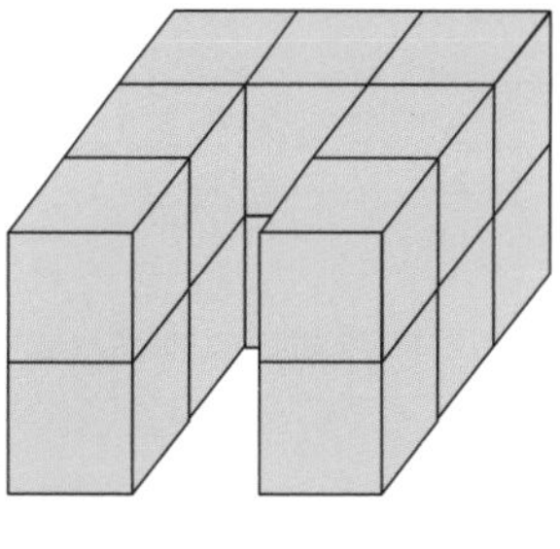

Volume = ________ cm^3

Find the volumes of the blocks. (4 marks)

(54)

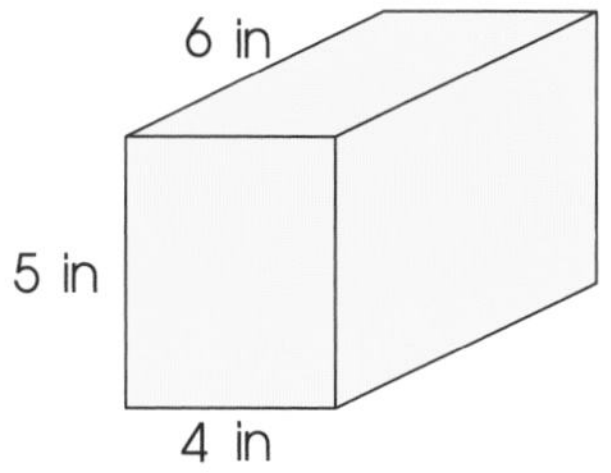

6 in
5 in
4 in

Volume = ________ in^3

(55)

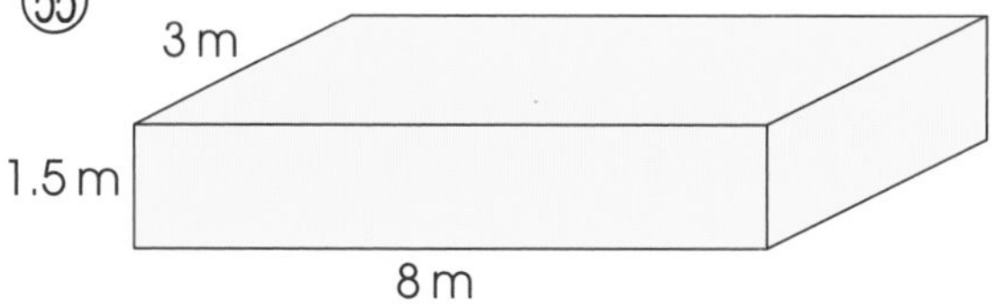

3 m
1.5 m
8 m

Volume = ________ m^3

Find the surface areas of the prisms. (3 marks)

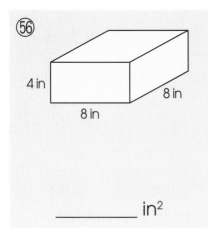

㊶

4 in
8 in
8 in

_____ in²

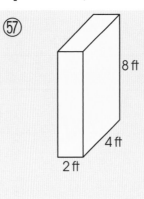

㊷

8 ft
4 ft
2 ft

_____ ft²

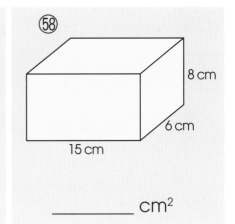

㊸

8 cm
6 cm
15 cm

_____ cm²

Draw the translation, reflection, or rotation images. Then write the ordered pairs of the transformed letters. (9 marks)

㊹

Flip over the dotted line.

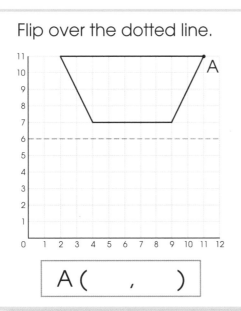

A

A (,)

㊿

Make $\frac{1}{2}$ turn about the turning point.

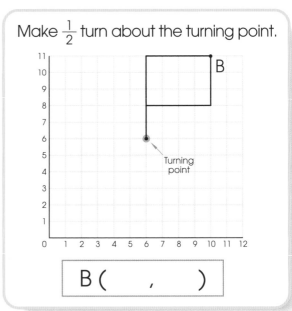

B

Turning point

B (,)

㊽

Slide 12 units right and 4 units up.

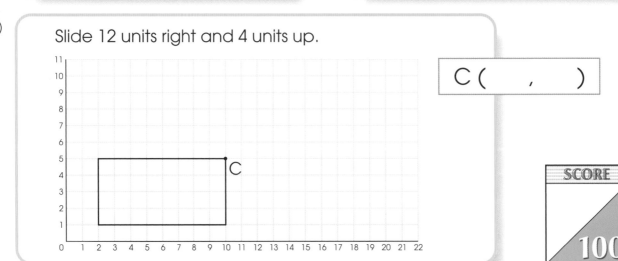

C

C (,)

SCORE

100

150

Section III

Overview

In the previous section, number skills were developed using whole numbers, fractions, and decimals. In this section, these skills are applied in order to solve word problems.

Students learn to recognize patterns and use these to solve problems. Careful reading is required and many solutions involve two steps.

Answers are written in full sentences using appropriate units.

Multiplication and Division of Whole Numbers

EXAMPLE

Gary ate 2 cookies each day and drank 28 glasses of milk per week. How many cookies and how much milk would he consume in 3 weeks?

Cookies Gary ate in 1 day : 2

Cookies he would eat in 3 weeks : $2 \times 7 \times 3 = 42$

Milk Gary drank in 1 week : 28

Milk he would drink in 3 weeks : $28 \times 3 = 84$

Answer : Gary would consume 42 cookies and 84 glasses of milk in 3 weeks.

Solve the problems. Show your work.

Frank's class has 28 pupils. There are 21 girls and 7 boys. Each pupil is given 3 pencils and 5 books at the beginning of the year. There are 2 extra chairs in the room.

① How many pencils are given out at the beginning of the year?

   Answer : _____ pencils are given out at the beginning of the year.

② How many more books than pencils are given out at the beginning of the year?

   Answer : _____

③ If all the chairs in the room were stacked in piles of 5 for cleaning, how many stacks would there be?

   Answer : _____

④ If the girls used 2 pencils each by the end of November, how many pencils belonging to girls would there be in the classroom?

   Answer : _____

⑤ For a special activity, the chairs that were being used by pupils in the classroom were to be put in rows of 7. How many rows would there be?

   Answer : _____

Donny moved into a new house with French doors. Each of these doors had 8 panes of glass. When Donny counted the doors, he found that there were 9 in all. There were also 19 windows with 2 panes of glass in each. The glass was all dirty from construction, and a cleaning company said that they would clean the windows for $5 each pane and the doors for $3 every 2 panes.

⑥ How many panes of glass were there in the doors?

Answer : _____

⑧ How much would it cost to clean the panes of glass in the doors?

Answer : _____

⑦ How many panes of glass were there in the house?

Answer : _____

⑨ How much would it cost to clean all the glass in the house?

Answer : _____

Sally was counting her collection of old coins. She had 34 pennies, 9 nickels, 31 dimes, and 19 quarters.

⑩ Sally was told that her pennies were worth 11¢ each. What was the value of Sally's pennies?

Answer : _____

⑬ Sally had 5 valuable quarters. They were worth 116¢ each. The rest were worth 76¢ each. What was the value of her quarters?

Answer : _____

⑪ Sally was told that her collection of nickels was worth 135¢. How much was each nickel worth?

Answer : _____

⑭ What was the value of her collection?

Answer : _____

⑫ Her dimes were only worth 14¢ each. What was the value of her collection of dimes?

Answer : _____

⑮ Would it be a good idea to sell her entire collection for 25¢ for each coin?

Answer : _____

September is the first month of school. Wanda's class had homework assigned every day of the month. It took 2 hours to complete the homework every night including weekends. All 17 girls in the class thought that this was too much. They only wanted to do 25 hours of homework every 15 days.

⑯ How many hours did Wanda spend on doing homework in September?

Answer : _____

⑰ How many hours did all the girls spend on doing homework in September?

Answer : _____

⑱ If there were 20 school days in September, how many hours of homework would be assigned each school day?

Answer : _____

⑲ If the teacher reduced the amount of homework as the girls requested, how many hours of homework would Wanda have to do in September?

Answer : _____

⑳ How many hours of homework would all the girls have to do in September then?

Answer : _____

On average, Lisa makes 4 long-distance phone calls a day with a payment of 2 calls for $3. Each week, Lisa tries to keep track of the amount of money she spends on making phone calls.

㉑ How much does Lisa spend each week on long-distance phone calls?

Answer : _____

㉒ How many long-distance phone calls would she make in January?

Answer : _____

㉓ How much would her long-distance phone calls cost in October?

Answer :

㉔ If each day, each call was to a different friend, how much could she save each day by sending them a letter if a stamp costs 39¢?

Answer :

㉕ If Lisa uses the service of another telephone company, the cost will be 4 calls for $5 on average. How much will she save each week by switching companies?

Answer :

There are 936 paperbacks and 882 hardcover books in a small library. It takes 36 seconds to dust each book. They are stored on shelves with 26 paperbacks or 21 hardcover books on each shelf.

㉖ How long does it take to dust all the paperback books?

Answer :

㉗ How long does it take to dust all the hardcover books?

Answer :

㉘ How many shelves of paperback books are there in the library?

Answer :

㉙ How many shelves of hardcover books are there in the library?

Answer :

㉚ If Uncle Bill uses 6 boxes to store the paperback and hardcover books, how many books are there in each box?

Answer :

Allan is taking stock of the items in his kitchen. He has 1,242 grams of raisins, 1,896 grams of peanuts, 4 bags of 63 figs each, 5 bags of 32 apricots each, and 486 cookies.

㉛ Allan divides his raisins into 6 bags. How many grams of raisins are there in each bag?

Answer : _____

㉜ Allan divides his peanuts into 8 servings. How many grams of peanuts are there in each serving?

Answer : _____

㉝ If each fig weighs 3 ounces, how heavy do Allan's figs weigh?

Answer : _____

㉞ Allan and his sister each eat 4 apricots after lunch every day. How long will Allan's apricots last?

Answer : _____

㉟ If Allan shares his cookies with 5 of his friends, how many cookies will each person get?

Answer : _____

㊱ Allan wants to put his cookies in bags of 5 or in bags of 7. Which way will there be more cookies left over?

Answer : _____

㊲ If Allan divides his figs into 3 bags, how many more figs will each bag hold than before?

Answer : _____

㊳ If Allan divides his peanuts into small bags each holding 25 grams, how many bags will he need to hold all the peanuts?

Answer : _____

㊴ If every 18 grams of raisins costs 12 cents, how much do Allan's raisins cost?

Answer : _____

- *Question 39 is* ← **Read this first.** *a 2-step problem. First, find how many portions of 18 grams each there are in 1,242 grams of raisins. Then multiply the number of portions by the cost.*

Solve the problems. Show your work.

④⓪ Karen was collecting pinecones on a park. After a couple of hours, she collected 308 pinecones. Karen wanted to take them home, but couldn't carry all those pinecones at once. She was going to be at the park for 4 days. How many pinecones would she have to carry each day?

Answer : _____

④① Larry had 17 CDs. He played them 4 times each on average in a month. If each CD was 1 hour long, how much time would he spend in a year listening to the CDs?

Answer : _____

④② Don's dad had 1,648 books. If he could fit 24 books on each shelf, how many shelves would he need?

Answer : _____

④③ Peter was planting pansies in his garden. The pansies were planted in rows of 35. There were 23 rows across the garden. How many plants did Peter need?

Answer : _____

④④ Peter uses about 45 quarts of water each day to water his plants. How much water will Peter use in a month of 31 days?

Answer : _____

CHALLENGE

The number of ants in Quincey's garden seems to double each day. Quincey saw 100 ants on Monday, how many ants might there be on Thursday?

Answer : _____

Operations with Whole Numbers

EXAMPLE

Two students were comparing their marks. Sylvia had 80 and Tim had half of Sylvia's mark plus 10. What was Tim's mark?

Tim's mark: $80 \div 2 + 10 = 40 + 10 = 50$

Answer: Tim's mark was 50.

Use the table below to solve the problems. Show your work.

A group of friends were playing a game. They threw a ball as far as they could in the park, and measured the distances. The person who threw the ball third farthest won 1 point, second farthest 3 points, and the farthest 5 points.

Name	Mario	Sandy	Danny	Jimmy	Dolores
Distance (yard)	12	18	14	19	16

① How much farther did Jimmy throw than Sandy?

Jimmy threw _____ farther
Answer: than Sandy. _____

② How far did everyone throw altogether?

Answer: _____

③ If Mario and Jimmy formed a team against Sandy and Dolores, which team threw the ball farther?

Answer: _____

④ If Danny got to double his distance because he had no one on his team, how much farther did the winning team throw than Danny did?

Answer: _____

⑤ The friends thought of a new game. They got to multiply their distance by their score. Who got the highest number? What is the number?

Answer: _____

Solve the problems. Show your work.

⑥ How many days are there in a leap year?

Answer: _____

⑦ If there were 56 marbles in a bag, how many marbles would Frank have if he bought 6 bags?

Answer: _____

⑧ A theater has 47 seats in each row. How many people will fill 12 rows?

Answer: _____

⑨ Bill's father buys paper in 250-sheet packages. If he wants to print 1,371 pages, how many packages of paper must he buy?

Answer: _____

⑩ George can ride his bike around a park in 4 minutes. How many times can he ride his bike around the park in 1 hour 20 minutes?

Answer: _____

⑪ Sally collects stamps. She has 482 stamps in her first album, 561 in her second one, and 398 in her third one. How many stamps does she have in all?

Answer: _____

⑫ A jacket costs $75. A pair of jeans costs $34. If John bought 2 jackets and 3 pairs of jeans, how much should he pay?

Answer: _____

Lorraine was helping out in a lumberyard. There were 2,352 pieces of pine, 598 pieces of oak, and 28 pieces of maple. Each piece of lumber was 2 yards long.

⑬ How many pieces of lumber were there in the lumberyard altogether?

Answer: _____

⑭ How many more pieces of pine than maple were there in the lumberyard?

Answer: _____

⑮ How many more pieces of pine than oak were there in the lumberyard?

Answer: _____

⑯ How many yards of lumber were there in the lumberyard?

Answer: _____

⑰ If 269 pieces of oak were sold on Wednesday, how many yards of oak would be left to sell?

Answer: _____

⑱ If 1,568 yards of pine were sold per day, how many days would it take to sell all the pine pieces?

Answer: _____

⑲ If there are 414 yards of oak left over, how many pieces of oak were sold?

Answer: _____

Solve these problems in your head and write the statements.

⑳ Jean works part-time at the mall. She works 2 hours a day for $9 an hour. How much did she earn in a five-day week?

Answer: _____

㉑ Matthew started his homework at 4:00 p.m. It took him 25 minutes to finish his math, 17 minutes for his social studies, and 28 minutes to read the next part of his English book. When did he finish his homework?

Answer: _____

㉓ It takes Sandy 20 minutes to walk to school and 14 minutes to run to school. How much time can she save each week if she runs to school and runs home each day instead of walking?

Answer: _____

㉒ Mario wanted two CDs. The first one was on sale for $15 and the other's regular price was $18. If all the prices included taxes and Mario had a twenty-dollar bill, a ten-dollar bill, and a five-dollar bill, could he afford the two CDs?

Answer: _____

㉔ Brian collects baseball cards. He read in a collector's magazine that one of his rare cards should double in price every seven years. How many times should its present value be worth in 21 years?

Answer: _____

CHALLENGE

① George was born in March in a leap year. If today is George's 11th birthday, how many days old is he?

Answer: _____

② A small company bills one of their clients $158,920 each quarter. How much money would the client pay them for 9 months' work?

Answer: _____

3 Comparing and Ordering Fractions

EXAMPLE

Sally walks $\frac{2}{3}$ of a block to school. Kari walks $\frac{3}{4}$ of a block. Who walks the farther? *(Hint: The LCM of 3 and 4 is 12.)*

Sally walks: $\frac{2}{3} = \frac{2 \times 4}{3 \times 4} = \frac{8}{12}$ Kari walks: $\frac{3}{4} = \frac{3 \times 3}{4 \times 3} = \frac{9}{12}$

Answer: Kari walks farther.

Solve the problems. Show your work.

① Peter and Joe were comparing hat sizes. Peter's hat was $6\frac{1}{2}$ and Joe's hat was $6\frac{3}{8}$. Who had the larger hat size?

Answer: _____ had the larger hat size. _____

② If Mary spent $\frac{1}{2}$ hour reading a history chapter and Jill spent 42 minutes, who read the chapter faster?

Answer: _____

③ Douglas had 1 quarter, 1 dime, and 3 pennies. Jill had 1 dime, 6 nickels, and 1 penny. Who had the larger fraction of a dollar?

Answer: _____

④ Mary's mother served $\frac{2}{7}$ of a cake and kept $\frac{1}{4}$ of it. Did she save more cake than she served?

Answer: _____

⑤ Henry and Ann each had a chocolate bar of the same size. Henry ate $\frac{1}{3}$ of his bar and Ann ate $\frac{2}{5}$ of her bar. Who ate less?

Answer: _____

The young people on Single Street wanted to raise money for charity. They decided that any time any member of their family raised their voice, they would have to put one coin in a special box. The louder the voice, the larger the coin. At the end of the month, they would meet and put all their coins together.

⑥ Patricia had 63 pennies. What fraction of a dollar did she have?

Answer: _____

⑦ Dolores brought in a dollar and 7 quarters. What fraction of a dollar did she have?

Answer: _____

⑧ Milly had 1 quarter, 4 dimes, and 12 nickels. What fraction of a dollar did she have?

Answer: _____

⑨ Gerry had 7 quarters, 2 dimes, and 6 nickels. What fraction of a dollar did he have?

Answer: _____

⑩ Who raised the most money for charity?

Answer: _____

⑪ How much money did they raise for charity in all?

Answer: _____

CHALLENGE

Sam had 147 trading cards, Hindy 216, Kelly 98, and Oliver 166. They went to a trading card show where an expert told them that Sam had 21 valuable cards, Hindy 54, Kelly 28, and Oliver 2.

① Who had the largest fraction of valuable cards in his or her collection?

Answer: _____

② Who had the second smallest fraction of valuable cards in his or her collection?

Answer: _____

③ List the people from the one with the largest fraction of valuable cards to the one with the smallest.

Answer: _____

Addition and Subtraction of Fractions

EXAMPLE

Frank had $\frac{1}{5}$ of a bag of marbles, Jerry had $\frac{3}{5}$ of a bag of marbles, and Kelly had $\frac{4}{5}$ of a bag of marbles. Yesterday they lost $\frac{2}{5}$ of a bag playing at recess. How many marbles do they still have in all?

No. of marbles they had in all : $\frac{1}{5} + \frac{3}{5} + \frac{4}{5} = \frac{8}{5}$

After losing, they still have : $\frac{8}{5} - \frac{2}{5} = \frac{6}{5} = 1\frac{1}{5}$

Answer : They still have $1\frac{1}{5}$ bags of marbles in all.

Solve the problems. Show your work and give your answers in simplest form.

Ann, Dolores, and Mario were working on a project together. Ann spent $1\frac{5}{6}$ hours, Dolores $1\frac{4}{6}$ hours, and Mario $\frac{1}{6}$ of an hour working on it.

① How many hours did they spend working on the project in all?

Answer : They spent _____ hours in all.

② How many more hours did Dolores spend on the project than Mario?

Answer : _____

③ How many more hours did Ann and Dolores spend on the project than Mario?

Answer : _____

④ How many hours did Ann and Mario spend on the project in all?

Answer : _____

⑤ Compare the number of hours Dolores spent on the project with that spent by Ann and Mario together.

Answer : _____

⑥ How much more time would Mario have to spend to equal the time spent by Ann?

Answer : _____

Harry's class was collecting bottles for recycling. They put them in large plastic bags. Harry filled $\frac{3}{7}$ of a bag the first day, $\frac{5}{7}$ the second, and $\frac{1}{7}$ the third. Barry filled $\frac{5}{7}$ of a bag the first day, $\frac{3}{7}$ the second, and $\frac{2}{7}$ the third. Mary filled $\frac{6}{7}$ of a bag the first day, $\frac{6}{7}$ the second, and 1 the third.

⑦ How many bags of bottles did Harry collect in all?

Answer : _____

⑧ How many bags of bottles did Barry collect in all?

Answer : _____

⑨ How many bags of bottles did Mary collect in all?

Answer : _____

⑩ Who collected the most bottles?

Answer : _____

⑪ How many bags of bottles did the children collect in all?

Answer : _____

⑫ How many more bags of bottles did Mary collect than Harry?

Answer : _____

⑬ How many more bags of bottles did Mary collect than Barry?

Answer : _____

⑭ How many more bags of bottles would Harry need to collect if he wanted to have 2 bags?

Answer : _____

⑮ How many more bags of bottles would Barry need to collect if he wanted to have 3 bags?

Answer : _____

⑯ How many more bags of bottles would Mary need to collect if she wanted to have 5 bags?

Answer : _____

- **To subtract from a whole number, change the whole number into a mixed number.**

  e.g. $5 = 4\frac{7}{7}$

Read this first.

Gary was looking at the breakfast cereals in his kitchen. He had $\frac{2}{5}$ of a box of corn flakes, $\frac{4}{5}$ of a box of bran flakes, and $\frac{3}{5}$ of a box of rice flakes.

⑰ How much cereal did he have in all?

Answer : _____

⑱ How much more bran flakes did he have than corn flakes?

Answer : _____

⑲ How much more rice and corn flakes did he have than bran flakes?

Answer : _____

⑳ If Gary's mother used $\frac{1}{5}$ of a box of each type of cereal to make healthy cookies, how much cereal would be left?

Answer : _____

㉑ If Gary bought a box of granola and ate $\frac{1}{5}$ of it, how much cereal would he have altogether?

Answer : _____

Kim's class was running for charity. Kim ran $2\frac{7}{20}$ kilometers. Lori ran $3\frac{19}{20}$ kilometers. Freda ran $2\frac{11}{20}$ kilometers. Toni ran 5 kilometers.

㉒ How far did they run in all?

Answer : _____

㉓ How much farther did the person who ran the farthest distance run than the one who ran the shortest?

Answer : _____

㉔ If Kim and Freda ran as a team, how far did their team run?

Answer : _____

㉕ If Lori and Freda ran as a team, how far did they run in total?

Answer : _____

㉖ How much farther did Toni run than Lori?

Answer : _____

㉗ How much farther did Freda run than Kim?

Answer : _____

Yvon has a collection of magazines. $\frac{7}{19}$ of his collection is from 1980 to 1989, $\frac{9}{19}$ from 1970 to 1979, $\frac{1}{19}$ from before 1970, and the rest new.

㉘ What fraction of his magazines are new?

Answer : _____

㉙ What fraction of his magazines were printed between 1980 and the present?

Answer : _____

㉚ What fraction of his magazines were printed between 1970 and 1990?

Answer : _____

㉛ Yvon was told that magazines printed before 1980 should be stored in protective envelopes. What fraction of his magazines need this protection?

Answer : _____

㉜ What fraction of his magazines do not need protective envelopes?

Answer : _____

㉝ If Yvon gives $\frac{3}{8}$ of his collection of magazines to his friends, what fraction of his magazines will be left?

Answer : _____

㉞ Yvon has 190 magazines. 113 of them are in English and the rest in French. What fraction of his magazines are in English?

Answer : _____

㉟ What fraction of his magazines are in French?

Answer : _____

CHALLENGE

Ralph's cat knocked a cup of hot chocolate over onto Ralph's math book. It stained the page with his homework. Ralph knew the answer to the last question was $\frac{9}{13}$, and that one of the two numbers was $\frac{3}{13}$. If he had to add to find the number, what was the fraction under the chocolate stain?

Answer : _____

Addition and Subtraction of Decimals

Frank's score on the English test was 79.8 and Jerry's was 92.3. How much higher was Jerry's score than Frank's?

Difference: 92.3 – 79.8 = 12.5

Answer : Jerry's score was 12.5 higher than Frank's.

Solve the problems. Show your work.

Franco was trying out a recipe. He needed 0.75 kilogram of egg-plants, 0.007 kilogram of salt, 1.28 kilograms of minced garlic, 0.95 kilogram of chopped tomatoes, and 0.01 kilogram of parsley to add to the liquid ingredients.

① How much would the solid ingredients weigh?

Answer : The solid ingredients would weigh _____ .

② Franco knew that he couldn't put more than 4 kilograms into a shopping bag or the handles would break. How much more weight could he add to his dry ingredients and still able to carry the bag by the handles?

Answer : _____

③ What weight of vegetables does this recipe require?

Answer : _____

④ What weight of herbs and spices does this recipe require?

Answer : _____

⑤ If Franco required 0.599 kilogram of liquid ingredients, how much would the entire dish weigh before cooking?

Answer : _____

168

Hortense received $7.50 each week for an allowance. She spent $3.49 on entertainment, $1.78 on snacks, $2.00 on transportation, and saved the rest.

⑥ How much money did she save each week?

Answer : _____

⑦ How much money did she spend on entertainment and snacks each week?

Answer : _____

⑧ How much more money did she spend on entertainment than transportation each week?

Answer : _____

⑨ If she got a $0.68 raise in allowance on the condition that she saved it all, how much would she save each week?

Answer : _____

⑩ If she needed $2.23 for snacks one week and wanted to take that money from her entertainment budget, how much would she have left for entertainment that week?

Answer : _____

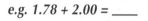

- **Align the decimal points when you add or subtract the decimal numbers.**

e.g. 1.78 + 2.00 = ____

Read this first.

```
   1. 78
 + 2. 00
 ─────────
      ↑
   align
```

CHALLENGE

① Kim wants to travel half of a 5.78-mile trip before stopping. If he has completed 1.97 miles, how much farther would he have to go?

Answer : _____

② Harriette made deposits of $5.78 and $1.99, and withdrawals of $3.14 and $2.67 from her bank account. If the bank charged her $0.15 per transaction and her initial balance was $15.02, what was her final balance?

Answer : _____

Multiplication and Division of Decimals

EXAMPLE

Every day for one week, Gary ate 2 cookies, each weighing 0.97 ounce. He also drank 10.5 quarts of milk that week. How many ounces of cookies and quarts of milk did he consume each day?

Cookies Gary ate each day : $2 \times 0.97 = 1.94$

Milk Gary drank each day : $10.5 \div 7 = 1.5$

Answer : Gary ate 1.94 ounces of cookies and drank 1.5 quarts of milk each day.

Solve the problems. Show your work.

Eddie was saving for a special game, which cost $75.60. He was planning on saving $5.75 per month for a year. His father suggested that he save $6.45 per month instead, but Eddie wasn't sure if he could afford that.

① Would Eddie save up enough money to buy the game by putting aside $5.75 per month for a year?

Answer : Eddie _____ save up enough money to buy the game. _____

② If he couldn't save the money within the year, how much would he be short of?

Answer : _____

③ Would his father's suggestion allow him to buy the game on time?

Answer : _____

④ How much extra would he have to save each month above the $5.75 a month to buy the game in a year?

Answer : _____

⑤ If the game went on sale for $59.88, how much less than $5.75 would he have to save each month to buy the game in a year?

Answer : _____

Jenny was building a project out of wood. She needed 2.16 yards of pine, 0.3 yard of oak, and 2.4 yards of walnut. Pine was $2 a yard, oak was $4.70 a yard, and walnut was $5.65 a yard.

⑥ How much would she spend on pine?

Answer : _____

⑦ How much would she spend on oak?

Answer : _____

⑧ How much would she spend on walnut?

Answer : _____

⑨ How much would she spend on wood altogether?

Answer : _____

⑩ If it cost $0.50 per yard for finishing the wood, what would be the total cost for finishing?

Answer : _____

⑪ What was the total cost for the wood plus finishing?

Answer : _____

⑫ If Jenny shared the total cost of the wood with 2 friends, how much would each person pay?

Answer : _____

⑬ If Jenny cut the pine into 3 equal parts, how long would be each part?

Answer : _____

⑭ If Jenny cut off 0.04 yard of the walnut and divided the rest into 4 equal parts, how long would be each part?

Answer : _____

⑮ How many yards of pine can you buy for $16.50?

Answer : _____

• *For decimals, multiply or divide as with whole numbers, but remember the rule for placing the decimal point in the product or quotient.*

Read this first.

171

Oliver traveled the following distances on his vacation. Read the table and solve the problems. Show your work.

Day	1	2	3	4	5
Distance traveled (mile)	271	305	652	186	395
Cost (per mile)	$0.04	$0.06	$0.05	$0.05	$0.04

⑯ What was the travel cost on day 2?

Answer : _____

⑰ What was the difference in travel cost between day 1 and day 4?

Answer : _____

⑱ On which day was his travel cost the lowest? What was the cost?

Answer : _____

⑲ On which day was his travel cost the highest? What was the cost?

Answer : _____

⑳ If Oliver had budgeted $12.00 per day for travel costs, would day 5 have exceeded his budget?

Answer : _____

㉑ Which days exceeded Oliver's travel budget?

Answer : _____

㉒ If the travel cost on day 6 was $4 and the distance traveled was 100 miles, what would be the cost per mile?

Answer : _____

㉓ The travel cost and the distance traveled on day 7 were the same as that on day 6, but Oliver had used a $2 gas coupon. What was the actual cost per mile?

Answer : _____

A quick way to do division in Questions 22 & 23 : **Read this first.**

- *Divided by 10 :*
  move the decimal point 1 place to the left.
  e.g. 7.96 ÷ 10 = 0. 796

- *Divided by 100 :*
  move the decimal point 2 places to the left.
  e.g. 7.96 ÷ 100 = 0. 0796

Solve the problems. Show your work.

㉔ Matthew paid $8.76 to buy 4 boxes of juice. How much does each box of juice cost?

Answer : _____

㉕ The capacity of a box of juice is 1.25 quarts. If the box of juice can fill up 5 glasses, what is the capacity of each glass?

Answer : _____

㉖ How much juice is there in 7 boxes?

Answer : _____

㉗ Which size is the better buy, regular size distilled water of 2 quarts for $1.38 or jumbo size of 10 quarts for $5.90?

Answer : _____

㉘ How much should Matthew pay for buying 8 bottles of regular size distilled water?

Answer : _____

㉙ If Matthew drinks 1.75 quarts of water a day, how much water will he drink in a week?

Answer : _____

CHALLENGE

Darlene is going to paint a wall 16.8 yards long and 2.4 yards high. If 1 quart of paint covers 32 square yards, how much paint will she need for 2 coats of paint for the wall?

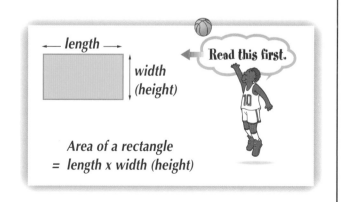

Answer : _____

173

Solve the problems. Show your work.

Last Sunday, Mr. Stanley held a Food Fair at Asna Park. His bakery baked different kinds of food for the Food Fair. Mr. Stanley decided to donate half of the money collected to the Children's Hospital.

① There were 9 groups of girls and 12 groups of boys helping out at the fair. Each group had 4 people. How many helpers were there?

Answer :

② The baker, Mrs. White, baked 64 cakes. If each cake was cut into 8 pieces, how many pieces of cake did Mrs. White make?

Answer :

③ Each piece of cake was sold for $0.75. How much did a whole cake cost?

Answer :

④ If it cost $2.16 to bake each cake, what would be the total cost for baking all the cakes?

Answer :

⑤ There were 1,064 chocolate doughnuts and 898 honey doughnuts. How many doughnuts were there in all?

Answer :

⑥ The chocolate doughnuts were sold in packages of 4. How many packages of chocolate doughnuts were there?

Answer :

⑦ At the end of the fair, 159 honey doughnuts were left. How many honey doughnuts had been sold?

Answer :

⑧ Gary bought 8 honey doughnuts for $5.04. How much did 1 honey doughnut cost?

Answer :

⑨ Each tray had 4 rows of 6 cookies. There were 15 trays altogether. How many cookies were there?

Answer :

⑩ 218 cookies were sold. How many cookies were left?

Answer :

⑪ The weight of a bag of 5 cookies was 17 ounces. How much did 1 cookie weigh?

Answer :

⑫ Gary bought $\frac{1}{8}$ of a cake and Sally bought $\frac{5}{8}$ of the same cake. How much of the cake did they buy in all?

Answer :

⑬ How much more of the cake did Sally buy than Gary?

Answer :

⑭ Jill paid $4.16 for the cake. What was her change from a $10 bill?

Answer :

⑮ A bag of 5 bagels cost $1.30 and a bag of 8 bagels cost $1.76. Which bag was a better buy?

Answer :

⑯ Each stall collected $459. There were 8 stalls at the Food Fair. How much money did the stalls collect in all?

Answer :

⑰ How much money did Mr. Stanley donate to the Children's Hospital?

Answer :

⑱ The total cost for organizing the fair was $1,285. Did Mr. Stanley make a profit after the donation?

Answer :

⑲ How much did Mr. Stanley gain or lose?

Answer :

Inger and her family want to redecorate their home. There are 4 bedrooms, 1 living room, 1 kitchen, and 3 bathrooms in the house.

⑳ If each bedroom needs 3.48 quarts of paint, how many quarts of paint are needed for all the bedrooms?

Answer : _____

㉑ A can of paint is 4 quarts. How many cans of paint does Inger need for all the bedrooms?

Answer : _____

㉒ Each bathroom needs $1\frac{3}{5}$ boxes of tiles. How many boxes of tiles are needed to cover all the bathrooms?

Answer : _____

㉓ If the tiles have to be bought in full boxes, how many boxes does Inger need to buy?

Answer : _____

㉔ How many boxes of tiles will be left over?

Answer : _____

㉕ For the living room, they want to buy a couch for $798.65 and a rug for $268.47. How much do they spend in all to furnish the living room?

Answer : _____

㉖ Inger wants to buy 6 chairs and 1 dining table. Store A charges $102 each for the chairs and store B charges $621 for 6 chairs. Which store offers a better buy?

Answer : _____

㉗ The dining table is priced at $1,295. How much will Inger pay for the dining table and 6 chairs at the lowest price?

Answer : _____

Circle the correct answer to each problem.

㉘ Mary drank $\frac{3}{7}$ of a bottle of milk. Kevin drank $\frac{5}{7}$ of a bottle and Lori drank an entire bottle. How many bottles of milk did they drink in all?

   A. $\frac{8}{7}$ B. $2\frac{1}{7}$ C. $2\frac{3}{7}$ D. None of the above

㉙ Peter spent \$1.68 on lunch. If he brought a \$1 bill, 2 quarters, and 4 dimes to school, how much would he have after lunch?

   A. \$2.20   B. \$0.32   C. \$0.22   D. \$0.02

㉚ Billy went shopping with 3 of his friends. Each of them bought 4 shirts. How many shirts did they buy altogether?

   A. 4   B. 8   C. 12   D. 16

㉛ Jim and Jane want to buy a gift for their parents and share the cost equally. The price of the gift is \$44.00. If they have a \$5 off coupon, how much will each person pay?

   A. \$19.50   B. \$19.05   C. \$24.50   D. \$24.05

㉜ Each cake cost \$8. If Kim paid for 3 cakes with 2 \$20 bills, how much change would he get?

   A. \$4   B. \$8   C. \$16   D. \$24

㉝ A pail of water weighs $3\frac{4}{5}$ pounds. A pail of sand weighs $1\frac{3}{5}$ pounds heavier. How heavy is a pail of sand?

   A. $5\frac{2}{5}$ pounds   B. $5\frac{1}{5}$ pounds   C. $4\frac{2}{5}$ pounds   D. $4\frac{1}{5}$ pounds

㉞ How heavy are the pail of water and the pail of sand together?

   A. $7\frac{2}{5}$ pounds   B. 8 pounds   C. $8\frac{3}{5}$ pounds   D. $9\frac{1}{5}$ pounds

㉟ Ray bought 24 packets of gum each containing 12 pieces. Ray gave his 18 classmates 4 pieces each. How many pieces of gum were left over?

   A. 206   B. 264   C. 216   D. 240

㊱ How many packets of gum were left over?

   A. 18   B. 22   C. 16   D. 20

7 Operations with Decimals

EXAMPLE

Ted wants to make a table 1.2 yards long and 0.6 yard wide. He wants to attach a rare wood edging around the table top. How many square yards would he need for the table top? How many yards of rare wood would he need for the edging?

Area of the table top : $1.2 \times 0.6 = 0.72$

Perimeter of the table top : $(1.2 + 0.6) \times 2 = 3.6$

1.2 yd   1.2 yd

0.6 yd   0.6 yd   0.6 yd

Area   1.2 yd

Perimeter

Answer : Ted would need 0.72 square yard of wood for the table top and 3.6 yards rare wood for the edging.

Solve the problems. Show your work.

The Orange and Black Department Store is having a sale. The prices shown below are taxes included.

① What will be the cost of 3 shirts and 1 CD?

   Answer : The cost will be _____ .

② What is the amount Joan will save if she buys 5 CDs on sale?

   Answer : _____

③ Can Mr. Ray buy a shirt and a 17" color TV with $230?

   Answer : _____

④ Jenny bought 2 pairs of running shoes. What was her change from $150?

   Answer : _____

Shirt
~~$14.95~~
$12.37 each

17" Color TV
~~$299.95~~
$227.36

Selected CDs
~~$19.99~~
$14.62 each

Ball Point Pens
~~$0.3 each~~
2 for **$0.59**

Running Shoes
~~$86.33~~
$67.99 a pair

Hi-Lighter
~~$0.99~~
$0.79 each

⑤ Mr. Winter bought a shirt, a CD, and a pair of running shoes. What was the average price of these 3 items?

   Answer : _____

Mary and Sally went shopping on Wednesday. They spent $5.88 on apples, $3.35 on lettuce, $4.32 on carrots, and $8.37 on candies.

⑥ How much did they spend in all?

Answer :

⑦ How much change should they receive from a $50 bill?

Answer :

⑧ Mary and Sally shared the bill. How much should each person pay?

Answer :

⑨ The store offers a special discount every Tuesday. Customers get $1.05 off every $10 spent. How much would Mary and Sally have paid by shopping one day earlier?

Answer :

⑩ The apples weighed 12 pounds. What was the cost of 1 pound of apples?

Answer :

⑪ The candies weighed 3 pounds. What was the cost of 1 pound of candies?

Answer :

⑫ They bought 5 heads of lettuce. What was the cost of 1 head of lettuce?

Answer :

⑬ A 5-pound bag of potatoes costs $6.45. An 8-pound bag of potatoes costs $9.28. Which bag is a better buy?

• *To compare the prices of 2 items, find the unit price first.*   Read this first.

Answer :

Use the map to solve the problems. Show your work.

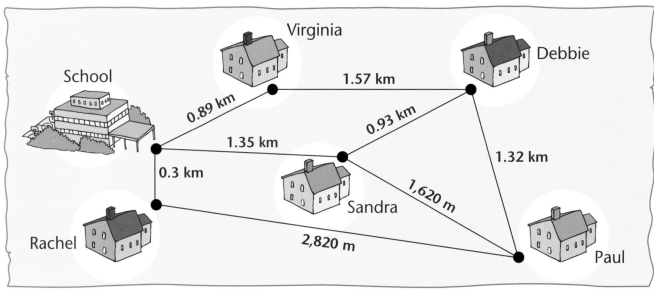

⑭ Who lives the closest to the school? What is the distance in meters?

Answer : _____

⑮ What is the distance in kilometers between Sandra's house and Paul's house?

Answer : _____

⑯ How far is it from Debbie's house to the school if she walks via Virginia's house?

Answer : _____

⑰ What is the shortest distance in meters from Debbie's house to the school?

Answer : _____

⑱ What is the shortest distance in kilometers from Rachel's house to Debbie's house?

Answer : _____

⑲ Yesterday Sandra walked to school in 5 minutes. What was the average distance she walked per minute?

Answer : _____

⑳ Debbie went from home to school passing Virginia's house in 6 minutes. What was the average distance she traveled per minute?

Answer :

㉑ Rachel went from home to Debbie's house passing Paul's house in 9 minutes. What was the average distance she traveled per minute?

Answer :

㉒ If Sandra shuttles between her house and school 4 times a day, how many kilometers will she travel in 5 days?

Answer :

㉓ Virginia and Sandra decide to meet at the school and walk over to Rachel's house together. How far do they walk in total?

Answer :

㉔ On a map, each centimeter represents 0.3 kilometer. What is the actual distance if it is 2.5 centimeters on the map?

Answer :

CHALLENGE

Mr. Headley's class was going to see a play. Each student ticket cost $3.75 and each adult ticket cost $6.90, taxes included. If 30 or more students attended, the theater would give them $12.60 off and a free ticket for the teacher.

① If 25 students attended, how much would the students and Mr. Headley have to pay in total?

Answer :

② If 35 students attended, how much would the students and Mr. Headley have to pay in total?

Answer :

Two-Step Problems

EXAMPLE

Mark bought 3 packages of trading cards for $0.99 each. He paid with a $5 bill. What was his change?

Cost of 3 packages of cards : 0.99 × 3 = 2.97

Change : 5.00 − 2.97 = 2.03

Answer : His change was $2.03.

Solve the problems. Show your work.

The theater has 26 rows of seats with 48 seats in each row. Tickets are $4.50 for adults and $3 for children. On Tuesdays, the $2 cup of popcorn is free with the purchase of 1 adult and 1 children's ticket.

① If 952 people attended a show, how many empty seats were there?

Answer : There were _____ empty seats .

② Yesterday the theater sold 462 adult tickets and the total amount from ticket sales was $2,475. How many children's tickets were sold?

Answer : _____

③ If the entire theater was filled with children and each bought a popcorn, how much money would be collected for that show?

Answer : _____

④ If the entire theater was filled with adults and each bought a popcorn, how much money would be collected for that show?

Answer : _____

⑤ If Mrs. Harris brought 4 children to the theater on Tuesday, and bought each child a popcorn, how much would she pay in all?

Answer : _____

There was a sale at Smirdley's Discount Department Store. All shirts were 2 for $9. All blouses were 3 for $18. All dresses were $19 each. All trousers were on sale for $14 each. The store decided to give a $4 discount for every 6 items bought. All the prices included taxes.

⑥ Peter bought 2 shirts and 1 pair of trousers. How much did he pay for his purchases?

Answer : _____

⑦ Miranda bought 6 blouses and 1 dress. She paid with a $100 bill. How much change did she get?

Answer : _____

⑧ Jerome's mother bought 4 shirts and 3 blouses for her children. She had a twenty-dollar bill and a ten-dollar bill in her wallet, and the rest of her money loose in her purse. How much money did she need from her purse?

Answer : _____

⑨ Wayne bought 2 pairs of trousers and 4 shirts. How much did he pay for his purchases?

Answer : _____

⑩ Mrs. Von bought 9 blouses and 3 pairs of trousers. How much did she pay for her purchases?

Answer : _____

⑪ Frances wanted to buy 4 dresses. She had saved up $50 for her clothing and would borrow the rest from her father. How much would she need to borrow from her father?

Answer : _____

⑫ What was the price difference between 6 blouses and 4 dresses?

Answer : _____

⑬ Amy paid $71 for buying a pair of trousers and some dresses. How many dresses did she buy?

Answer : _____

⑭ There were 128 blue shirts and 224 white shirts. If the salesman put them in packages of 4, how many packages of 4 would he make?

Answer : _____

⑮ If the salesman put them in packages of 3, how many packages of 3 would he make?

Answer : _____

A radio station plays music and ads according to a formula. Every half hour, they play 8 minutes of ads, 16 minutes of music, and the rest is talk. The station broadcasts 16 hours a day.

⑯   How much talk is there every hour?

Answer : _____

⑰   If an ad costs $120 per 30 seconds, how much will the station earn per hour?

Answer : _____

⑱   If the average song is 4 minutes long, how many songs can be played between 4:00 p.m. and 9:00 p.m.?

Answer : _____

⑲   How many minutes of non-ad time are there in a day?

Answer : _____

⑳   If a disc jockey speaks at a rate of 36 words every 10 seconds, how many words will he say in each hour's talk time?

Answer : _____

Anna received a chain letter telling her to make 4 copies of it and send them to 4 friends. Each of her friends was to do the same, and so on. Stamps cost $0.39 each.

㉑   Anna had no stamps at home and had to buy them to send her letters. How much change did she get from a $5 bill?

Answer : _____

㉒ If Anna sent out her letters and her 4 friends sent out their letters, how much would be spent on postage by all of them?

Answer :

㉓ If Anna's chain was 3 friends long, how many people would be involved in the chain?

Answer :

㉔ If Anna's chain was 3 friends long, and everybody did as they were requested, how much would they all pay for postage?

Answer :

㉕ If it took 6 minutes to copy the letter and 2 minutes to fold and put it in an envelope, how much time would be spent by Anna and her 4 friends in doing this?

Answer :

CHALLENGE

① Ellen reads 38 pages each night before going to sleep and 29 pages each morning before breakfast. If she was reading a 249-page book, and started it on a Monday afternoon, how many pages would she have left to read on Thursday at noon?

Answer :

② A television set is on sale for $2,120.50. It can also be bought for 24 payments of $92.60 each. How much more does Wayne pay by purchasing it on the instalment plan?

Answer :

9 *Patterns*

Gary entered a contest. The skill-testing question was:

Take a number. Multiply it by 8. Subtract 6. Divide by 2. Add 15. Divide by 4.
Subtract 3. What pattern did you find in Gary's number and the answer?

If Gary chose 14 as his number:

$14 \times 8 = 112$ ➡ $112 - 6 = 106$ ➡ $106 \div 2 = 53$ ➡ $53 + 15 = 68$ ➡

$68 \div 4 = 17$ ➡ $17 - 3 = 14$

Answer : Gary's number and the answer are the same.

Solve the problems. Show your work.

Dorothy and Gladys were playing a pattern game. Dorothy would think of a pattern like "add 2 and multiply by 3" and keep it secret. Gladys would say a number like "2" and Dorothy would answer "12". Gladys would have to guess the pattern.

① If Gladys said "4", what would Dorothy answer?

Answer : Dorothy would answer _____ .

② If Gladys said "6", what would Dorothy answer?

Answer : _____

③ If Gladys said "5.5", what would Dorothy answer?

Answer : _____

④ Gladys wanted a turn to think of a pattern. When Dorothy said "4", she would answer "14". Which of the following is Gladys's pattern?

A. Divide by 2. Add 10.

B. Multiply by 6. Subtract 10.

C. Subtract 3. Multiply by 10.

D. Add 8. Divide by 2.

Answer : _____

⑤ If Dorothy said "2.4", what would Gladys answer?

Answer : _____

Billy was practicing shooting hoops. He kept track of the number of baskets he scored each day he played.

Day	1st	2nd	3rd	4th	5th
Number of Baskets	1	3	5	7	9

⑥ Was Billy improving as the week progressed?

Answer : _____

⑦ There was a pattern in his improvement. Look at the data and write out the pattern in words.

Answer : _____

⑧ Following the pattern, how many baskets would Billy score on the 6th day?

Answer : _____

⑨ On which day would Billy score 19 baskets?

Answer : _____

⑩ What was the total number of baskets Billy scored in the first 2 days?

Answer : _____

⑪ What was the total number of baskets Billy scored in the first 3 days?

Answer : _____

⑫ What was the total number of baskets Billy scored in the first 4 days?

Answer : _____

⑬ What was the total number of baskets Billy scored in the first 5 days?

Answer : _____

⑭ If this pattern were to continue, what would be the total number of baskets Billy scored in the first 9 days?

Answer : _____

⑮ If this pattern were to continue, how many days would Billy take to get 121 baskets in all?

Answer : _____

Sandy and Andy were on a long walk. To make sure that they did not get bored, they made up some problems for each other to solve.

⑯ Sandy gave Andy this list of numbers : 1, 3, 9, 27, ... She asked Andy to tell her the pattern and the next 2 numbers.

Answer :
_____

⑰ Andy wanted to stump Sandy. He used this list of numbers : 1, 1.9, 2.8, 3.7, ... What is the pattern? What are the next 2 numbers?

Answer :
_____

⑱ Sandy wanted to find a series that Andy could not figure out. She asked him to try this one : a, c, f, j, ... What is the pattern? What are the next 2 letters?

Answer :
_____

⑲ Andy was in trouble. He could not stump Sandy, so he tried this one : 3, 6, 10, 15,... What is the pattern? What are the next 2 numbers?

Answer :
_____

⑳ Andy used this list of numbers : 1, 1, 2, 2, 2, 4, 3, 3, 6, ... to stump Sandy. What is the pattern? What are the next 6 numbers?

Answer :
_____

㉑ Sandy had the last laugh. She said : 1, 2, 3, 5, 8, 13, 21, ... What is the pattern? What are the next 2 numbers?

Answer :
_____

Solve the problems. Show your work.

22 Hortense's parents have strange ideas about allowances. They offered her $0.10 the first day and doubled that each day for a week or Hortense could receive $12 per week. Which was a better deal for Hortense's parents?

Answer : _____

23 Karen got only 52 in math. The math teacher, Mr. Finley, said that if she worked hard to improve, he would double any improvement she made on the next test to reach a final mark. Karen got 58 on the next test. What score would Mr. Finley give her?

Answer : _____

24 On Jerry's 12th birthday, he received a gift from his grandparents. It was a $25 bond that doubled in value every 10 years. What will the bond be worth when Jerry is 72 years old?

Answer : _____

CHALLENGE

Donald and Ronald invented a pattern machine. It had a door to put numbers in, 4 dials to set, and a door to take numbers out. The first example would be : (5 + 12) × 3 = 51. Help them complete the table.

	Number in	1st Operation		2nd Operation		Number out
		Number	Operation	Number	Operation	
	5	12	Addition	3	Multiplication	51
①	8	4	Multiplication	8	Addition	
②	45	3	Division	7		8
③	1	17		9	Division	2

 **Using Patterns**

EXAMPLE

A magic rabbit jumps 1.6 yards with its first jump, and half that distance each jump after. The problem is that the magic rabbit cannot jump less than 0.3 of a yard. How many jumps can the magic rabbit take?

1st jump	2nd jump	3rd jump	4th jump
1.6	$1.6 \div 2 \rightarrow 0.8$	$0.8 \div 2 \rightarrow 0.4$	$0.4 \div 2 \rightarrow 0.2$

But 0.2 < 0.3, so the magic rabbit can only take 3 jumps.

Answer: The magic rabbit can take 3 jumps.

Solve the problems. Show your work.

The price of a savings bond doubles every 10 years. Use this fact to complete the table.

①

Year	1940	1950	1960	1970	1980	1990	2000
Price ($)			250.00		1,000.00		

② What will the price of the savings bond be in 2020?

Answer: _____

③ In which year will the price of the savings bond be $64,000.00?

Answer: _____

④ How many times more was the price of the bond in 1960 than that in 1940?

Answer: _____

⑤ How much would you earn if you bought the bond in 1980 and sold it in 2020?

Answer: _____

Matthew buys trading cards every week. He buys as many as he can with the money left over after paying for everything else.

⑥ Complete the table to see what pattern you can find.

Week	1	2	3	4	5	6	7
No. of cards bought	5	6	8	5		8	
Money spent ($)	2.25	2.70	3.60		2.70		2.25
No. of cards in collection	5	11					

⑦ How many cards will Matthew buy in week 9?

Answer : _____

⑧ How much money will Matthew spend in week 10 on buying cards?

Answer : _____

⑨ How many cards will Matthew collect in the first 3 weeks?

Answer : _____

⑩ How many cards will Matthew collect in the first 6 weeks?

Answer : _____

⑪ How many cards will Matthew collect from week 1 to week 9?

Answer : _____

⑫ How many cards will Matthew collect from week 1 to week 30?

Answer : _____

⑬ If Matthew buys 5 cards in week 22, how many cards will he buy in week 23?

Answer : _____

⑭ How much money will Matthew spend in the first 3 weeks?

Answer : _____

⑮ How much money will Matthew spend in the first 6 weeks?

Answer : _____

Tony has 12 yellow marbles and 5 blue marbles. Each day Tony buys 2 yellow marbles and 3 blue marbles.

⑯ Help Tony complete the table.

Day	1st	2nd	3rd	4th	5th	6th
No. of yellow marbles	12					
No. of blue marbles	5					

⑰ How many yellow marbles will Tony have on the 7th day?

Answer : Tony will have _____ yellow marbles on the 7th day.

⑱ How many blue marbles will Tony have on the 7th day?

Answer : _____

⑲ How many days will Tony take to have 32 yellow marbles?

Answer : _____ .

⑳ How many days will Tony take to have 32 blue marbles?

Answer : _____

㉑ How many days will Tony take to have the same number of yellow and blue marbles?

Answer : _____

㉒ How many marbles will Tony have in all in the first 6 days?

Answer : _____

㉓ What is the pattern of increase in the number of marbles?

Answer : _____

Mrs. Faam's class is studying a table. The numbers in column or row follow a pattern.

24 Help them complete the table.

Row \ Column	1	2	3	4	5	6
1	0	0	0		0	
2	2	4		8		12
3					20	
4			18			36
5	8			32	40	
6	10	20	30			60

25 What is the pattern in column 3? What will the next 3 numbers be after 30?

Answer : _____

26 What is the pattern in row 3? What will the next 3 numbers be after 24?

Answer : _____

27 Which of the columns has the same pattern as that in row 6? What is the pattern?

Answer : _____

28 Joe has 10 cards. The total number of cards that Joe has collected increases by 10 each day. Which of the rows above can show the counting pattern of Joe's cards? How many cards will he have after 5 days?

Answer : _____

29 Raymond uses $8 every day. Which of the rows above can show the total amount of money he has spent? How much money will Raymond have spent after 4 days?

Answer : _____

The Johnson twins are setting up an agency to take care of dogs. Read the rate card.
Then complete the table and answer the questions.

Simple care : $4 for the first hour; $5 per hour thereafter

Walking   : $2 each time, plus $0.50 per mile

Washing   : 2 times total charges

Drying   : Free with care over 3 hours; $2 otherwise

㉚ Simple care :

Time (h)	1	2	3	4	5	6
Charge ($)						

㉛ Walking :

Distance (mi)	1	2	3	4	5	6
Charge ($)						

㉜ Tina had the twins look after her dog, Dorfus, for 10 hours. What was the charge?

Answer : _____

㉝ Kevin asked the twins to look after his dog for 4 hours and take her for a 3-mile walk.
How much did the twins earn for the service?

Answer : _____

㉞ Lily wanted her poodle walked for 4 miles and washed. What was her bill?

Answer : _____

㉟ Dolly's parents asked the twins to look after their dog for 8 hours. They wanted the
dog washed and dried. What was their total bill?

Answer : _____

Keri and Harry were so impressed with the Johnson twins' business that they decided to start one of their own. They would look after cats. Use the following tables to complete their rate card and answer the questions.

Simple Care

Time (h)	1	2	3	4
Charge ($)	3.50	8.00	12.50	17.00

Feeding

No. of meals	1	2	3	4
Charge ($)	5.00	10.00	15.00	20.00

③⑥

Simple care : $_____ for the first hour;

$_____ per hour thereafter

Chasing cat : $12.00 per hour, plus $0.75 a mile

Feeding cat : $_____ per meal

③⑦ Ralph had a cat that was a little wild. His bill showed 3 hours' care and 1 hour and 6 miles of chasing. What was his total bill?

Answer : _____

③⑧ Mr. and Mrs. Quorley had a very well-behaved cat. They wanted it cared for 7 hours and fed 2 meals. What was their total bill?

Answer : _____

CHALLENGE

Willy and Billy set up a baby-sitting service. They charged $1.00 for the first hour and $1.50 per hour after that. If the children were under 3, there was a surcharge of $2.00 for the first hour.

Mr. and Mrs. Jones wanted them to babysit their two children for 5 hours. One was 2 years old and the other 4 years old. How much would their bill be?

Answer : _____

Solve the problems. Show your work.

This is a map of a section of Squaretown. Each block in Squaretown is 1.96 square miles and each side of the block is 1.4 miles. On this map, Allan lives at A. Bobby lives at B. Carol lives at C and Doris lives at D.

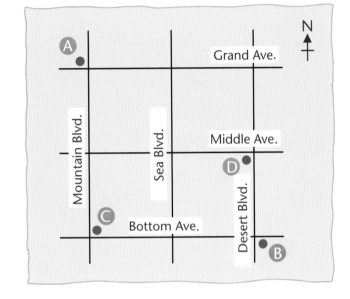

① What is the area bounded by Grand Ave. on the north, Bottom Ave. on the south, Mountain Blvd. on the west, and Desert Blvd. on the east?

Answer : _____

② If Doris walks along Middle Ave. and then turns right on Mountain Blvd. to Allan's house, how far will she walk?

Answer : _____

③ If Bobby walks along Desert Blvd., and then turns left on Grand Ave. to Allan's house, how far will he walk?

Answer : _____

④ If both Allan and Carol walk to Doris's house by the shortest route, how far will they travel in all?

Answer : _____

⑤ Carol was walking to Bobby's house by the shortest route. If she completed 1.86 miles, how much farther would she have to walk?

Answer : _____

⑥ If Bobby walked to Doris's house in 5 minutes, how far would he travel in 1 minute?

Answer : _____

⑦ If Doris walked to Bobby's house in 4 minutes, how much farther would she walk in 1 minute than Bobby?

Answer : _____

Bobby was cycling along Desert Blvd. He kept track of the time it took him to travel each block.

⑧ Complete the table.

No. of blocks	1	2	3	4	5	6
Distance traveled (mi)	1.4	2.8	4.2			
Time (min)	3	6	9			

⑨ What is the pattern of the time taken by Bobby to travel each block?

Answer : _____

⑩ What is the pattern of the distance traveled by Bobby?

Answer : _____

⑪ How long would Bobby take to travel 8 blocks?

Answer : _____

⑫ If Bobby rode for 36 minutes, how many blocks would he pass?

Answer : _____

⑬ If Bobby passed 9 blocks, how many miles would he travel?

Answer : _____

⑭ If Bobby drank $\frac{1}{4}$ quart of water every 15 minutes, how many quarts of water would he have drunk after 75 minutes?

Answer : _____

⑮ If Bobby drank $1\frac{3}{4}$ quarts of water, for how long would he have traveled on his bike?

Answer : _____

SuperSave Department Store is having a sale and all the prices include taxes. They take $3.25 off purchase between $10 and $20, $7.15 off purchase between $20.01 and $40, and $15.50 off purchases $40.01 and over.

⑯ The price of a sweater is $29.45. How much do you have to pay?

Answer :

⑰ Jane paid $53.25 for a pair of jeans. What was its original price?

Answer :

⑱ Tim buys 3 packs of socks at $10.80 each. How much can he save?

Answer :

⑲ The regular price of a book is $15.99. If Jim buys 2 books, how much will he pay?

Answer :

⑳ Billy pays $50 for 2 CDs at $22.99 each. How much change will he get?

Answer :

㉑ May pays $60 for 1 pair of shoes at $59.99 and 1 pair of socks at $3.99. How much change will she get?

Answer :

㉒ A box of chocolates costs $19.87. If Gary has 1 $10 bill, 6 $1 bills, and 3 quarters, will he have enough money to buy a box of chocolates?

Answer :

㉓ There are 329 customers in the store. If 251 customers are female, how many male customers will there be?

Answer :

㉔ On average, each customer spends $5 in the store. How much money can be collected from 215 customers?

Answer :

㉕ Ray wants to buy either sweater A or sweater B. The price of sweater A is $34.87. The price of sweater B is $40.05. What is the price difference between sweater A and sweater B after the discount?

Answer :

㉖ Which sweater should Ray buy? Explain.

Answer :

Circle the correct answer to each problem.

Frank has invented a machine. If he drops a number in the top, a related number comes out from the side.

㉗ If you drop a 1 in the top, a 5 comes out from the side. A 2 produces an 8 and a 3 produces an 11. Which of the following is the machine's pattern?

A. Add 4

B. Multiply by 3 and add 2

C. Add 2 and multiply by 3

D. Multiply by 2 and add 3

㉘ If you drop a 4 in the top, what number will come out from the side?

A. 8   B. 11   C. 14   D. 18

㉙ Frank dreams of a machine that works on the same pattern, but turns 1 $1 bill into 5, 2 $1 bills into 8 and so on. How much money would he make if he dropped 7 $1 bills into his machine?

A. 23   B. 42   C. 17   D. 11

㉚ To make 29 $1 bills, how many $1 bills would Frank have to drop into the machine?

A. 8   B. 9   C. 25   D. 13

㉛ What pattern would Frank have to create for the machine to turn 2 quarters into $11 and 3 quarters into $12?

A. Add 3 and multiply by 3

B. Multiply by 5 and add 3

C. Multiply by 4 and add 9

D. Multiply by 5 and subtract 3

㉜ If the machine made $14, how many quarters would Frank have dropped into the machine?

A. 7   B. 6   C. 5   D. 4

㉝ What pattern would Frank have to create for the machine to turn 6 nickels into $9 and 8 nickels into $10?

A. Multiply by 1.5

B. Multiply by 10 and add 6

C. Multiply by 1.25 and add 1.5

D. Add 4.2 and multiply by 2

There are 72 seats in the Virtual Reality Game Center. Each adult ticket costs $6.49 and each children's ticket is $2.90 less than an adult ticket.

③④ If all the seats were occupied by adults, how much money would the center collect?

A. $467.28   B. $487.28   C. $457.28   D. $367.28

③⑤ If all the seats were occupied by children, how much money would the center collect?

A. $248.48   B. $258.48   C. $348.48   D. $358.48

③⑥ If 46 seats were occupied by children and the rest by adults, how much money would the center collect?

A. $391.88   B. $398.78   C. $268.98   D. $333.88

③⑦ Mrs. Faam buys 8 tickets for $46.12. The number of children's tickets she intends to buy is fewer than 5, how many adult tickets does she buy?

A. 4   B. 5   C. 6   D. 7

③⑧ How many children's tickets does she buy?

A. 1   B. 2   C. 3   D. 4

③⑨ Game A lasts $6\frac{7}{12}$ minutes and Game B lasts $5\frac{11}{12}$ minutes. How long do these two games last altogether?

A. $11\frac{2}{3}$ minutes   B. $12\frac{1}{2}$ minutes

C. $11\frac{3}{4}$ minutes   D. $13\frac{2}{3}$ minutes

④⓪ By how many minutes is Game A longer than Game B?

A. $1\frac{2}{3}$ B. $\frac{3}{4}$ C. $1\frac{1}{4}$ D. $\frac{2}{3}$

④① Joe played Game A twice. How long did he play Game A?

A. $12\frac{1}{12}$ minutes   B. $12\frac{14}{24}$ minutes   C. $12\frac{7}{12}$ minutes   D. $13\frac{2}{12}$ minutes

Overview

In the previous section, problem-solving strategies were applied in the context of the four arithmetic operations and pattern recognition.

In this section, word problems involve finding perimeter, area, volume, speed, and time. The geometry units include applications of coordinate systems and transformations. The statistics topics covered are the interpretation of circle graphs and line graphs. Students also practice solving problems involving mean and mode, and probability.

Operations with Money

Mary buys 2 desk pads at $14.95 each and 5 binders at $2.97 each. If Mary gets a $2.18 discount on desk pads and a $1.48 discount on binders, how much will she spend in all?

Cost of desk pads : (14.95 × 2) − 2.18 = 27.72

Cost of binders : (2.97 × 5) − 1.48 = 13.37

Cost in all : 27.72 + 13.37 = 41.09

Answer : Mary will spend $41.09 in all.

Solve the problems. Show your work.

Ben wants to make some money by doing odd jobs.

Excellent Service	
Call Ben • 725-JOBS	
Raking Leaves	$ 4.98
Sweeping Sidewalks	$ 2.84
Mowing Lawns	$12.49
Cleaning Garages	$20.18
Washing Cars	$ 5.39
* $4.50 off for 3 jobs or more at the same time.	

① If Mrs. Donovan hired Ben to rake her leaves and mow her lawn, what would her bill be?

Answer : Her bill would be _____ .

② If Mr. Kell hired Ben to clean his garage and wash his car, what would his bill be?

Answer : _____

③ If Mr. Ryan hired Ben to do all the jobs except car washing, what would his bill be?

Answer : _____

④ If Mr. Ryan gave Ben a $100 bill, how much change would he get?

Answer : _____

⑤ Mrs. Winter hired Ben to do 2 jobs and her bill was $23.02. Which 2 jobs did Ben do?

Answer : _____

⑥ If Mrs. Winter gave Ben a $50 bill, how much change would she get?

Answer : _____

⑦ If it took Ben 2 hours to clean a garage, how much money would he earn per hour?

Answer :

⑧ Ben decided to give a quarter of his earnings to charity. He earned $37.65 the first week, $35.94 the second, and $31.53 the third. How much would he have after his donation?

Answer :

Edward's Emporium is having a year-end sale. There is a $1.50 rebate for every $10 spent. If a customer spends over $100, he or she gets an additional $0.30 off every $10. All prices include taxes.

⑨ Ann buys a blouse at $82.97. What is her change from a $100 bill?

Answer :

⑩ Tim buys a shirt at $120.45. What is his change from a $100 bill?

Answer :

⑪ Ray buys 3 sweaters at $16.99 each. How much rebate does he get? What is his change from a $50 bill?

Answer :

⑫ A pair of boots costs $92.85. If Sally wants to buy 2 pairs of boots, should she buy them separately or together? Explain.

Answer :

⑬ Jacket A costs $98.27. Jacket B costs $102.95. If Eric wants to buy a cheaper jacket, which one should he buy?

Answer :

Donna and her friends went to a new candy store to buy their favorite candies. The prices included taxes.

⑭ Donna wanted to buy some lollipops. It was $0.97 each or $10.80 for a package of 12. How much would Donna save by buying a package of lollipops?

Answer : _____

⑮ Donna bought 2 packages of lollipops. What was her change from $25?

Answer : _____

⑯ Gary wanted some jellybeans. A box of 6 packages was sold at $3.24. How much did 1 package cost?

Answer : _____

⑰ Christopher bought 18 packages of jellybeans. What was his change from a $20 bill?

Answer : _____

⑱ Ted paid $23.76 to buy a package of lollipops and a few boxes of jellybeans. How many boxes of jellybeans did Ted buy?

Answer : _____

⑲ There was a sign in the shop. 'Buy 2 chocolate bars at $1.26 each and get the third one free'. How much did each chocolate bar cost on average?

Answer : _____

⑳ Alexander took 9 chocolate bars. How much did he pay?

Answer : _____

㉑ Each jar of candies cost $12.96. Jeffrey had $40. Would he have enough money to buy 3 jars of candies?

Answer : _____

㉒ If Jeffrey bought 2 jars of candies, how much money would he have left?

Answer : _____

• For Question 18, follow the pattern to find the answer, e.g.

Read this first.

No. of boxes of jellybeans	1	2
Cost ($)	3.24	6.48

Help the candy store owner write out the profits in the past 4 weeks in numbers and in words. Then put the weeks in order.

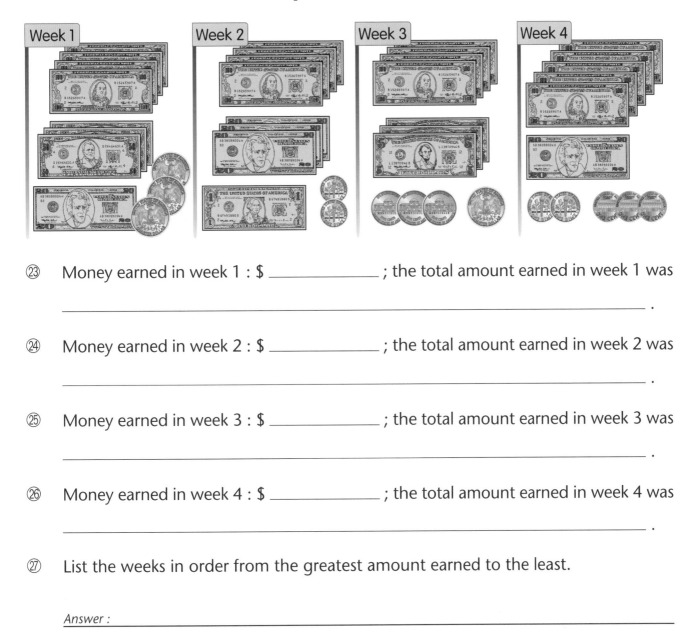

㉓   Money earned in week 1 : $ _____ ; the total amount earned in week 1 was

_____ .

㉔   Money earned in week 2 : $ _____ ; the total amount earned in week 2 was

_____ .

㉕   Money earned in week 3 : $ _____ ; the total amount earned in week 3 was

_____ .

㉖   Money earned in week 4 : $ _____ ; the total amount earned in week 4 was

_____ .

㉗   List the weeks in order from the greatest amount earned to the least.

Answer : _____

CHALLENGE

Mr. Tiff buys 12 toy cars for $187.20 and re-sells them at $20.94 each.

①   How much money will Mr. Tiff get?   ②   How much will he gain or lose?

Answer : _____   *Answer :* _____

2 Perimeter and Area

What is the perimeter and area of this figure?

Perimeter : 1.5 + 1.2 + 2 + 0.8 + 3.5 +2 = 11

Area : (1.5 × 2) + (2 × 0.8) = 4.6

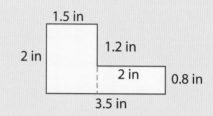

Answer : The perimeter of this figure is 11 inches and its area is 4.6 square inches.

The diagrams below are the drawings of 6 gardens. Use the diagrams to solve the problems. Show your work.

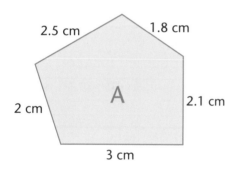

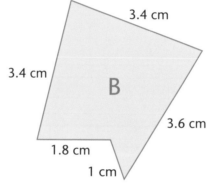

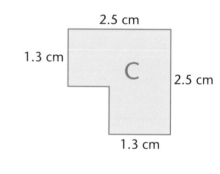

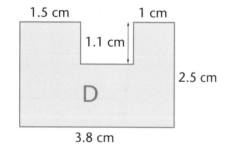

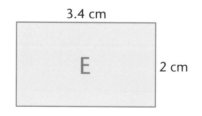

① What is the perimeter of A?

Answer : Its perimeter is _____ .

② What is the perimeter of B?

Answer : _____

③ What is the perimeter of C?

Answer : _____

④ What is the perimeter of D?

Answer : _____

⑤ What is the perimeter of E?

Answer : _____

⑥ What is the perimeter of F?

Answer : _____

• Use these formulas to find the perimeter of a square and a rectangle.

Read this first.

length

Perimeter of a square = length × 4

length

width

Perimeter of a rectangle = (length + width) × 2

⑦ The actual dimensions of each garden are 100 times that of the diagram. Find the actual perimeter of each garden and write in meters.

Garden	A	B	C	D	E	F
Actual Perimeter						

Darren wants to divide his backyard into parts. The actual dimensions are 100 times that of the diagram below. Measure the diagram to solve the problems. Show your work.

Q

T

P

R

S

⑧ What is the actual perimeter of P?

Answer : _____

⑨ What is the actual perimeter of Q?

Answer : _____

⑩ What is the actual perimeter of R?

Answer : _____

⑪ What is the actual perimeter of S?

Answer : _____

⑫ What is the actual perimeter of T?

Answer : _____

⑬ Put the parts in order from the part with the greatest perimeter to the one with the smallest.

Answer : _____

Look at the floor plan and dimensions of the first floor of Darren's house. All the ceilings are 2.8 yards high. Solve the problems. Show your work.

	Dimension		Dimension
Library	5 yd × 6.5 yd	Side Garden	2.3 yd × 5 yd
Porch	5 yd × 2.9 yd	Wash-room	2.6 yd × 5 yd
Dining Room	5 yd × 13 yd	Living Room	7.9 yd × 7.9 yd
Hall	3 yd × 7.3 yd	Kitchen	5 yd × 6.4 yd

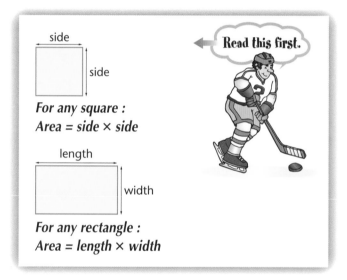

⑭ What is the area of the library?

Answer :

⑮ What is the area of the hall?

Answer :

⑯ What is the area of the living room?

Answer :

⑰ How many times of the area of the washroom is the area of the dining room?

Answer :

⑱ What is the area of the first floor of Darren's house?

Answer :

⑲ How many square yards of carpet would cover the living room and the library?

Answer :

⑳ If 1 square yard of carpet costs $2, how much does Darren need to pay for the carpet for his living room and library?

Answer :

㉑ Darren wants to paint 2 adjacent walls in the kitchen. If 1 quart of paint covers 4 square yards, how many quarts of paint are needed for the 2 walls?

Answer :

㉒ If paint comes in 2-quart cans, how many cans of paint does Darren need to buy?

Answer :

Solve the problems. Show your work.

㉓ A flag is 2.5 yards long and 1.2 yards wide. What is its perimeter and area?

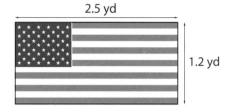

Answer : _____

㉔ The length of a square coffee table is 30 inches. What is its perimeter and area?

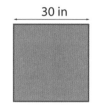

Answer : _____

㉕ A square has a perimeter of 12 feet. How long is each side?

Answer : _____

㉖ A rectangular backyard has an area of 450 square yards. If its length is 25 yards, what is its width?

Answer : _____

㉗ A piece of rectangular cardboard has a perimeter of 45 inches. If its width is 5 inches, what is its area?

Answer : _____

CHALLENGE

The outside dimensions of a framed picture are 12 inches by 20 inches. If the border is 1 inch wide,

① what is the length and width of the picture?

Answer : _____

② what is the area and perimeter of the picture?

Answer : _____

Time

EXAMPLE

School starts at 8:45 a.m. and finishes at 3:20 p.m. How long is the school day?

1st ▶ From 8:45 a.m. to noon : 3 hours 15 minutes

2nd ▶ From noon to 3:20 p.m. : 3 hours 20 minutes

Total time : 3 h 15 min + 3 h 20 min = 6 h 35 min

Answer : The school day is 6 hours 35 minutes.

1st	
	12 h 00 min
−	8 h 45 min
	3 h 15 min

2nd	
	3 h 20 min
−	0 h 00 min
	3 h 20 min

Solve the problems. Show your work.

Jimmy and his grandparents like to walk for exercise. Last Saturday, they left home at 9:40 a.m. for the park, which took them 57 minutes at their usual pace. After spending 40 minutes there, they walked to the convenience store for groceries, which took them 32 minutes. After shopping, they arrived home at 12:42 p.m.

① At what time did Jimmy and his grandparents reach the park?

They reached the park
Answer : at _____ .

② At what time did they leave the park?

Answer : _____

③ At what time did they reach the convenience store?

Answer : _____

④ They shopped in the store for 35 minutes. At what time did they leave the store?

Answer : _____

⑤ How long did it take them to walk home after shopping?

Answer : _____

⑥ Jimmy's grandma took 26 minutes to cook their lunch. If she finished cooking at 1:17 p.m., at what time did she start?

Answer : _____

⑦ Larry has an assignment due on November 29. If he starts to work on it on November 3, how many days does he have to complete the assignment?

Answer : _____

⑧ If Larry starts doing his assignment at 8:16 a.m. and stops at 4:05 p.m., how long has he worked on it?

Answer : _____

⑨ Larry spent 2 hours 20 minutes looking for reference materials in the school library. He left at 5:32 p.m. When did he start working in the library?

Answer : _____

⑩ Mrs. Smith has an appointment with her doctor at 2:15 p.m. It takes her 23 minutes to walk to the doctor's office. If Mrs. Smith leaves home at 1:48 p.m., will she be there on time?

Answer : _____

⑪ Ben's favorite TV show starts at 11:45 a.m. and lasts 1 hour 35 minutes. When will the show be over?

Answer : _____

⑫ Movie A lasts 1 hour 43 minutes; movie B lasts 1 hour 16 minutes. If movie A starts at 11:45 a.m. and movie B starts at 12:10 p.m., which movie finishes first?

Answer : _____

⑬ Peter traveled from City A to City B in 170 hours. How many days and hours did he spend on traveling?

Answer : _____

⑭ Gary wanted to go to the theater. He left home at 11:26 a.m. First he took a bus for 37 minutes. Then he walked for 16 minutes. At what time did he reach the theater?

Answer : _____

CHALLENGE

A flight from Jonesville to Littletown takes 2 hours 16 minutes. A flight from Norhead to Littletown takes 1 hour 45 minutes. If flight A leaves Jonesville for Littletown at 11:55 a.m., about what time must flight B leave Norhead to reach Littletown at the same time as flight A?

Answer : _____

Speed

EXAMPLE

. . . .

Mr. Ford drove his car at an average speed of 40 miles per hour. Mr. Coleman drove his car at an average speed of 45 miles per hour. They both started at the same time from the same place but drove in opposite directions. How far apart would they be after 3 hours?

Distance traveled by Mr. Ford : 40 × 3 = 120

Distance traveled by Mr. Coleman : 45 × 3 = 135

Distance apart : 120 + 135 = 255

40 mph   45 mph
←   →

Answer : They would be 255 miles apart after 3 hours.

Solve the problems. Show your work.

Sally and her family were going on a motoring trip. They planned to drive to Centertown, a distance of 400 miles, and from there to Middleberg, a distance of 550 miles and then drove 480 miles home.

①   If they drove at an average speed of 40 mph, how long would it take to drive from home to Centertown?

Answer : It would take _____ .

②   If they drove at an average speed of 50 mph, how long would it take to drive from Centertown to Middleberg?

Answer : _____

③   The trip from Middleberg to home took 10 hours. What was their average speed on this part of the trip?

Answer : _____

④   If they drove at an average speed of 40 mph, how long would it take to drive from Middleberg to home?

Answer : _____

⑤   If they drove at an average speed of 50 mph, how long would it take to drive the whole trip?

Answer : _____

⑥   If it took them 20 hours to complete the trip, what would be the average speed?

Answer : _____

Doris can cycle at 20 miles per hour and run at 12 miles per hour. Use the diagram to solve the problems. Show your work.

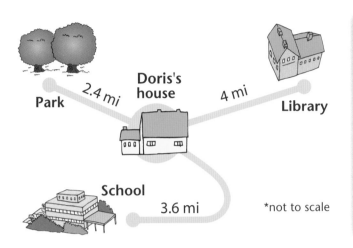

Park — 2.4 mi — Doris's house — 4 mi — Library

School — 3.6 mi

*not to scale

• **Don't forget :**

1 h = 60 min ;

$$h \underset{\div 60}{\overset{\times 60}{\rightleftarrows}} min$$

← Read this first.

e.g. 0.3 h = 18 min

$$\begin{array}{r} 0.3 \\ \times\ 6\,0 \\ \hline 1\,8.0 \end{array}$$

42 min = 0.7 h

$$\begin{array}{r} 0.7 \\ 6\,0\,\overline{)4\,2.0} \\ \underline{4\,2\,0} \end{array}$$

⑦ How long will it take Doris to cycle to and from the library?

Answer : _____

⑧ How long will it take Doris to run to the park from home?

Answer : _____

⑨ How many minutes can Doris save by riding the bicycle to the park instead of running?

Answer : _____

⑩ How many minutes will it take Doris to cycle to school?

Answer : _____

⑪ Last Thursday, it took Doris 15 minutes to cycle to school. What was her cycling speed in miles per minute?

Answer : _____

⑫ What was her cycling speed in miles per hour?

Answer : _____

CHALLENGE

Ricky, Raymond, and Sam each have a 180-page storybook. Ricky plans to read 20 pages each day. Raymond plans to read 36 pages every 2 days. Sam plans to read 15 pages every half day. How many days will it take each of them to finish the whole book? Who will be the first to finish the book?

Answer : _____

Volume and Surface Area

EXAMPLE

Gary has a box 20 inches long, 12 inches wide, and 18 inches high. What is its volume? What is its surface area?

Volume : 20 × 12 × 18 = 4,320

Surface area : 20 × 12 + 20 × 18 × 2 + 12 × 18 × 2 = 1,392

Answer : The volume of his box is 4,320 cubic inches. Its surface area is 1,392 square inches.

Solve the problems. Show your work.

Sandy had a new aquarium 25 inches long, 10 inches wide, and 15 inches high. She was told to fill it with water to a depth of 4 inches on Monday, 8 inches on Wednesday, and 12 inches on Friday. On Saturday, she could put her fish in the aquarium.

① Before filling the aquarium with water, what was the volume of air inside?

Answer : _____

② What volume of water would be needed to fill up the aquarium?

Answer : _____

③ What was the volume of water in the aquarium on Monday?

Answer : _____

④ What was the increase in volume of water in the aquarium on Wednesday?

Answer : _____

The space above the water is still occupied by air.   ◄— **Read this first.**

water

⑤ What volume of air would be in the aquarium on Friday?

Answer : _____

⑥ After putting in the fish, water level in the aquarium rose to 13 inches high. What was the volume of the fish?

Answer : _____

Alan has a tank 30 inches long, 16 inches wide, and 20 inches high. It is full of water. He is trying to empty it with a pail which can hold 320 cubic inches of water.

⑦   What is the volume of the water in the tank?

Answer : _____

⑧   How many times of the volume of the water held by the pail can be held by the tank?

Answer : _____

⑨   How many pailfuls of water are required to empty the tank?

Answer : _____

⑩   After Alan has removed 8 pailfuls of water, how much water has been removed?

Answer : _____

⑪   What volume of water will remain in the tank?

Answer : _____

⑫   How many pailfuls of water must be removed to half empty the tank?

Answer : _____

⑬   If Alan was emptying the water into an aquarium 4 feet long and 20 inches wide, how high would it be to just hold all the water from the tank?

Answer : _____

⑭   If Alan puts 5 metal cubes into the tank and 320 cubic inches of water overflows, what is the volume of each metal cube?

Answer : _____

⑮   If the length of each cube is 4 inches, what is its surface area?

Answer : _____

Carol has 2 aquariums. The big one is 1 meter long, 0.5 meter wide, and 0.6 meter high. The small one is only 0.6 meter long, but has the same height and width as the big one.

⑯　What is the volume of the big aquarium?

Answer : _____

⑰　What is the volume of the small aquarium?

Answer : _____

⑱　By how much is the volume of the big aquarium larger than that of the small one?

Answer : _____

⑲　Each side of a cube is 10 centimeters long. If Carol tries to put the cubes into the small aquarium, how many cubes can the small aquarium hold?

Answer : _____

⑳　If Carol put the cubes into the big aquarium, how many cubes can the big aquarium hold?

Answer : _____

㉑　If it takes Carol 30 minutes to fill up the big aquarium with water, how long will it take her to fill up the small aquarium with water flowing at the same rate?

Answer : _____

• **For Questions 19 and 20:**
  Assume the given dimensions
  are those of the inside of the
  aquariums.

Small aquarium

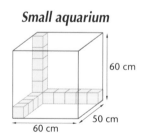

60 cm

50 cm

60 cm

Read this first.

• **For Question 21, first find the volume of water flows in 1 minute. Then**
  use this rate of water flow to find the answer.

Look at the floor plan of Francis's new house. All the ceilings are 3 meters high. Use the table to solve the problems. Show your work.

Washroom

| Bedroom 1 |
| Living Room |
| Bedroom 2 | Hall |
| Dining Room | Kitchen |

	Dimension
Bedroom 1	4 m × 7 m
Bedroom 2	8 m × 7 m
Washroom	2.3 m × 2.8 m
Dining room	4 m × 6.4 m
Kitchen	4 m × 5 m
Living room	5.6 m × 8.6 m

㉒ What volume of air is there in the living room?

Answer : _____

㉓ What volume of air is there in bedroom 2?

Answer : _____

㉔ How much more air is there in bedroom 1 than in the washroom?

Answer : _____

㉕ Francis's father has built a store room in the kitchen. The area of the store room is one-eighth of the kitchen. What is its volume in cubic meters?

Answer : _____

㉖ What is the volume of the store room in cubic centimeters?

Answer : _____

CHALLENGE

Tina used cubes of length 1 centimeter to build 2 models as shown. Help her find the volumes and surface areas of the models.

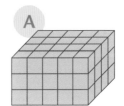
A

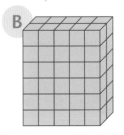
B

	Model	Volume (cm³)	Surface area (cm²)
①	A		
②	B		

6 Coordinate Systems

EXAMPLE

Kari was at position (2, 1). First she went 6 units right and 4 units up. Then she went 4 units left and 3 units down. Finally, she went 1 unit right and 2 units up. Show Kari's route on the grid and tell where she is now.

1st : 6 units right and 4 units up ⟶ (8, 5)

2nd : 4 units left and 3 units down ⟶ (4, 2)

Final: 1 unit right and 2 units up ⟶ (5, 4)

Answer : She is at position (5, 4) now.

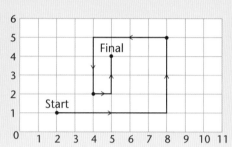

Solve the problems.   Show your work.

Help Lori graph each set of ordered pairs called out by Jerry. Join them to form polygons. Then identify each polygon.

① (9, 5), (9, 1), (1, 1), (1, 5)

Answer : It is a _____ .

② (6, 1), (9, 4), (2, 5)

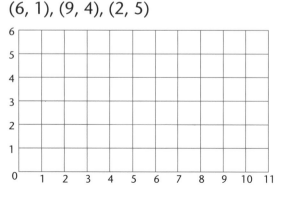

Answer : _____

③ (3, 5), (10, 5), (9, 1), (2, 1)

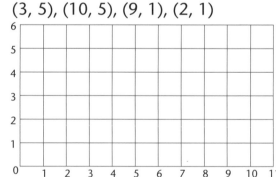

Answer : _____

④ (2, 5), (8, 5), (6, 1), (4, 1)

Answer : _____

Jerry draws some incomplete shapes on the grid. Help Lori find the missing vertex to complete each shape and solve the problems.

⑤ The missing vertex is 3 units right and 2 units up from (7, 3).

a.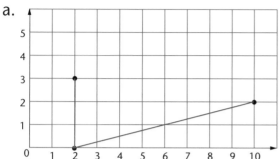

b. What is the ordered pair of the missing vertex?

Answer : _____

c. What shape is it?

Answer : _____

⑥ The missing vertex is 2 units right and 3 units up from (0, 2).

a.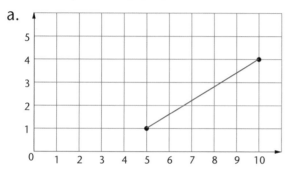

b. What is the ordered pair of the missing vertex?

Answer : _____

c. What shape is it?

Answer : _____

⑦ The missing vertex is 2 units up from (3, 0).

a.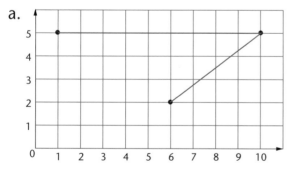

b. What is the ordered pair of the missing vertex?

Answer : _____

c. What shape is it?

Answer : _____

⑧ The missing vertex is midway between the ordered pairs (0, 4) and (4, 4).

a.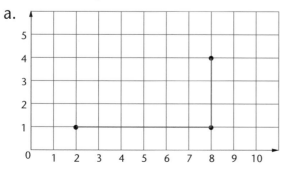

b. What is the ordered pair of the missing vertex?

Answer : _____

c. What shape is it?

Answer : _____

Dory's class is having a treasure hunt. They have a grid drawn over the map of an island. To find the treasure, they should follow Dory's instructions. Help the children find the coordinates of all the places and locate the traps on the grid. Then complete Dory's instructions and draw the route on the grid.

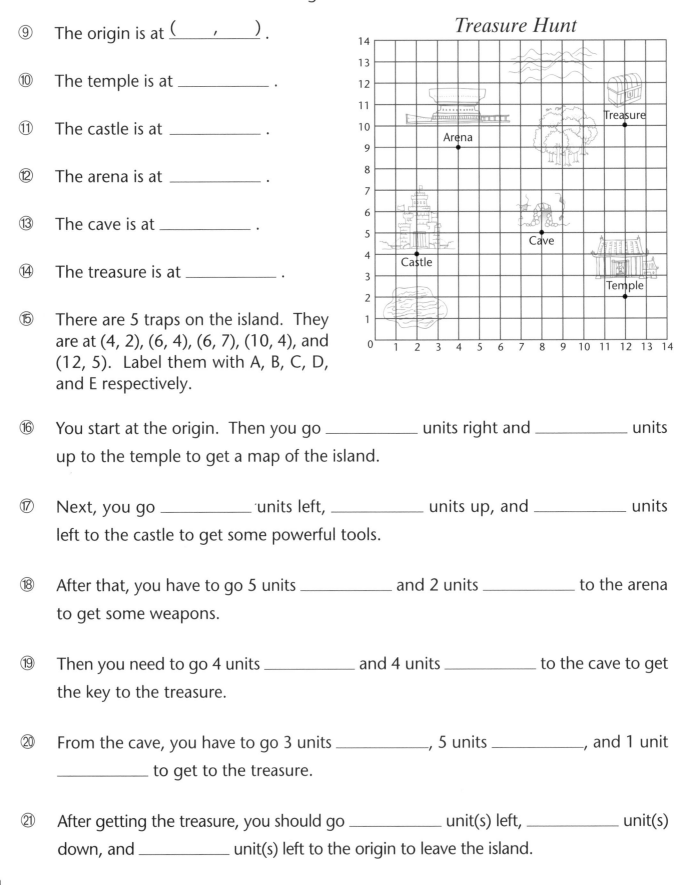

Treasure Hunt

⑨ The origin is at (____ , ____).

⑩ The temple is at _____ .

⑪ The castle is at _____ .

⑫ The arena is at _____ .

⑬ The cave is at _____ .

⑭ The treasure is at _____ .

⑮ There are 5 traps on the island. They are at (4, 2), (6, 4), (6, 7), (10, 4), and (12, 5). Label them with A, B, C, D, and E respectively.

⑯ You start at the origin. Then you go _____ units right and _____ units up to the temple to get a map of the island.

⑰ Next, you go _____ units left, _____ units up, and _____ units left to the castle to get some powerful tools.

⑱ After that, you have to go 5 units _____ and 2 units _____ to the arena to get some weapons.

⑲ Then you need to go 4 units _____ and 4 units _____ to the cave to get the key to the treasure.

⑳ From the cave, you have to go 3 units _____, 5 units _____, and 1 unit _____ to get to the treasure.

㉑ After getting the treasure, you should go _____ unit(s) left, _____ unit(s) down, and _____ unit(s) left to the origin to leave the island.

Use the clues to find the seats for the children. Write their names in the boxes and find the ordered pairs.

- Mary is sitting 2 units left from Lori; Daisy is sitting 2 units right from Lori.

- Matthew is sitting between Daisy and Jerry.

- George is sitting 2 units up from the origin; Susan is sitting 1 unit down from George.

- Alvin is sitting between Mary and Gary; Ray is sitting 1 unit left from Alvin.

- Walk 2 units down and 1 unit left from Michael and you can find Amy's seat.

- Emily is sitting between Michael and Sarah; Jessica is sitting 1 unit right from Emily.

- John is sitting 1 unit up from Jessica, and Emily is sitting between John and Elaine.

㉒
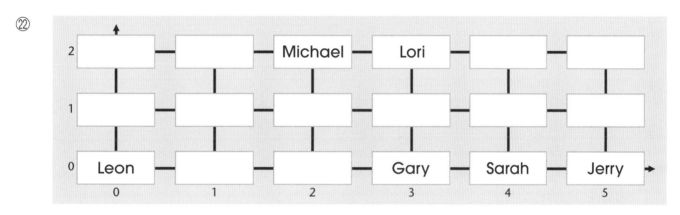

㉓ George _____

㉔ Susan _____

㉕ Elaine _____

㉖ Alvin _____

㉗ Jessica _____

㉘ Mary _____

CHALLENGE

A and B are two vertices of a square. Write out the possible coordinates for the other two vertices and plot them on the grid.

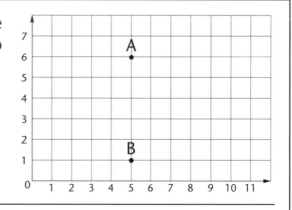

Answer : _____

Solve the problems. Show your work.

Wilma went to the mall to buy some containers and an aquarium. She left home at 10:47 a.m. and traveled at an average speed of 30 mph to get to the mall.

① Wilma reached the mall at 11:11 a.m. How long did it take her to go from her home to the mall?

Answer : _____

② How far away was the mall from her house?

Answer: _____

③ Wilma shopped in the mall for 2 hours and 18 minutes. She then had lunch there for 45 minutes. At what time did she leave the mall?

Answer : _____

④ Wilma traveled at 24 mph back home. At what time did she reach home?

Answer : _____

⑤ Wilma bought 1 box and 1 aquarium. The box cost $18.27 and the aquarium cost $52.49. What was her change from a $100 bill?

Answer : _____

⑥ How much more did the aquarium cost than the box?

Answer : _____

⑦ The box was 20 inches wide, 24 inches long, and 20 inches high. Wilma wanted to cover the bottom of the box with felt. How much felt would she need?

Answer : _____

⑧ Wilma wanted to decorate the edges of the top sides of the box by drawing a border. How long would her border be?

Answer : _____

⑨ What was the volume of the box?

Answer : _____

⑩ A box of tissues was 4 inches wide, 8 inches long, and 5 inches high. How many boxes of tissues could the box hold?

Answer : _____

⑪ The aquarium was 8 inches wide, 16 inches long, and 12 inches high. What volume of water could the aquarium hold?

Answer : _____

⑫ Wilma turned on the tap to fill the aquarium with water from 4:29 p.m. until 4.34 p.m. How long did it take to fill up the whole aquarium?

Answer : _____

⑬ Wilma poured some water from the aquarium until the water level in the aquarium dropped 2 inches. What volume of water was in the aquarium?

Answer : _____

⑭ Wilma put 8 pebbles into the aquarium and the water level rose 0.5 inch. On average, what was the volume of each pebble?

Answer : _____

Darlene has a grid drawn over the map of her neigborhood. Follow Darlene's instructions to write the places in the boxes.

⑮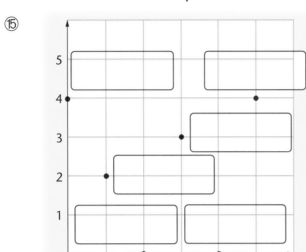

- The library is 1 unit up and 2 units right of Darlene's house.
- The park is 5 units left of the shopping mall.
- The school is 2 units down and 3 units right of Darlene's house.
- The shopping mall is 1 unit right and 4 units up of the school.
- The convenience store is 2 units left of the school.

⑯ Darlene's house is at (___ , ___) .

⑰ The park is at _____ .

⑱ The shopping mall is at _____ .

⑲ The convenience store is at _____ .

⑳ The school is at _____ .

㉑ The library is at _____ .

㉒ If the bus travels at an average speed of 30 mph and it takes Darlene 15 minutes to get to the mall, how far away is the mall from the bus stop?

Answer : _____

㉓ When will Darlene arrive at the mall if she gets on the bus at 11:56 a.m.?

Answer : _____

㉔ A student ticket costs $1.28 each or 10 for $10.40. How much will Darlene save if she buys 10 tickets?

Answer : _____

㉕ Darlene buys 12 student tickets. How much does she pay?

Answer : _____

㉖ Darlene spends $12.84 on food and $31.39 on stationery. How much does she spend in all?

Answer : _____

㉗ Darlene has spent $32.97 altogether. Now she has $22.81 left. How much did she have at the beginning?

Answer : _____

Circle the correct answer to each problem.

㉘ Gary is drawing a square on a grid. The vertices of the square are at (2, 0), (6, 0), and (2, 4). Where is the 4th vertex?

A. (4, 6)   B. (0, 6)   C. (6, 4)   D. (0, 4)

㉙ John is drawing a rectangle on a grid. The vertices of the rectangle are at (6, 2), (3, 5), and (1, 3). Where is the 4th vertex?

A. (0, 4)   B. (4, 0)   C. (5, 0)   D. (0, 5)

㉚ What is the surface area of a rectangular box 1.6 meters long, 0.6 meter wide, and 0.8 meter high?

A. 5.44 m^2 B. 4.48 m^2 C. 4.16 m^2 D. 4.96 m^2

㉛ A bicycle and a car start at the same time from Bayville to Meadowview. The average speeds of the bicycle and the car are 12 mph and 34 mph respectively. How far ahead is the car after 1 hour and 30 minutes?

A. 22 miles   B. 18 miles   C. 33 miles   D. 51 miles

㉜ It takes a car 3 hours 16 minutes to travel from Bayville to Meadowview. It leaves Bayville at 3:47 p.m. When will it arrive at Meadowview?

A. 6:33 p.m.   B. 8:03 p.m.   C. 6:03 p.m.   D. 7:03 p.m.

㉝ Georgia is planting her garden. Her plot is 4.2 yards long and 3.5 yards wide. She wants to put a fence around her plot. What length of fencing will she need?

A. 7.7 yards   B. 14.7 yards   C. 16.1 yards   D. 15.4 yards

㉞ If the fence costs $2.50 per yard, what will the cost of fencing be?

A. $19.25   B. $38.50   C. $36.75   D. $40.25

㉟ Georgia wants to plant one-seventh of her garden with lettuce. How much space will the lettuce take up?

A. 2.1 yd^2 B. 7.7 yd^2 C. 13 yd^2 D. 14.7 yd^2

7 *Transformations*

What motion is shown in each set of diagrams? Write translation, reflection, or rotation to describe each motion.

a.   Before   After

b.   Before   After

c.   Before   After

Answer :   a. Translation   b. Rotation   c. Reflection

Solve the problems. Show your work.

① Draw the reflection image of each polygon.

a.

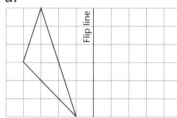

b.

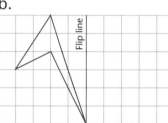

c.

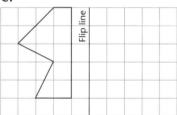

② Draw the rotation image of each polygon.

a. $\frac{1}{4}$ turn clockwise   b. $\frac{1}{2}$ turn clockwise   c. $\frac{1}{4}$ turn counterclockwise

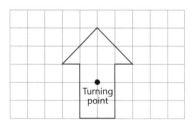

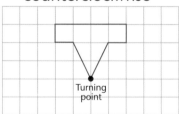

③ Draw the translation image of each polygon.

a. 2 units right
   1 unit down

b. 3 units right
   1 unit up

c. 3 units left
   2 units down

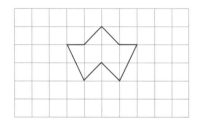

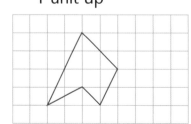

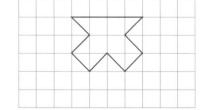

④ Draw the flip line for the reflection image of each colored polygon.

a.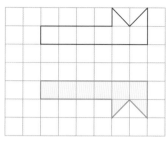

b.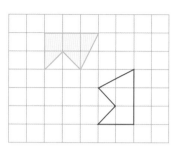

c.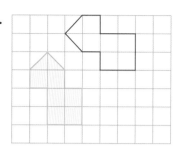

⑤ Draw the turning point for the rotation image of each colored polygon and tell whether the turn is $\frac{1}{4}$ turn, $\frac{1}{2}$ turn, or $\frac{3}{4}$ turn clockwise.

a.

Answer : _____

b.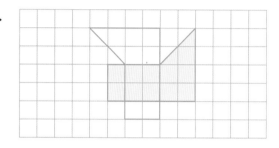

Answer : _____

⑥ Describe the translation image of each colored polygon.

a.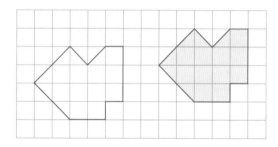

Answer : _____

b.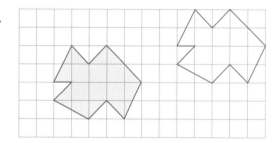

Answer : _____

⑦ Draw the reflection image of each colored polygon over the flip lines l, m, and n.

a.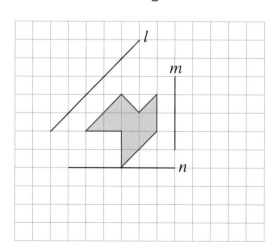

b.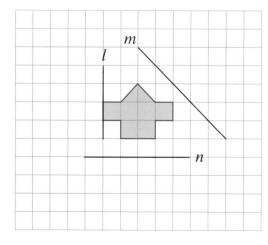

Draw the images.

⑧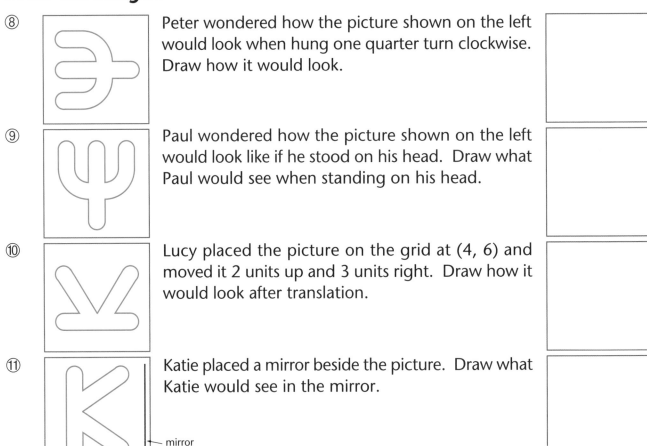

Peter wondered how the picture shown on the left would look when hung one quarter turn clockwise. Draw how it would look.

⑨ Paul wondered how the picture shown on the left would look like if he stood on his head. Draw what Paul would see when standing on his head.

⑩ Lucy placed the picture on the grid at (4, 6) and moved it 2 units up and 3 units right. Draw how it would look after translation.

⑪ Katie placed a mirror beside the picture. Draw what Katie would see in the mirror.

– mirror

Look at the polygons on the grid. Solve the problems.

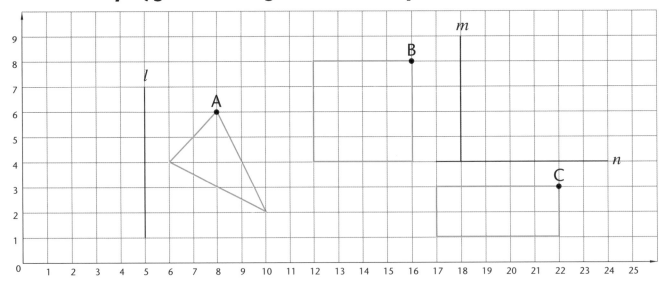

⑫ If Darren makes a $\frac{1}{4}$ turn clockwise about the vertex (6, 4) of the triangle, what will be the ordered pair of vertex A of the rotation image?

Answer : _____

⑬ If Darren flips the triangle over line *l*, what will be the ordered pair of vertex A of the reflection image?

Answer : _____

⑭ If the ordered pair of the translation image of vertex B is (10, 6), describe how Terry translates the square to its image.

Answer : _____

⑮ If Terry flips the square over the line *m*, what will be the ordered pair of vertex B of the reflection image?

Answer : _____

⑯ If Grace makes a $\frac{1}{4}$ turn counterclockwise about the vertex (17, 3) of the rectangle, what will be the ordered pair of vertex C of the rotation image?

Answer : _____

⑰ If the ordered pair of the translation image of vertex C is (23, 7), describe how Grace translates the rectangle to its image.

Answer : _____

⑱ If Grace flips the rectangle over line *n*, what will be the ordered pair of vertex C of the reflection image?

Answer : _____

CHALLENGE

Sam is turning his sticker counterclockwise. Which set of the diagrams below shows the movement of the sticker? Circle the correct answer.

A.

B.

C.

D.

Line Graphs

Mary used a line graph to show the number of stamps she had. How many more stamps did Mary have in December than in August?

No. of stamps in December : 25

No. of stamps in August : 5

Difference : 25 – 5 = 20

Answer : Mary had 20 more stamps in December than in August.

Use the graphs to solve the problems. Show your work.

Larry recorded the number of toy cars produced by the factory last week.

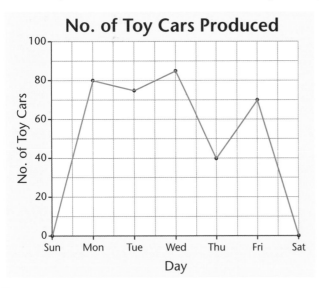

① How many toy cars were produced last Monday?

                   toy cars were produced

Answer : last Monday.

② How many toy cars were produced last Friday?

Answer :

③ How many more toy cars were produced on Wednesday than on Thursday?

Answer :

④ One of the production lines in the factory broke down last week. Which day did it happen? Explain.

Answer :

⑤ On which days was the factory closed? Explain.

Answer :

⑥ On average, how many toy cars were produced each working day?

Answer :

Larry's factory produces 3 types of toy cars. He kept track of the production in the past year.

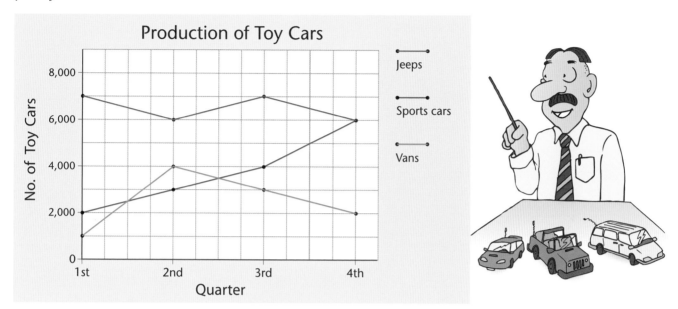

⑦ How many sports cars were produced in the 1st quarter?

Answer : _____

⑧ How many vans were produced in the 2nd quarter?

Answer : _____

⑨ How many Jeeps were produced in the 3rd quarter?

Answer : _____

⑩ How many more vans were produced in the 4th quarter than in the 1st quarter?

Answer : _____

⑪ How many Jeeps were produced from the 1st quarter to the 4th quarter?

Answer : _____

⑫ How many vehicles were produced in the 4th quarter?

Answer : _____

⑬ In which quarter was the number of Jeeps 3 times the number of vans?

Answer : _____

⑭ In which quarter did Larry's factory produce more vans than sports cars?

Answer : _____

⑮ What did the line for sports cars indicate?

Answer : _____

⑯ If Larry wanted to cut one of his production lines, which one should be cut? Explain.

Answer : _____

Darcy and Horace wanted to buy a gift for their sister. They used a table to record their savings. Use their table to make a line graph and solve the problems.

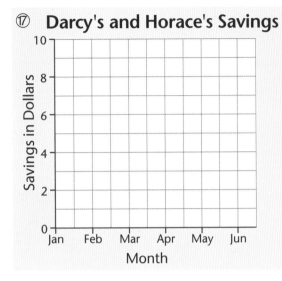

⑰ **Darcy's and Horace's Savings**

	Darcy's savings	Horace's savings
JAN	$4.50	$4.50
FEB	$2.00	$6.00
MAR	$8.50	$3.50
APR	$4.50	$7.00
MAY	$7.00	$6.00
JUN	$6.50	$5.50

⑱ How much more did Darcy save than Horace in March?

Answer :

⑲ How much more did Horace save than Darcy in February?

Answer :

⑳ In which months did Darcy save more than Horace?

Answer :

㉑ How many months were Darcy's savings more than Horace's?

Answer :

㉒ In which month were their savings the same?

Answer :

• *Don't forget to label the lines on the line graph.* e.g.

Read this first.

Amy
John

㉓ How much did Darcy save in the six months?

Answer :

㉔ How much did Horace save in the six months?

Answer :

㉕ If the birthday gift for their sister cost $65.39, would they have enough money to buy it?

Answer :

Mrs. Harding sold her nuts in bags. She recorded the sales of cashew nuts and almonds in the past year. Use her table to make a line graph and solve the problems.

	JAN	FEB	MAR	APR	MAY	JUN	JUL	AUG	SEP	OCT	NOV	DEC
Cashew nuts sold (bag)	250	350	300	450	350	300	250	250	250	300	200	200
Almond sold (bag)	150	150	100	150	200	250	300	300	350	400	400	450

㉖
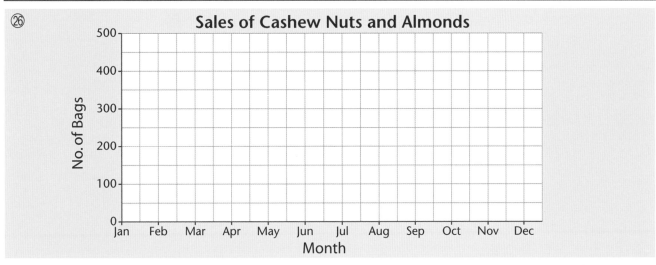

㉗ How many more bags of cashew nuts were sold than almonds in April?

Answer : _____

㉘ How many more bags of almonds were sold than cashew nuts in September?

Answer : _____

㉙ How many bags of nuts did Mrs. Harding sell in June?

Answer : _____

㉚ In which month did the sales of cashew nuts increase the most?

Answer : _____

CHALLENGE

Look at the above line graph. Describe the trend of sales of cashew nuts and the trend of sales of almonds.

Answer :

Circle Graphs

Dora's parents were looking at Dora's circle graph. It showed the time she was awake and the time she spent sleeping. They said that Dora should get more sleep. How did they know?

Dora's Day

Answer: They found that only $\frac{1}{4}$ of the circle represented sleeping. Since $\frac{1}{4}$ of 24 hours is 6 hours, they thought that Dora did not have enough sleep.

Solve the problems. Show your work.

Karin loves fruit. She kept track of the amount of money she spent on fruit each week and drew the circle graph.

① Which fruit did Karin spend the most money on?

Karin spent the most money

Answer: on _____ .

② Which section represents the fruit that Karin spent the most money on? Color it red.

③ Which fruit did Karin spend the least money on?

Answer: _____

④ Which section represents the fruit that Karin spent the least money on? Color it green.

⑤ If Karin spent $100 on fruit, how much would she spend on pears?

Karin's Spending on Fruit

Banana

Pear

Grape

Apple

⑥ List the fruits from the one Karin spent the most money on to the one she spent the least money on.

Answer: _____

Answer: _____

Gary's teacher, Mr. Milne, made a circle graph to show the number of students in each group that scored an A on the test.

⑦ Which group had the most As?

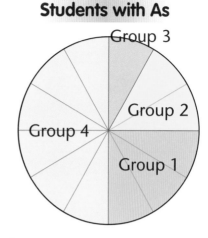

Students with As

Answer : _____

⑧ Which group had the fewest As?

Answer : _____

⑨ Altogether, there were 12 students who scored an A. How many students with an A were in group 4?

Answer : _____

⑩ How many students with an A were in group 1?

Answer : _____

⑪ Half of the students in group 4 got an A on the test. How many students were there in group 4?

Answer : _____

⑫ Each group had the same number of students. How many students took the test?

Answer : _____

⑬ There were 5 students with Bs in group 1, 1 in group 2, 4 in group 3, and 2 in group 4. Color the circle graph and the boxes with matching colors to show the number of students in each group that scored a B on the test.

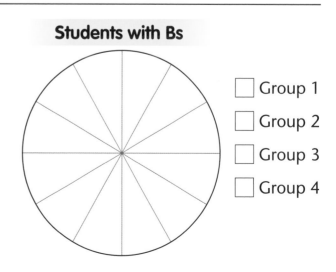

Students with Bs

☐ Group 1

☐ Group 2

☐ Group 3

☐ Group 4

Four groups of children sold apples to raise money for charity. Lori, John, Mario, and Shirley were the group representatives. Their teacher, Mrs. Carter, recorded the results in the circle graph.

⑭ Which group raised the second most money?

Answer : _____

⑮ Which group raised the least money?

Answer : _____

⑯ List the group representatives from the most money raised to the least.

Answer : _____

⑰ John's group raised $24. How much money did Mario's group raise?

Answer : _____

⑱ How much money did Shirley's group raise?

Answer : _____

⑲ How much money did Lori's group raise?

Answer : _____

⑳ How much money did the children raise altogether?

Answer : _____

Money Raised in Apple Sale

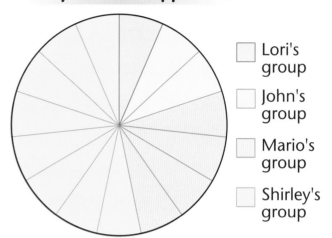

- Lori's group
- John's group
- Mario's group
- Shirley's group

㉑ If the cost of each apple was the same, which group sold the most apples? Explain.

Answer : _____

㉒ Which group sold the second most apples? Explain.

Answer : _____

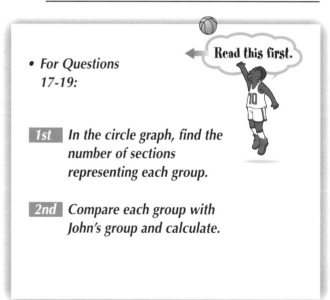

- **For Questions 17-19:**

Read this first.

1st *In the circle graph, find the number of sections representing each group.*

2nd *Compare each group with John's group and calculate.*

Willy drew a circle graph to show how much time he spent on video games each day last week.

㉓ Which day did Willy spend the most time on video games?

Answer : _____

㉔ Which day did he spend the second most time on video games?

Answer : _____

㉕ Which days did he not play video games?

Answer : _____

㉖ Willy spent 1 hour playing video games on Friday. How many hours did he play video games on Monday?

Answer : _____

Time Spent on Video Games

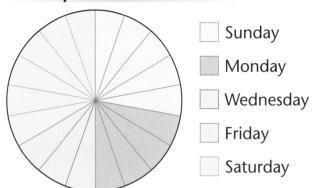

☐ Sunday
▨ Monday
☐ Wednesday
☐ Friday
☐ Saturday

㉗ How many hours did he play video games on Saturday?

Answer : _____

㉘ How many more hours did he play video games on Sunday than on Wednesday?

Answer : _____

CHALLENGE

Katie had $20. She spent $8 on clothing, $5 on entertainment, $3 on food, and $4 on transportation. Which of the circle graphs below is the best to show Katie's spending? Explain.

A. **Kate's Spending**

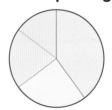

B. **Kate's Spending**

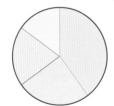

C. **Kate's Spending**

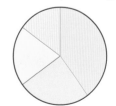

☐ Clothing
☐ Entertainment
☐ Transportation
☐ Food

Answer : _____

 **Mean and Mode**

EXAMPLE

Ken got his report card with the following marks : 87, 75, 78, 56, 78, and 88. What were his mean and mode marks?

Mean : (87 + 75 + 78 + 56 + 78 + 88) ÷ 6 = 462 ÷ 6 = 77

Mode : 87, 75, 78, 56, 78, 88 ———— 78 occurs the most often.

Answer : His mean mark was 77 and his mode mark was 78.

Solve the problems. Show your work.

Lori was practicing to improve her running speed. She ran the same distance in the park every morning for the past 4 weeks. Her times were recorded in the table.

① What was Lori's mean running time in the 1st week?

Her mean running time was
Answer :   seconds.

Lori's Running Time (second)

Day \ Week	1st	2nd	3rd	4th
Sun	127	110	124	100
Mon	117	126	106	125
Tue	120	112	98	105
Wed	105	104	110	104
Thu	110	108	106	100
Fri	105	110	106	104
Sat	100	121	106	104

② What was her mean running time in the 2nd week?

Answer :

③ What was her mean running time in the 3rd week?

⑤ What was her mode running time in the 3rd week?

Answer :

Answer :

④ What was her mean running time in the 4th week?

⑥ What was her mode running time in the 4th week?

Answer :

Answer :

Mr. Layton grouped the children and listed their allowances.

Group A		**Group B**		**Group C**		**Group D**	
Frank	$5.00	Ron	$6.80	George	$3.83	Lily	$4.75
Kelly	$6.75	Amy	$9.15	Ringo	$7.37	Donny	$8.13
Ray	$5.37	Rachel	$4.16	Elaine	$3.83	Terry	$4.75
Peter	$5.00	Beatrice	$4.16			Cindy	$4.75
		Tim	$4.18			Mark	$8.13
						Wayne	$0.69

⑦ Who had the highest allowance in the class?

Answer : _____

⑧ Who had the lowest allowance in the class?

Answer : _____

⑨ What was the mean allowance received by the students in group A?

Answer : _____

⑩ What was the mean allowance received by the students in group C?

Answer : _____

⑪ Was the mean allowance received by the students in group B higher than that in group D?

Answer : _____

⑫ What was the mode allowance in group B?

Answer : _____

⑬ What was the mode allowance in group D?

Answer : _____

⑭ If Tim was placed in group A, what would the mean allowance of group A be?

Answer : _____

⑮ If one of the students in group D joined group C and changed the mean allowance of group C to $5.79, who were the possible students?

Answer : _____

Henry, Larry, Michael, and Elaine were comparing their trading cards. Henry had 258 cards, Larry 426, Michael 426, and Elaine 678.

⑯ What was the mean number of cards that the 4 children had?

Answer : _____

⑰ What was the mode number of cards that the 4 children had?

Answer : _____

⑱ If Elaine gave Henry 126 cards, what would be the mean number of cards that the 4 children had?

Answer : _____

⑲ What would be the mode number of cards that the 4 children had?

Answer : _____

⑳ If Larry gave Michael 252 cards, what would be the mean number of cards that the 4 children had?

Answer : _____

㉑ What would be the mode number of cards that the 4 children had?

Answer : _____

㉒ If Michael gave Larry 60 cards and Henry gave Elaine 40 cards, what would be the mean number of cards that the 4 children had?

Answer : _____

㉓ If Larry bought 28 cards and Henry bought 120 cards, what would be the mean number of cards that the 4 children had?

Answer : _____

㉔ If Elaine lost 88 cards, what would be the mean number of cards that the 4 children had?

Answer : _____

㉕ If the 4 children gave 160 cards to their friend, Ray, what would be their mean number of cards afterward?

Answer : _____

㉖ If Michael lost 48 cards and Henry bought 12 cards, what would be the mean number of cards that the 4 children had?

Answer : _____

㉗ Tim has an average of 135 cards in 4 boxes. Which 4 of these boxes are his?

Ⓐ 110   Ⓑ 150   Ⓒ 120   Ⓓ 130   Ⓔ 180

Answer :

㉘ If all the above boxes belonged to Tim, what would be the mean number of cards in each box?

Answer :

㉙ Elaine has an average of 12.35 kilograms of flour in 4 bags. Which 4 of these bags are hers?

Ⓐ Flour 10.68 kg   Ⓑ Flour 12.37 kg   Ⓒ Flour 13.25 kg   Ⓓ Flour 11.89 kg   Ⓔ Flour 14.46 kg

Answer :

㉚ If all the above bags belonged to Elaine, what would be the mean amount in each bag?

Answer :

CHALLENGE

Don spilled some hot chocolate onto his report card, covering his mark in math. He got 78 in English, 86 in social studies, 92 in science and 68 in physical education. His average mark was 76.

① What was his mark in math?

Answer :

② If he wanted an average mark of 77, how much would he have to get in math?

Answer :

Probability

Harry has a bag with 5 red balls and 7 blue balls. If he takes out one ball, what is the probability that the ball will be red?

Think : There are 12 balls altogether; 5 out of 12 balls are red.

Answer : The probability that the ball will be red is 5 out of 12, or $\frac{5}{12}$.

Solve the problems. Show your work.

Donny and Sari drew a circle on a piece of cardboard and divided it into 4 sections. Then they mounted a pointer at its center and spun it 100 times.

Outcome	Ice cream	Pop	Lollipop	Popsicle
No. of times occurred	40	10	30	20

① Complete the bar graph to show the number of times each outcome occurred.

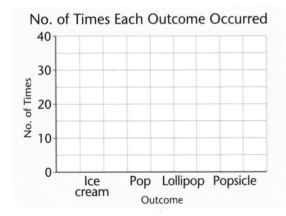

No. of Times Each Outcome Occurred

② What fraction of times did the spinner stop on 'ice cream'?

Answer : _____

③ What fraction of times did the spinner stop on 'pop'?

Answer : _____

④ What fraction of times did the spinner stop on 'lollipop'?

Answer : _____

⑤ On which section do you think the spinner is least likely to stop?

Answer : _____

⑥ On which section do you think the spinner is most likely to stop?

Answer : _____

See how many marbles each child has. Help them solve the problems. Show your work.

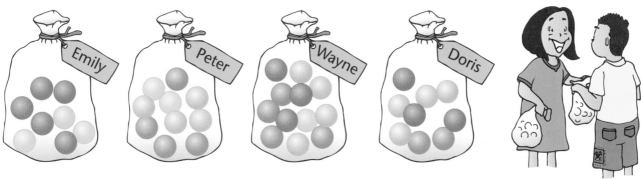

⑦ If Emily draws out a marble from her bag, what is the probability that the marble will be red?

Answer : _____

⑧ If Peter draws out a marble from his bag, what is the probability that the marble will be blue?

Answer : _____

⑨ If Wayne draws out a marble from his bag, what is the probability that the marble will be green?

Answer : _____

⑩ If Doris draws out a marble from her bag, what is the probability that the marble will be yellow?

Answer : _____

⑪ If Emily puts all her marbles into Peter's bag and draws out a marble from his bag, what is the probability that the marble will be blue?

Answer : _____

⑫ Doris says, 'If I draw out a marble from my bag, it is most likely that the marble will be red'. Is she correct? Explain.

Answer : _____

Solve the problems. Show your work.

The Fisher King Restaurant is holding a 'Spin and Win' event to attract customers. For every ten dollars spent, a customer can spin one of the spinners once to see what he or she can get.

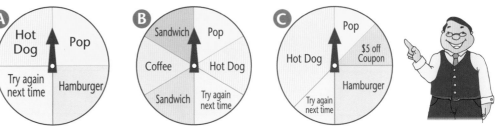

⑬ For spinner A, what is the probability that the spinner will stop on 'Hamburger'?

Answer : _____

⑭ For spinner B, what is the probability that the spinner will stop on 'Sandwich'?

Answer : _____

⑮ For spinner C, what is the probability that the spinner will stop on 'Pop'?

Answer : _____

⑯ For spinner C, what is the probability that the spinner will stop on 'Hot Dog'?

Answer : _____

⑰ Which spinner has the greatest probability that it will stop on 'Hot Dog'?

Answer : _____

⑱ Which spinner has the least probability that it will stop on 'Try again next time'?

Answer : _____

⑲ Michael spends $20.08 in the restaurant. How many times can he spin?

Answer : _____

⑳ If Michael wants to have a free hot dog, which spinner should he spin? Explain.

Answer : _____

㉑ If Michael chooses spinner A, what is the probability that the spinner will stop on 'Hot Dog', 'Pop', 'Hamburger', or 'Try again next time'?

Answer : _____

㉒ If Michael chooses spinner C, what is the probability that the spinner will stop on 'Coffee'?

Answer : _____

• **The sum of the probability of all possible outcomes must be equal to 1.**

• **If an event never occurs, then the probability is zero.**

Read this first.

Joe has 1 yellow marble, 1 blue marble, and 1 red marble in his bag. Tim has a penny. They try to take a marble from the bag and flip the coin once.

㉓ Complete the tree diagram to show all the possible outcomes.

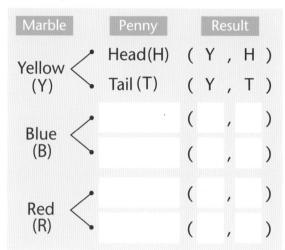

Marble	Penny	Result
Yellow (Y)	Head (H)	(Y , H)
	Tail (T)	(Y , T)
Blue (B)		(,)
		(,)
Red (R)		(,)
		(,)

㉔ How many possible outcomes are there?

Answer :

㉕ What is the probability that they will get a red marble and a head?

Answer :

㉖ What is the probability that they will get a blue marble and a tail?

Answer :

㉗ Joe says, 'The probability of getting a blue marble and a head is greater than the probability of getting a red marble and a tail'. Is he correct? Explain.

Answer :

㉘ If Joe and Tim played the games 60 times, about how many times would they get a yellow marble and a head?

Answer :

CHALLENGE

Which 2 of the 4 spinners below show the same probability of getting each letter? Explain.

Spinner A

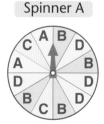

Spinner B

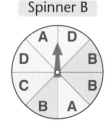

Spinner C

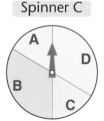

Spinner D

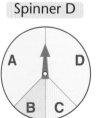

Answer :

Solve the problems. Show your work.

Mrs. Quinn, the convenience store owner, was packing cereal boxes into a carton 20 centimeters wide, 60 centimeters long, and 90 centimeters high.

① What was the volume of the carton?

Answer : _____

② Each cereal box was 5 centimeters wide, 15 centimeters long , and 30 centimeters high. How many boxes of cereal would the carton hold?

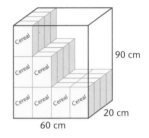

Answer : _____

③ If each box of cereal cost $2.99, how much would the carton cost when it was packed full?

Answer : _____

④ Mrs. Quinn filled the carton with 18 boxes of bran flakes, 8 boxes of rice flakes, 10 boxes of corn flakes, and some boxes of granola. How many boxes of granola were there?

Answer : _____

⑤ If Mrs. Quinn took out 1 box of cereal from the carton, what would be the probability that it was a box of rice flakes?

Answer : _____

⑥ If Mrs. Quinn took out 1 box of cereal from the carton, what would be the probability that it was not a box of corn flakes?

Answer : _____

⑦ Which type of cereal had the greatest probability that it would be taken out by Mrs. Quinn? Explain.

Answer : _____

⑧ Mrs. Quinn wanted to use a circle graph to show the different kinds of cereal in the carton. Each sector in the circle graph represents 2 boxes. Color the circle graph and the boxes with matching colors to show the number of each kind of cereal in the carton.

Number of Boxes of Cereal

☐ Bran Flakes
☐ Rice Flakes
☐ Corn Flakes
☐ Granola

Mrs. Quinn recorded the number of cartons of cereal sold last year. Use the table to make a line graph.

	Jan	Feb	Mar	Apr	May	Jun	Jul	Aug	Sep	Oct	Nov	Dec
Cereal sold (carton)	125	100	150	50	25	75	150	125	100	100	75	125

⑨

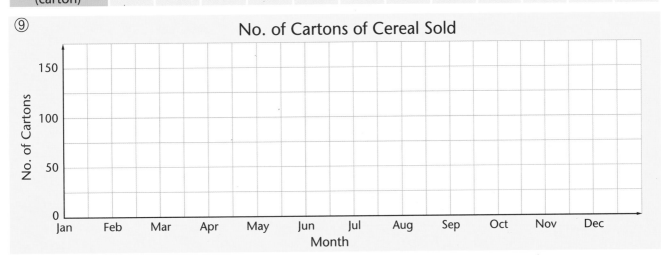

No. of Cartons of Cereal Sold

⑩ How many more cartons were sold in August than in May?

Answer : _____

⑪ On average, how many cartons were sold each month?

Answer : _____

⑫ If the delivery charge for 1 carton was $0.25, how much would be the cost of delivery in November?

Answer : _____

247

Look at the report cards of some of the students in Miss Bliss's class.

Sarah			Molly			Stanley			Elaine		
English	:	80	English	:	78	English	:	76	English	:	82
Math	:	86	Math	:	91	Math	:	88	Math	:	97
French	:	86	French	:	78	French	:	97	French	:	69
Art	:	75	Art	:	65	Art	:	72	Art	:	96
Science	:	79	Science	:	85	Science	:	76	Science	:	80
Drama	:	86	Drama	:	89	Drama	:	83	Drama	:	80

⑬ What was Sarah's mean mark?

Answer :

⑭ What was Molly's mean mark?

Answer :

⑮ What was Stanley's mean mark?

Answer :

⑯ What was Elaine's mean mark?

Answer :

⑰ What was Sarah's mode mark?

Answer :

⑱ Which students had their mean mark higher than their mode mark?

Answer :

⑲ What was the mean mark in English for these 4 students?

Answer :

⑳ What was the mean mark in drama for these 4 students?

Answer :

㉑ The children shuffled their report cards and placed them face down. If Elaine picked a card, what was the probability that she would pick her own card?

Answer :

㉒ If Molly picked a card, what was the probability that she would not pick her own card?

Answer :

㉓ If Stanley played the game 40 times, about how many times would he get his own card?

Answer :

Circle the correct answer to each problem.

㉔ Which of the diagrams below is the same as its reflection image?

A. ⊚ | Filp line   B. ¢ | Filp line   C. ⊄ _____ Filp line   D. $ _____ Filp line

㉕ Which set of the diagrams below shows a translation?

A.   B.   C.   D.

㉖ Which set of the diagrams below shows a $\frac{1}{2}$ turn clockwise about the turning point?

A.   B.   C.   D.

㉗ Gary started doing his homework at 7:15 p.m. He finished at 9:04 p.m. How long did it take him to do his homework?

A. 1 h 49 min   B. 1 h 39 min   C. 1 h 19 min   D. 49 min

㉘ Mr. Louis took 2 hours 30 minutes to complete his trip of 120 miles. What was his average speed per hour?

A. 300 mph   B. 40 mph   C. 60 mph   D. 48 mph

㉙ Marcus puts 3 red balls, 2 yellow balls, and 4 blue balls into a bag. If Marcus draws a ball from the bag, what is the probability that he will get a red ball?

A. $\frac{2}{3}$ B. $\frac{2}{9}$ C. $\frac{4}{9}$ D. $\frac{1}{3}$

㉚ What is the probability that Marcus will get either a red ball or a blue ball?

A. $\frac{2}{3}$ B. $\frac{5}{9}$ C. $\frac{7}{9}$ D. $\frac{1}{3}$

③ How many minutes are there from 11:49 a.m. to 1:07 p.m.?

   A. 68 minutes   B. 78 minutes   C. 18 minutes   D. 118 minutes

③ Paul is looking at his watch. The 6 is nearest to him. If he gives the watch a quarter turn counterclockwise, what number will be farthest away from him?

   A. 3   B. 6   C. 9   D. 12

③ Kelly has a swimming pool 16 meters long, 12 meters wide, and 2 meters deep. She wants to fill it right up to the top with water. How many cubic meters of water will she need?

   A. 384 m³   B. 192 m³   C. 30 m³   D. 768 m³

③ The hose carries 6 cubic meters of water a minute. How many minutes will it take to fill Kelly's swimming pool?

   A. 5 minutes   B. 32 minutes   C. 64 minutes   D. 128 minutes

③ Look at the shape on the right. What is the perimeter of the shape?

   A. 10.4 in   B. 9.7 in

   C. 7.9 in   D. 12.2 in

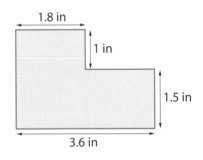

③ What is the area of the shape?

   A. 4.5 in²   B. 7.2 in²   C. 6.48 in²   D. 5.4 in²

③ The heights of three boys are 3 feet 2 inches, 3 feet 7 inches, and 3 feet 9 inches. What is their average height?

   A. 3 ft 4 in   B. 3 ft 5 in   C. 3 ft 7 in   D. 3 ft 6 in

Parents' Guide

1. Large Numbers

- Children learn how to write and read large numbers up to a hundred million.
- Advise children to start writing a number from the ones digit, and put a comma between every three numerals counted from the right.

  <u>Example</u>   Write 14,803,765 instead of 14803765.

- When rounding a number to a certain place value, the digit immediately to the right of that place has to be considered.

  <u>Example</u>   Round 14,803,765 and 2,497,382 to the nearest thousand.

  14,803,765 ← The hundreds digit 7 is greater than 5, so round up to 14,804,000.

  2,497,382 ← The hundreds digit 3 is less than 5, so round down to 2,497,000.

2. Distributive Property of Multiplication

- Encourage children to apply the distributive property of multiplication to simplify their calculation.

  <u>Example</u> $42 \times 7 + 42 \times 3$ $42 \times 7 + 42 \times 3$

  $= 294 + 126$ ← Multiply in the usual $= 42 \times (7 + 3)$ ← Apply the distributive
  way; then add.   property of multiplication.
  $= 420$ $= 42 \times 10$

  $= 420$

- Remind children that the distributive property does not apply to division.

  <u>Example</u> $24 \div 2 + 24 \div 4$ $24 \div 2 + 24 \div 4$

  $= 12 + 6$ $= 24 \div (2 + 4)$

  $= 18$ ✔ $= 24 \div 6$

  $= 4$ ✘

3. Prime and Composite Numbers

- Children learn the difference between prime and composite numbers. Parents may emphasize the following points:
  a. 1 is neither a prime number nor a composite number.
  b. All prime numbers except 2 are odd numbers.
  c. All numbers with the ones digit equal to 5 are composite numbers except 5.
  d. A number with only 1 and itself as factors is a prime number.
  e. A number with more than two factors is a composite number.
  f. A number which can form a rectangle is a composite number.

4. Fractions

- Remind children that the value of a fraction equals 1 if its numerator and denominator are equal, and that any whole number can be written as an improper fraction.
- Make sure children understand equivalent fractions have the same numerical value.

Parents' Guide

- To add or subtract fractions with like denominators, children should add or subtract the numerators only and keep the denominator the same. To add or subtract mixed numbers, they can either add or subtract the whole numbers and fractions separately, or change the mixed numbers to improper fractions before calculation.

- Reduce 1 to an improper fraction if necessary when subtracting fractions.

- To multiply two fractions, multiply their numerators and denominators respectively. To divide a fraction by another fraction, invert the fraction immediately after the ÷ sign and change ÷ to x.

- If the divisor is a whole number, remind children to change it to a fraction with a denominator that equals 1 before doing the division.

  <u>Example</u>
  $$\frac{4}{5} \div 2 = \frac{4}{5} \div \frac{2}{1} = \frac{\overset{2}{\cancel{4}}}{5} \times \frac{1}{\underset{1}{\cancel{2}}} = \frac{2}{5}$$

5. Decimals

- Remind children to align the decimal points when doing vertical addition or subtraction.

- The number of decimal places in the product is the same as that in the question. Add enough "0"s before the non-zero digits if necessary to locate the decimal point, and the "0"s at the end of the product can be deleted after locating the decimal point.

  <u>Example</u> 0.5 x 0.08 = ?

  $$\begin{array}{r} 0.0\,8 \\ \times \quad 0.5 \\ \hline 4\,0 \end{array} \quad \rightarrow \quad \begin{array}{r} 0.0\,8 \\ \times \quad 0.5 \\ \hline 0.0\,4\,0 \end{array}$$

  This "0" can be deleted after locating the decimal point.

  Add 2 "0"s to locate the decimal point.

- When dividing, don't forget to add a "0" if necessary to locate the decimal point. If there is a remainder, add "0"s to the right of the dividend after the decimal point and continue to divide until the remainder is zero or there are enough decimal places.

  <u>Example</u> 4.8 ÷ 5 = ?

  $$\begin{array}{r} 9 \\ 5\,\overline{)\,4.8} \\ 4\,5 \\ \hline 3 \end{array} \rightarrow \begin{array}{r} 9 \\ 5\,\overline{)\,4.8\,0} \\ 4\,5 \\ \hline 3\,0 \end{array} \rightarrow \begin{array}{r} 9\,6 \\ 5\,\overline{)\,4.8\,0} \\ 4\,5 \\ \hline 3\,0 \\ 3\,0 \end{array} \rightarrow \begin{array}{r} 0.9\,6 \\ 5\,\overline{)\,4.8\,0} \\ 4\,5 \\ \hline 3\,0 \\ 3\,0 \end{array}$$

  There is a remainder.   Add a "0" to the right of the dividend and bring down.   Continue to divide until the remainder is zero.   Add a "0" to locate the decimal point.

- Encourage children to check if their answers are reasonable by rounding the decimals to the nearest whole number and estimating the answers.

6. Decimals and Fractions

- Remind children that a decimal is another way to represent a fraction, with a denominator of 10, 100, 1,000, etc., and that a fraction can be changed to a decimal by first writing its equivalent fraction with a denominator of 10, 100, 1,000, etc.

- A fraction can also be converted to a decimal by dividing the numerator by the denominator.

Examples

$$7.5 = 7\frac{5}{10}$$

$$(0.5 = \frac{5}{10})$$

$$7\frac{1}{4} = 7\frac{25}{100} = 7.25 \quad \leftarrow \quad (\frac{25}{100} = 0.25)$$

$$(\frac{1}{4} = \frac{1 \times 25}{4 \times 25} = \frac{25}{100})$$

7. Percents

- Children learn the conversion among percents, decimals, and fractions. Parents should encourage them to make observations of the application of percents in everyday situations.

- Children should note that $1 = 100\%$ (one hundred percent) $= \frac{100}{100}$.

8. Simple Equations

- Children may encounter difficulties in determining the value of an unknown in an equation using guess-and-test method. Parents can explain to them the balance principle in solving simple equations, and encourage them to check the answer by substituting the answer for the unknown.

Examples

1.
$$y + 30 = 70 \quad \leftarrow \text{ an addition equation}$$
$$y + 30 - 30 = 70 - 30 \leftarrow \text{ subtract the same amount from both}$$
$$y = 40 \qquad \text{sides of the equation}$$

2.
$$y \times 4 = 28 \quad \leftarrow \text{ a multiplication equation}$$
$$y \times 4 \div 4 = 28 \div 4 \quad \leftarrow \text{ divide both sides of the equation}$$
$$y = 7 \qquad \text{by the same number}$$

9. Time and Speed

- Children recognize how to write the time and find a duration on a 12-hour clock and a 24-hour clock. Parents may remind children that when calculating a duration, they should trade 1 hour for 60 minutes if necessary.

10. Perimeter and Area

- Children practice using formulas to find the perimeter and area of some 2-D shapes. They may sometimes mistake the hypotenuse of a triangle or the slanted side of a parallelogram for the height. Remind them that the height of a 2-D shape must make a right angle with its base.

11. Factorization

- Children learn how to write a number as a product of prime factors, and determine the GCF and LCM of two numbers.

12. Inverse Proportion

↝ Make sure that children understand the difference between direct and inverse proportions. Encourage them to think and estimate whether one quantity is increasing or decreasing while the other quantity is increasing before writing the mathematical sentence for calculation. Remind them to check if their answers are reasonable.

13. Circles

↝ Children recognize the circumference, center, radius, and diameter of a circle. At this stage, parents should not introduce to children the concept of π and the relationship between circumference and diameter/radius.

14. Volume and Surface Area

↝ Children use a formula to calculate the volume of a cube. The method of determining the volume of an irregular object using the amount of water displaced is also introduced.

↝ Point out to children that the unit cubic centimeter (cm^3) is used to measure smaller volumes while cubic meter (m^3) is used to measure larger volumes.

↝ Remind children that the total surface area of a rectangular prism is the sum of the areas of all its six faces and each pair of opposite faces have the same area.

15. Graphs

↝ Children learn to read bar graphs presenting data in large numbers.

↝ Besides learning to read and draw line graphs, children should be encouraged to make predictions following the trend of a line graph, and estimate data which have not been collected.

↝ At this stage, children learn to read and complete circle graphs divided into simple fractions only.

16. Transformations and Coordinate Systems

↝ When reading coordinates on a grid, children should read the number on the horizontal axis first, and then the number on the vertical axis.

17. Money

↝ Children practice how to write the amount of money using decimals and perform mathematical operations to find the change or money spent.

18. Probability

↝ At this stage, children are required to represent the probability of an event happening as a simple fraction.

   <u>Example</u>   The probability of getting a 2 by rolling a dice is $\frac{1}{6}$.

1 Operations with Whole Numbers

1. 700   2. 570   3. 800   4. 70,000
5. 290   6. 90   7. 200   8. 620
9. 100   10. 300   11. 1,000   12. 40
13. 6,580   14. 111   15. 6,753   16. 8,229
17. 85   18. 2,512   19. 73

20.
```
        6 5
    5 ) 3 2 5
        3 0
        2 5
        2 5
```
21.
```
        2 9 1
    3 ) 8 7 3
        6
        2 7
        2 7
        3
        3
```
22.
```
        9 2
    8 ) 7 3 6
        7 2
        1 6
        1 6
```

23. 4,833   24. 5,124   25. 1,065
26. 7,002 + 499 = 7,501   27. 984 – 578 = 406

28.
```
  A      G
  2   1    0
  5   2         3   0
          D
      2   0   7   0
  E            F
  4       7   5   0
  6       6
```

29. 2   30. 0   31. 1   32. 0
33. 4   34. 2   35. 9 ; 9
36. 11 – 7 = 4 ; 4
37. 12 + 12 + 2 + 2 = 28 ; Its perimeter is 28 feet.
38. 66 x 60 = 3,960 ; It beats 3,960 times in an hour.
39. 240 ÷ 12 = 20 ; 20 x 2 = 40 ; He earns $40 per day.

Just for Fun

1a. 110 , 121 , 132   b. 108 , 120 , 132
2. 5,790 ; 4,563

2 Introducing Decimals

1. $\frac{52}{100}$ 2. 0.05   3. 0.3   4. $\frac{9}{100}$

5. 7.2   6. $4\frac{1}{10}$

7.
```
  |--•---•----•-•-------|---|---|---|---•---|
  0 D   C    A B                       E   1
```

8. 0.01 , 0.02 , 0.1 , 0.15 , 0.2   9. 1.05 , 1.4 , 1.45 , 1.50 , 1.54
10. 5.88 , 5.80 , 5.08 , 0.58 , 0.55 , 0.50
11. 3.2 , 2.93 , 2.9 , 2.39 , 2.3 , 2.09
12. 0.05   13. 0.10   14. 0.75   15. 0.40
16. 3.16   17. 3.7   18. T   19. F
20. T   21. T   22. F   23. F
24. 7.02   25. 3.57   26. 0.16   27. 2.35
28. 0.05   29. 0.25   30. 0.7   31. 1.15
32. 1.75   33. 2   34. tenths ; 0.5
35. hundredths ; 0.07   36. tens ; 20
37. ones ; 3   38. hundredths ; 0.06
39. hundreds ; 100   40. 5.7
41. 0.9   42. 2.0   43. 12.3   44. 5.94
45. 2.70   46. 3.10   47. 6.01   48. <
49. <   50. >   51. >
52a. 3 hours 58.5 minutes b. Yes
53. She spent $64.
54. (Suggested answers)
a. 8 (10¢)   b. 1 (25¢) ; 4 (10¢) ; 3 (5¢)
55. One hundred ninety-five dollars and fifty-five cents.

Just for Fun

▪ = 3 or 1   ♠ = 1 or 3
◆ = 7   ♥ = 8

3 Adding Decimals

1. 1.5   2. 10.6   3. 46.8   4. 65.0
5. 22.9   6. 13.7   7. 58.21   8. 34.23
9. 30.91   10. 107.14   11. 8.83   12. 108.10
13. 6.40   14. 326.00   15. 158.01   16. 26.23
17. 12.8   18. 6.68   19. 7.63   20. 8.23
21. 14.63   22. 7.93   23. 52.57   24. 29.15
25. 162.13   26. 811.82   27. 167.45   28. 370.42
29. 16.18   30. 115.9   31. 30.65   32. 9.09
33. 21.83   34. 21.14   35. 980
36. 20 + 5 + 0.8 + 0.07   37. 10 + 2 + 0.9 + 0.03
38. 570.8   39. 108.64   40. $10.27   41. $11.17
42. $11.32   43. $11.14   44. $60.07   45. $71.44
46. $69.83   47. $11.17 , $11.32 , $60.07 , $71.44
48. $154   49. $154   50. 18.7   51. 24.6
52. 23.3   53. 17.4   54. + ; +
55. 5.50 + 5.50 + 3.75 + 1.2 + 1.2 = 17.15 ; $17.15
56. 6.75 + 5.90 + 6.50 + 5 = 24.15 ;
    She gets $24.15 over the 4-week period.
57. 25.2 + 22.1 + 24.8 + 28.2 = 100.3 ;
    He cycled 100.3 miles during the week.

Just for Fun

5 ; 7 ; 5

4 Subtracting Decimals

1. 0.5   2. 56.5   3. 6.3   4. 1.2
5. 28.4   6. 33.8   7. 5.04   8. 0.69
9. 3.06   10. 579.16   11. 23.71   12. 1.98
13. 5.03   14. 3.77   15. 8.27   16. 3.02
17. 11.38   18. 7.87   19. 1.82   20. 0.88
21. 0.22   22. 0.26   23. 0.81   24. 0
25. 0.06   26. 32.47   27. 26.4   28. 150.77
29. 50   30. 19.78   31. 199.4   32. 3
33. 1   34. 40   35. 9   36. 14
37. 14   38. 2.7   39. 1.8   40. 11.1
41. 18.4   42. 34.3   43. 12.6   44. 1.4
45. 8   46. 3.36   47. 2.4   48. 1.9
49. 2.61   50. 4.2   51. 1.23   52. 7
53. 0.6   54. 7.7   55. 7.38   56. 14.13
57. 9.46

58.
11.4	7.7	7.38	7.0	6.94
17.0	5.8	1.4	10.6	9.17
7.5	0.2	14.13	5.2	3.61
15.1	9.3	4.2	14.0	15.2
14.8	3.63	9.46	41.11	12.3
12.3	22.3	2.61	2.60	11.36
2.63	0.6	8.0	1.23	3.27

59. I
60. 35 – 32.85 ; 2.15 ; $2.15
61. 99.7 – 91.5 = 8.2 ; Sue is 8.2 pounds heavier than her sister.
62. 0.55 – 0.19 = 0.36 ; The CN Tower is 0.36 kilometer taller.
63. 12.13 – 11.87 = 0.26 ; Carl took 0.26 second longer.

Just for Fun

4	9	2
3	5	7
8	1	6

5 More Addition and Subtraction of Decimals

1. 19.5   2. 2   3. 6.99   4. 14
5. 10.5   6. 1.5   7. 0   8. 15
9. 10   10. 28   11. 0.5   12. 17.5
13. 10   14. 100   15. 15.45   16. 3.28
17. 8.8   18. 5.01   19. 4.69   20. 4.8
21. 109.25   22. 20.33   23. 243.6   24. 1,003.8

25. 0.93 26. 100.27 27. 14.56 28. 10.66
29. $15.44 30. $73.10 31. $24.80 32. $98
33. $10.24 34. $11.52 35. 59¢ 36. 33¢
37. 22¢ 38. 7¢ 39. 8.1 40. 1.67
41. 1.5 42. 20 43. 0.65 44. 3.44
45. 25 – 4.55 – 6.99 = 13.46 ; $13.46
46. 35 – 5.95 – 17.45 = 11.60 ; She has $11.60 left.
47. 6.50 + 19.95 + 7.50 – 2 = 31.95 ; Each of them spent $31.95.
48. 17.5 + 17.5 + 17.5 = 52.50 ; 20.95 + 20.95 + 2.10 = 44 ;
They have enough money.

Just for Fun

1¢ + 2¢ + 4¢ + 8¢ + 16¢ + 32¢ + 64¢ = 127¢ ($1.27)

6 Multiplying Decimals by Whole Numbers

1. 1 2. 32 3. 0.7 4. 0.08
5. 12 6. 9.9 7. 24.06 8. 540
9. 91.5 10. 0.1 11. 10 12. 93
13. 200.8 14. 8 15. 6.2 16. 1
17. 248 18. 1 19. 14.1 20. 10.76
21. 54.5 22. 45.29 23. 44.40 24. 65.7
25. 34.3 26. 97.6 27. 28.60 28. 59.34
29. 10.8 30. 3.92 31. 33.81 32. 1.62
33. 29.25 34. 9.66 35. 23.2 36. 506.1
37. 29.97 38. 4.56 39. 35 ; 36.4
40. 8 ; 7.4 41. 50 ; 49.05 42. 48 ; 49.38
43. 12 ; 11.25 44. 3.2 ; 2.88 45. 1.8 ; 1.53
46. 32 ; 33.76 47. 13.86 48. ✓ 49. 3.09
50. 100 51. 3 52. 10 53. 100
54. 159 55. 30.9 56. 23.99 x 3 ; 71.97 ; $71.97
57. 89.50 x 4 = 358 ; The total cost is $358.
58. 1.4 x 5 = 7 ; He walks 7 miles in a 5-day week.
59. 1.25 x 8 = 10 ; They occupy 10 inches.
60. 12.95 x 3 = 38.85 ; 39.99 x 2 = 79.98 ; 38.85 + 79.98 = 118.83 ;
She pays $119 altogether.

Just for Fun

444 + 44 + 4 + 4 + 4 = 500

7 Dividing Decimals by Whole Numbers

1. 0.98 2. 0.032 3. 0.75 4. 0.0092
5. 0.328 6. 0.0005 7. 0.008 8. 1.5493
9. 3.1645 10. 17.6 11. 0.12 12. 2.04
13. 0.52

14.

15.
```
       7 . 4
  9 ) 6 6 . 6
       6 3
        3  6
        3  6
```

16.
```
      1 0 . 5
  7 ) 7 3 . 5
        3  5
        3  5
```

17.
```
      1 . 4 2
  6 ) 8 . 5 2
      6
      2 5
      2 4
        1 2
        1 2
```

18.
```
      0 . 0 6
  4 ) 0 . 2 4
          2 4
```

19.
```
      2 0 . 1
  8 ) 1 6 0 . 8
      1 6
           8
           8
```

20.
```
      4 . 0 3
  3 ) 1 2 . 0 9
      1 2
           9
           9
```

21.
```
      1 0 . 5 3
  5 ) 5 2 . 6 5
      5
        2  6
        2  5
           1 5
           1 5
```

22.
```
      4 . 5 5
  8 ) 3 6 . 4
      3 2
        4  4
        4  0
           4 0
           4 0
```

23.
```
      1 7 . 6
  4 ) 7 0 . 4
      4
      3 0
      2 8
        2  4
        2  4
```

24.
```
      2 . 0 8
  5 ) 1 0 . 4
      1 0
         4 0
         4 0
```

25.
```
      2 . 1 5
  9 ) 1 9 . 3 5
      1 8
        1  3
           9
           4 5
           4 5
```

26.
```
      2 . 3
  4 ) 9 . 2
      8
      1 2
      1 2
```

27.
```
      0 . 1 9
  3 ) 0 . 5 7
      3
      2 7
      2 7
```

28.
```
      2 . 5 5
  2 ) 5 . 1
      4
      1 1
      1 0
        1 0
        1 0
```

29.
```
      5 . 1 2
  7 ) 3 5 . 8 4
      3 5
          8
          7
         1 4
         1 4
```

30.
```
      1 5 2 . 1
  5 ) 7 6 0 . 5
      5
      2 6
      2 5
        1 0
        1 0
           5
           5
```

31.
```
      7 . 0 1
  5 ) 3 5 . 0 5
      3 5
           5
           5
```

32.
```
      1 . 3
  8 ) 1 0 . 4
      8
      2 . 4
      2 . 4
```

33.
```
      5 4 . 3
  7 ) 3 8 0 . 1
      3 5
      3 0
      2 8
        2  1
        2  1
```

34.
```
      1 2 5 . 8 5
  4 ) 5 0 3 . 4
      4
      1 0
       8
       2 3
       2 0
         3 . 4
         3 . 2
           2 0
           2 0
```

35.
```
      0 . 0 9
  5 ) 0 . 4 5
          4 5
```

36.
```
      6 . 5 3
  9 ) 5 8 . 7 7
      5 4
        4  7
        4  5
           2 7
           2 7
```

37.
```
      8 3 . 7 3
  6 ) 5 0 2 . 3 8
      4 8
        2  2
        1  8
           4 3
           4 2
             1 8
             1 8
```

38. LITTLE STARS
39. 71.7 ÷ 10 ; 7.17 ; 7.17 pounds
40. 4,570 ÷ 100 = 45.7 ; He traveled 45.7 miles each hour.
41. 36.4 ÷ 8 = 4.55 ; Each part is 4.55 yards.
42. 394 ÷ 8 = $49.25 ; Each student pays $49.25.
43. 13.5 ÷ 3 = 4.5 ; The length of each side is 4.5 centimeters.

Just for Fun

21 ; 34 ; 55

8 More Multiplying and Dividing of Decimals

1. 73.4 2. 0.923 3. 1.234 4. 1.21
5. 12.3 6. 120 7. 0.03 8. 10.1
9. 3.429 10. 34,290 11. 125 12. 0.002
13. 4 14. 11.8 15. 4 16. 0.0125
17. 0.2 18. 635

19.
```
      2 3 . 6
  4 ) 9 4 . 4
      8
      1 4
      1 2
        2  4
        2  4
```

20.
```
      1 . 0 4
  7 ) 7 . 2 8
      7
        2  8
        2  8
```

21.
```
      1 5 . 0 3
  3 ) 4 5 . 0 9
      3
      1 5
      1 5
           9
           9
```

22.
```
      3 . 9 2
  x       4
  1 5 . 6 8
```

23.
```
     1 0 . 3
  x       7
  7 2 . 1
```

24.
```
      5 . 9 1
  x       6
  3 5 . 4 6
```

25.
```
    1.32
6)7.92
    6
    1 9
    1 8
      12
      12
```

26.
```
    1.9
9)17.1
    9
    8 1
    8 1
```

27.
```
    1.24
5)6.2
    5
    1 2
    1 0
      20
      20
```

28.
```
    0.47
  x    8
    3.76
```

29.
```
    18.2
  x     9
   163.8
```

30.
```
-   36.7
  x      2
    73.4
```

31. 10   32. 7   33. 0.17   34. 2.6
35. 27.72   36. 25.6   37. 89   38. 190
(39., 44. : products < 15)
40. 15.8   41. 15.2   42. 17.1   43. 15.5
(46., 47. : quotients > 2)

45.
```
    1.4
9)12.6
    9
    3 6
    3 6
```

48.
```
    1.9
3)5.7
    3
    2 7
    2 7
```

49.
```
    1.8
6)10.8
    6
    4 8
    4 8
```

50.
```
    1.9
7)13.3
    7
    6 3
    6 3
```

51. 100   52. 10   53. 3.42   54. 2
55. 6.2   56. 9.1   57. 100   58. 10
59. 58.2 ÷ 3 = 19.4 ; $19.40
60. 19.95 x 3 = 59.85 ; 12.45 x 2 = 24.90 ; 1.25 x 10 = 12.50 ;
    59.85 + 24.90 + 12.50 = 97.25 ; She pays $97.25 altogether.
61. 12.99 x 2 = 25.98 ; 1.29 x 2 = 2.58 ; 1.49 x 2 = 2.98 ;
    25.98 + 2.58 + 2.98 = 31.54 ; 31.54 ÷ 5 = 6.308 ;
    They must pay $6.31 each.
62. 29.40 ÷ 6 = 4.90 ; 39.50 ÷ 10 = 3.95 ;
    A 10-pound bag for $39.50 is the better buy.

Just for Fun

0.5

Midway Review

1. 18.95   2. 11.76   3. 67.2   4. 1.05
5. 16.26   6. 0.62   7. 209.04   8. 3.2
9. 954.1   10. 14.59   11. 968.69   12. 149.5
13. 54.19   14. 95.31   15. 520 ; 5.2   16. 7 ; 0.07
17. 1.2 ; 0.012 18. 7.5 ; 0.75 19. 0.3 ; 0.03 20. 8 ; 80
21. 150 ; 1,500 22. D   23. C   24. C
25. C   26. B   27. D   28. B
29. C   30. A   31. B   32. B
33. C   34. C   35. 9.0 + 3.2 + 3.2 = 15.4 ; 15.4
36. 20 x 15.4 = 308 ; The total cost is $308.
37. 9 + 3.2 + 9 + 3.2 = 24.4 ; The perimeter is 24.4 yards.
38. 9 x 3.2 = 28.8 ; The area is 28.8 square yards.
39a. New length = 9 x 2 = 18 ; New width = 3.2 x 2 = 6.4 ;
     18 + 18 + 6.4 + 6.4 = 48.8 = 24.4 x 2 ;
     The perimeter is doubled as well.
  b. 9 x 2 x 3.2 x 2 = 9 x 3.2 x 2 x 2 = 28.8 x 4 ;
     The area is 4 times the original area.

9 Introducing Fractions

1. $\frac{1}{6}$ 2. $\frac{1}{3}$ 3. $\frac{2}{3}$ 4. $\frac{5}{6}$

5. $\frac{1}{6}$ 6. $\frac{4}{6} = \frac{2}{3}$ 7. $\frac{5}{8}$ 8. $\frac{6}{16} = \frac{3}{8}$

9. $\frac{3}{8}$ 10. $\frac{1}{4}$

11.   12.   13.

14.   15.   16.

17.

18. $\frac{5}{9}$ 19. $\frac{5}{8}$ 20. $\frac{8}{11}$

21.   22.   23.

24. 5   25. 12   26. 6   27. 2

28. 2   29. 4   30. $\frac{3}{4}$ 31. $\frac{1}{3}$

32. $\frac{1}{2}$ 33. $\frac{2}{3}$ 34. $\frac{3}{8}$ 35. $\frac{4}{5}$

36. (Suggested answers) $\frac{1}{8}$; $\frac{1}{4}$; $\frac{1}{3}$

37a. $\frac{35}{100} = \frac{7}{20}$ b. $\frac{60}{100} = \frac{3}{5}$ 38. $\frac{3}{24} = \frac{1}{8}$ 39. $\frac{2}{8} = \frac{1}{4}$

40. $\frac{50}{250} = \frac{1}{5}$ 41. $\frac{15}{45} = \frac{1}{3}$ 42. $\frac{21}{26}$ 43. $\frac{18}{30} = \frac{3}{5}$

44. $\frac{50}{120} = \frac{5}{12}$ 45. $\frac{12}{16} = \frac{3}{4}$ 46a. $\frac{87}{100}$ b. $\frac{13}{100}$

Just for Fun

1. $\frac{1}{16}$; $\frac{1}{32}$; $\frac{1}{64}$ 2. No

10 Equivalent Fractions and Ordering of Fractions

1. 25   2. 25   3. 15   4. 75
5. 2   6. 77   7. $\frac{5}{6}$ 8. $\frac{1}{2}$

9. $\frac{2}{11}$ 10. $\frac{3}{7}$ 11. $\frac{1}{4}$ 12. $\frac{2}{3}$

13. $\frac{3}{4}$ 14. $\frac{1}{3}$ 15. $\frac{1}{6}$ 16. $\frac{2}{3}$

17. $\frac{8}{21}$ 18. $\frac{11}{15}$ 19. $\frac{1}{10} < \frac{1}{5} < \frac{1}{2} < \frac{3}{5} < \frac{7}{10} < \frac{4}{5}$

20. $\frac{1}{4} < \frac{1}{3} < \frac{2}{4} < \frac{2}{3} < \frac{3}{4}$ 21. T   22. F

23. T   24. F   25. 3 ; 12
26. 5 ; 2   27. 2 ; 4   28. 55 ; 4

29. – 32. (Suggested answers)   29. $\frac{2}{16}$; $\frac{3}{24}$; $\frac{4}{32}$

30. $\frac{4}{6}$; $\frac{6}{9}$; $\frac{8}{12}$ 31. $\frac{2}{8}$; $\frac{3}{12}$; $\frac{4}{16}$ 32. $\frac{10}{14}$; $\frac{15}{21}$; $\frac{20}{28}$

33. $\frac{7}{8} > \frac{3}{4} > \frac{5}{8} > \frac{1}{2} > \frac{3}{8} > \frac{1}{4} > \frac{3}{16}$

34. $\frac{5}{6} > \frac{13}{18} > \frac{2}{3} > \frac{1}{2} > \frac{7}{18} > \frac{1}{3} > \frac{1}{6}$

35. <   36. =   37. >   38. <
39. <   40. >   41. $\frac{3}{4}$ 42. $\frac{3}{5}$

43. $\frac{5}{6}$ 44. $\frac{4}{9}$ 45. $\frac{7}{9}$ 46. $\frac{6}{7}$

47. $\frac{200}{450}$; $\frac{75}{125}$; $\frac{15}{20}$; $\frac{14}{18}$; $\frac{45}{54}$; $\frac{150}{175}$

48. 14 ; 14   49. 8 ; 8   50. 88 ; 88
51. Nadine : $\frac{9}{12} = \frac{27}{36}$; Danielle : $\frac{14}{18} = \frac{28}{36}$; Danielle

52a. $\frac{682}{5,421}$; $\frac{1,583}{8,474}$ b. Increasing

  c. $\frac{512}{5,421}$; $\frac{542}{8,474}$ d. Decreasing

Just for Fun

$\frac{1}{16}$; $\frac{1}{25}$; $\frac{1}{36}$

11 Adding Fractions with Like Denominators

1. 1
2. 1
3. $\frac{2}{3}$
4. $\frac{2}{5}$

5. $\frac{5}{9}$
6. $\frac{4}{7}$
7. $\frac{4}{5}$
8. 1

9. 1
10. $\frac{8}{9}$
11. $\frac{11}{13}$
12. $\frac{8}{11}$

13. $\frac{7}{8}$
14. $\frac{13}{20}$
15. $\frac{9}{17}$
16. $\frac{9}{19}$

17. $\frac{21}{25}$
18. $\frac{10}{12}=\frac{5}{6}$
19. $\frac{17}{21}$
20. $\frac{8}{15}$

21. $\frac{6}{16}=\frac{3}{8}$
22. $\frac{2}{4}=\frac{1}{2}$
23. $\frac{12}{18}=\frac{2}{3}$
24. $\frac{22}{23}$

25. $\frac{4}{6}=\frac{2}{3}$
26. $\frac{25}{27}$
27. $\frac{13}{20}$
28. $\frac{12}{15}=\frac{4}{5}$

29. $\frac{3}{9}=\frac{1}{3}$
30. $\frac{12}{14}=\frac{6}{7}$
31. $\frac{6}{8}=\frac{3}{4}$
32. $\frac{6}{10}=\frac{3}{5}$

33. $\frac{8}{16}=\frac{1}{2}$
34. $\frac{6}{12}=\frac{1}{2}$
35. $\frac{4}{20}=\frac{1}{5}$
36. $\frac{2}{6}=\frac{1}{3}$

37. $\frac{4}{7}$
38. $\frac{3}{18}=\frac{1}{6}$
39. $\frac{6}{24}=\frac{1}{4}$
40. $\frac{8}{32}=\frac{1}{4}$

41. $\frac{7}{7}=1$
42. $\frac{11}{11}=1$

43. $\frac{4}{8}=\frac{1}{2}$

44. $\frac{1}{3}+\frac{2}{3}=\frac{3}{3}=1$

45. $\frac{3}{6}+\frac{1}{6}=\frac{4}{6}=\frac{2}{3}$

46. $\frac{1}{4}+\frac{1}{4}=\frac{2}{4}=\frac{1}{2}$

47. $\frac{1}{3}+\frac{2}{3}=\frac{3}{3}=1$

48. $\frac{1}{5}+\frac{2}{5}=\frac{3}{5}$

49. $\frac{2}{7}$
50. $\frac{1}{11}$
51. $\frac{5}{6}$
52. $\frac{7}{8}$

53. $\frac{1}{4}$
54. $\frac{1}{8}$
55. $\frac{1}{15}$
56. $\frac{1}{10}$

57. $\frac{11}{20}$
58. $\frac{5}{12}$
59. $\frac{11}{25}$
60. $\frac{2}{9}$

61. $\frac{1}{4}+\frac{1}{4}+\frac{1}{4}=\frac{3}{4}$; $\frac{3}{4}$

62a. $\frac{2}{6}+\frac{2}{6}+\frac{1}{6}=\frac{5}{6}$; They eat $\frac{5}{6}$ of the pizza.

b. $\frac{5}{6}<1$; There is some pizza left.

63a. $\frac{5}{8}+\frac{1}{8}=\frac{6}{8}=\frac{3}{4}$; She needs $\frac{3}{4}$ foot altogether.

b. $\frac{3}{4}<1$; She will have enough ribbon.

64a. $\frac{3}{10}+\frac{1}{10}=\frac{4}{10}=\frac{2}{5}$; She has spent $\frac{2}{5}$ of her allowance.

b. $\frac{2}{5}+\frac{3}{5}=1$; She has $\frac{3}{5}$ of her allowance left.

Just for Fun

$\frac{8}{15}$	$\frac{1}{15}$	$\frac{6}{15}$
$\frac{3}{15}$	$\frac{5}{15}$	$\frac{7}{15}$
$\frac{4}{15}$	$\frac{9}{15}$	$\frac{2}{15}$

12 Improper Fractions and Mixed Numbers

1. $2\frac{1}{7}$
2. $\frac{27}{8}$
3. $3\frac{2}{3}$
4. $\frac{45}{4}$

5. $1\frac{2}{5}$
6. $\frac{4}{7}$; $\frac{5}{20}$; $\frac{7}{9}$; $\frac{11}{12}$

7. $\frac{9}{9}$; $\frac{25}{20}$; $\frac{15}{8}$; $\frac{16}{7}$
8. $3\frac{3}{10}$; $3\frac{1}{2}$; $1\frac{5}{20}$; $1\frac{2}{5}$

9. $2\frac{2}{3}$; $\frac{8}{3}$
10. $1\frac{1}{6}$; $\frac{7}{6}$

11.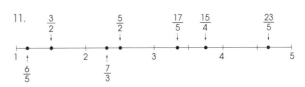

12. $\frac{8}{6}$; $1\frac{1}{3}$
13. $\frac{13}{6}$; $2\frac{1}{6}$
14. $\frac{15}{6}$; $2\frac{1}{2}$
15. $\frac{16}{6}$; $2\frac{2}{3}$

16. $\frac{20}{6}$; $3\frac{1}{3}$
17. $\frac{23}{6}$; $3\frac{5}{6}$
18. $\frac{15}{4}>\frac{7}{2}>\frac{7}{3}>\frac{9}{4}>\frac{5}{3}$

19. $\frac{17}{2}>\frac{17}{3}>\frac{17}{4}>\frac{17}{5}>\frac{17}{6}$
20. $\frac{23}{6}$; $\frac{19}{6}$; $\frac{7}{2}$

21. $\frac{60}{7}$; $\frac{49}{6}$; $\frac{25}{3}$

22.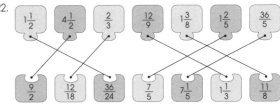

23a. $\frac{5}{2}$
b. $2\frac{1}{2}$
24. 9

25. $1\frac{3}{5}$
26. 9

27. False. Since $\frac{15}{4}=3\frac{3}{4}$, $\frac{13}{3}=4\frac{1}{3}$; so $\frac{13}{3}>\frac{15}{4}$

Just for Fun

56

13 Adding Improper Fractions and Mixed Numbers

1. 2
2. 3
3. 5
4. 3
5. 7
6. 3
7. 6
8. 7
9. 3
10. 2
11. 2
12. 3

13. 4
14. 2
15. $2\frac{1}{4}$
16. $6\frac{3}{5}$

17. $3\frac{2}{5}$
18. $5\frac{1}{2}$
19. $3\frac{2}{5}$
20. $3\frac{1}{2}$

21. $1\frac{1}{2}$
22. $4\frac{1}{3}$
23. $1\frac{3}{5}$
24. $2\frac{7}{8}$

25. $3\frac{1}{4}$
26. 2
27. $4\frac{3}{4}$
28. $2\frac{1}{3}$

29. $9\frac{2}{5}$
30. 6
31. $\frac{3}{4}$
32. $\frac{5}{8}$

33. $1\frac{4}{5}$
34. $1\frac{1}{2}$
35. $\frac{1}{2}$
36. $\frac{3}{5}$

37. $\frac{2}{3}$
38. $\frac{7}{6}$
39. $3\frac{1}{5}$
40. $\frac{3}{4}$

41. T
42. T
43. F
44. T

45. T
46. F
47. T
48. F

50, 51, 55 : sum < 3
49. $3\frac{1}{3}$
52. $3\frac{1}{2}$

53. $3\frac{1}{2}$
54. $3\frac{1}{5}$
56. $3\frac{5}{9}$

57. $1\frac{1}{4}+2\frac{1}{4}+1\frac{3}{4}=5\frac{1}{4}$; They eat $5\frac{1}{4}$ cans of food per week.

58. $45\frac{3}{8}+2\frac{1}{8}=47\frac{1}{2}$; The new selling price is $47\frac{1}{2}$ ¢.

59a. $3\frac{1}{8} + 4\frac{3}{4} = 7\frac{7}{8}$; She must buy $7\frac{7}{8}$ yards.　　b. Yes.

60. $1\frac{1}{4} + 1\frac{1}{4} + \frac{3}{4} + 1\frac{1}{4} + 2 + 1\frac{3}{4} + 2\frac{3}{4} = 11$;

She watched TV for 11 hours during the week.

Just for Fun

16

14 Subtracting Fractions with Like Denominators

1. $\frac{2}{7}$　　2. $\frac{1}{12}$　　3. $\frac{7}{9}$　　4. $\frac{2}{11}$

5. $\frac{2}{7}$　　6. $\frac{1}{10}$　　7. $\frac{3}{17}$　　8. 0

9. $\frac{1}{15}$　　10. $\frac{1}{4}$　　11. $\frac{2}{13}$　　12. $\frac{2}{7}$

13.　　14.　　15.　　16.

17. $\frac{1}{2}$　　18. $\frac{1}{2}$　　19. $\frac{1}{3}$　　20. $\frac{1}{4}$

21. $\frac{2}{3}$　　22. $\frac{3}{4}$　　23. $\frac{1}{2}$　　24. $\frac{4}{7}$

25. $\frac{2}{3}$　　26. $\frac{1}{4}$　　27. $\frac{3}{4}$　　28. $\frac{3}{5}$

29. $\frac{1}{3}$　　30. $\frac{2}{5}$　　31. $\frac{1}{2}$　　32. $\frac{1}{4}$

33. $\frac{3}{4}$　　34. $\frac{1}{7}$　　35. $\frac{4}{7}$　　36. $\frac{2}{4}$

37. $\frac{1}{4}$　　38. $\frac{8}{9}$　　39. $\frac{1}{5}$　　40. $\frac{4}{9}$

41. $\frac{1}{6}$　　42. $\frac{3}{4}$　　43. $\frac{6}{9}$　　44. $\frac{2}{9}$

45. $\frac{2}{3}$　　46. $\frac{2}{5}$　　47. $\frac{3}{10}$　　48. $\frac{5}{11}$

49. $\frac{2}{5}$　　50. $\frac{1}{8}$　　51. $\frac{2}{7}$

52. $\frac{4+7-5}{12}$; $\frac{6}{12} = \frac{1}{2}$　　53. $\frac{11-7+1}{18}$; $\frac{5}{18}$

54. $\frac{5}{8} - \frac{3}{8} = \frac{2}{8} = \frac{1}{4}$; $\frac{1}{4}$

55. $\frac{3}{4} - \frac{1}{4} = \frac{1}{2}$; It takes Ben $\frac{1}{2}$ hour longer.

56. $\frac{5}{6} - \frac{1}{6} = \frac{4}{6} = \frac{2}{3}$; It takes Dave $\frac{2}{3}$ hour less.

57a. $\frac{10}{40} = \frac{1}{4}$; She has done $\frac{1}{4}$ of the job.

b. $1 - \frac{1}{4} = \frac{3}{4}$; $\frac{3}{4}$ of the job still remains.

58a. $\frac{2}{10} = \frac{1}{5}$; $\frac{4}{10} = \frac{2}{5}$; $\frac{1}{5}$ are violet, $\frac{2}{5}$ are red.

b. $1 - \frac{2}{5} - \frac{1}{5} = \frac{2}{5}$; $\frac{2}{5}$ are neither red nor violet.

Just for Fun

A = 8 ; B = 7 ; C = 8 ; D = 8 , E = 3 , F = 8

15 Subtracting Improper Fractions and Mixed Numbers

1. $2\frac{1}{7}$　　2. $2\frac{2}{5}$　　3. $\frac{7}{9}$　　4. $\frac{1}{8}$

5. $\frac{3}{4}$　　6. $\frac{3}{4}$　　7. 0　　8. $\frac{2}{9}$

9. 3　　10. $\frac{1}{9}$　　11. $\frac{3}{13}$　　12. 1

13. $\frac{7}{8}$　　14. $\frac{2}{3}$　　15. $\frac{4}{6} = \frac{2}{3}$　　16. 5

17. 0　　18. $2\frac{1}{2}$　　19. 1　　20. $1\frac{1}{2}$

21. $\frac{1}{2}$　　22. $\frac{1}{4}$　　23. 2　　24. $\frac{2}{5}$

25. $\frac{1}{3}$　　26. 1　　27. $1\frac{1}{4}$　　28. 0

29. 1　　30. $1\frac{2}{3}$　　31. 3　　32. $1\frac{1}{5}$

33. $\frac{1}{2}$　　34. $\frac{4}{5}$　　35. $\frac{1}{3}$　　36. 5

37. $1\frac{1}{2}$　　38. $\frac{3}{4}$　　39. 4　　40. $\frac{5}{3} = 1\frac{2}{3}$

41. $\frac{3}{4}$　　42. $2\frac{3}{7}$　　43. $\frac{2}{5}$　　44. $3\frac{1}{2}$

45. $\frac{2}{3}$　　46. 1　　47. $\frac{1}{2}$　　48. $\frac{4}{5}$

49. $5\frac{1}{2}$　　50. $9 + 1 - 3 + \frac{2-1}{8}$; $7\frac{1}{8}$

51. $4 + 1 - 3 + \frac{1+4-3}{6}$; $2\frac{1}{3}$　　52. $3 + 2 - 1 + \frac{2+4-5}{7}$; $4\frac{1}{7}$

53. $3\frac{1}{4} - 2\frac{3}{4} = \frac{1}{2}$; Pat spent $\frac{1}{2}$ hour longer.

54. $8\frac{3}{8} - 6\frac{5}{8} = 1\frac{3}{4}$; He ran $1\frac{3}{4}$ miles farther.

55. $3\frac{1}{5} - 2\frac{4}{5} = \frac{2}{5}$; The difference is $\frac{2}{5}$ dollar.

56. $1 - \frac{3}{8} - \frac{1}{8} = \frac{1}{2}$; The length of the third side is $\frac{1}{2}$ meter.

57. $15\frac{1}{4} - 1\frac{1}{2} - 1\frac{1}{2} = 12\frac{1}{4}$; $10\frac{1}{2} - 1\frac{1}{2} - 1\frac{1}{2} = 7\frac{1}{2}$;

The dimensions of the unframed part of the picture are $12\frac{1}{4}$ inches by $7\frac{1}{2}$ inches.

Just for Fun

$\frac{1}{4}$

16 Relating Decimals and Fractions

1. 0.1　　2. 0.7　　3. 0.03　　4. 0.49

5. 0.09　　6. 0.73　　7. $\frac{3}{10}$　　8. $\frac{7}{10}$

9. $\frac{9}{10}$　　10. $\frac{1}{100}$　　11. $\frac{9}{100}$　　12. $\frac{7}{100}$

13. $\frac{31}{100}$　　14. $\frac{19}{100}$　　15. $\frac{47}{100}$　　16. $\frac{3}{100}$

17. 0.5　　18. 0.2　　19. 0.75　　20. 0.6

21. 0.125　　22. 0.625　　23. 0.375　　24. 0.8

25. 1.63　　26. 3.57　　27. 12.8　　28. 2.38

29. 3.83　　30. 5.44　　31. 1.67　　32. 2.6

33. 4.25　　34. 10.4　　35. 8.86　　36. 6.7

37. $\frac{13}{20}$　　38. $\frac{75}{100}$; $\frac{3}{4}$　　39. $\frac{5}{100}$; $\frac{1}{20}$　　40. $\frac{12}{100}$; $\frac{3}{25}$

41. $\frac{45}{100}$; $\frac{9}{20}$　　42. $\frac{36}{100}$; $\frac{9}{25}$　　43. $1\frac{45}{100}$; $1\frac{9}{20}$　　44. $6\frac{55}{100}$; $6\frac{11}{20}$

45. $2\frac{8}{10}$; $2\frac{4}{5}$　　46. $2\frac{25}{100}$; $2\frac{1}{4}$　　47. 25　　48. 75

49. 40　　50. 60　　51. 70　　52. 90

53. 0.65　　54. 0.9　　55. $1\frac{2}{5}$　　56. $\frac{2}{3}$

57. 4.26　　58. 0.57　　59. 3.69　　60. 8.38

61. $6\frac{3}{8}$　　　　62. 1.54 ; $1\frac{7}{8}$; $1\frac{8}{9}$

63. $2\frac{4}{7}$; $2\frac{3}{5}$; 2.68　　　　64. $5\frac{4}{5}$; 5.83 ; $5\frac{9}{10}$

65. 0.125 ; 0.25 ; 0.75 ; 0.375 ; 0.875 ; 0.2 ; 0.7

66. $\frac{1}{8}$; $\frac{1}{5}$; $\frac{1}{4}$; $\frac{3}{8}$; $\frac{7}{10}$; $\frac{3}{4}$; $\frac{7}{8}$　　67. $\frac{6}{25}$

68a. $\frac{5}{8}$　　b. 0.625　　69a. 0.2　　b. $0.6 (60¢)

Just for Fun

$\frac{3}{9}$; $\frac{3}{8}$; 0.56 ; $\frac{5}{6}$; $\frac{8}{9}$

Final Review

1. B 2. C 3. D 4. A
5. B 6. D 7. A 8. C
9. B 10. $\frac{3}{4}$; 0.75 11. $1\frac{2}{5}$; 1.4 12. $\frac{1}{5}$; 0.2

13. $\frac{3}{20}$; $\frac{1}{4}$; $\frac{1}{2}$; $\frac{3}{5}$; $\frac{4}{5}$ 14. 0.15; 0.25; 0.5; 0.6; 0.8

15. $3\frac{3}{4}$ 16. $1\frac{1}{2}$ 17. $3\frac{2}{5}$ 18. $2\frac{1}{9}$
19. $1\frac{1}{3}$ 20. $3\frac{1}{2}$ 21. $4\frac{2}{3}$ 22. $4\frac{1}{6}$
23. $4\frac{3}{8}$ 24. $1\frac{3}{4}$ 25. $2\frac{3}{5}$ 26. $4\frac{4}{5}$

27.

28. 0 29. 2 30. 4 31. $1\frac{1}{4}$

32. $4\frac{2}{5}$ 33. 9 34. $\frac{1}{2}$ 35. $\frac{3}{5}$

36. $8.00 – $5.15 = $2.85
37a. $8.00 x 5 ; $40   b. $5.15 x 5 ; $25.75
38. $40 – $25.75 = $14.25
39a. $7\frac{1}{4}$ b. $\frac{29}{4}$ 40. $7.25 + $0.50 ; $7.75

41a. 1990 , $248\frac{4}{5}$; 2000 , $281\frac{2}{5}$

b. 281.4 – 248.8 = 32.6 or $32\frac{3}{5}$;

The increase was 32.6 or $32\frac{3}{5}$ million.

c. 281.4 + 32.6 = 314

The population of the U.S. in 2010 will be 314 million.

42a. $\frac{35}{100} = \frac{7}{20} = 0.35$; He has run $\frac{7}{20}$ or 0.35 of his monthly goal.

b. 100 – 35 = 65 ; He still has to run 65 miles.

c. $1 - \frac{7}{20} = \frac{13}{20} = 0.65$;

He still has to run $\frac{13}{20}$ or 0.65 of the total distance.

d. $\frac{65 - 35}{100} = \frac{30}{100} = \frac{3}{10}$;

The difference between the fractions of the total distance
run in the first week and during the rest of the month is $\frac{3}{10}$.

43a. $2\frac{1}{4} + 3\frac{3}{4} = 6$; They drink 6 cups of tea.

b. $3\frac{3}{4} - 2\frac{1}{4} = 1\frac{1}{2}$; The difference is $1\frac{1}{2}$ cups.

c. $2\frac{1}{4} = 2.25$; 2.25 x 7 = 15.75 ;

Mr. King will drink 15.75 cups per week.

d. $3\frac{3}{4} = 3.75$; 3.75 x 7 = 26.25 ;

Mrs. King will drink 26.25 cups per week.

44a. $8\frac{1}{5} + 9\frac{3}{5} + 7\frac{1}{5} = 25$; They watch TV for 25 hours in a week.

b. $9\frac{3}{5} - 8\frac{1}{5} = 1\frac{2}{5}$; David watches TV for $1\frac{2}{5}$ hours longer
than Peter.

c. $9\frac{3}{5} - 7\frac{1}{5} = 2\frac{2}{5}$; David watches TV for $2\frac{2}{5}$ hours longer
than Ruth.

d. $7\frac{1}{5} - 1\frac{3}{5} = 5\frac{3}{5}$; She can watch TV for $5\frac{3}{5}$ hours now.

1 Large Numbers

1. 282,000
2. 164,300
3. 1,343,200
4. 275,300
5. 5,000,000
6. 600,000
7. 20,000,000
8. 70,000

	hundred	thousand	ten thousand
9.	123,200	123,000	120,000
10.	174,200	174,000	170,000
11.	246,500	247,000	250,000
12.	477,100	477,000	480,000
13.	1,205,100	1,205,000	1,210,000
14.	985,800	986,000	990,000

Activity

A, D

2 Prime and Composite Numbers

1. 8; composite
2. 7; prime
3. 5; prime
4. 4; composite
5. composite
6. prime
7. composite
8. composite
9. prime
10. prime

11 – 13.

14. 25; prime
15. composite
16. True
17. True
18. False

Activity

1. 7 + 13 (or 17 + 3)
2. 5 + 19 (or 17 + 7 ; 13 + 11)
3. 13 + 19 (or 29 + 3)
4. 31 + 67 (or 19 + 79 ; 37 + 61)

3 Fractions

1. $\dfrac{4 \times 2}{1 \times 3}$

$\dfrac{8}{3} = 2\dfrac{2}{3}$

$2\dfrac{2}{3}$

2. $\dfrac{3}{2}$

$\dfrac{1 \times 3}{2 \times 2} = \dfrac{3}{4}$

$\dfrac{3}{4}$

3. $1\dfrac{1}{5}$
4. $1\dfrac{2}{7}$
5. $\dfrac{1}{6}$
6. $\dfrac{4}{27}$
7. $8\dfrac{1}{2}$
8. $\dfrac{1}{2}$
9. $\dfrac{1}{6}$
10. $1\dfrac{3}{7}$
11. 16
12. $\dfrac{1}{2}$
13. $\dfrac{1}{15}$
14. $\dfrac{2}{7}$
15. $\dfrac{1}{18}$
16. $\dfrac{1}{12}$
17. $\dfrac{2}{3}$
18. $\dfrac{2}{5}$
19. 4
20. 6
21. 12
22. 20
23. $7\dfrac{1}{2}$
24. $4\dfrac{1}{2}$
25. 10
26. $\dfrac{6}{7}$
27. 6
28. $3\dfrac{1}{2}$
29. $\dfrac{5}{6}$

Activity

1. +
2. x
3. ÷
4. –

4 Distributive Property of Multiplication

1. 10 + 6
   16
2. 2 x 8
   16
3. Yes
4. 7 x 3 + 7 x 5
   21 + 35
   56
5. 4 x 18 – 4 x 7
   72 – 28
   44
6. 5 x (12 – 7)
   5 x 5
   25
7. 5 x (70 + 3)
   5 x 70 + 5 x 3
   350 + 15
   365
8. 6 x (100 – 2)
   6 x 100 – 6 x 2
   600 – 12
   588

9. 714   10. 441   11. 558

12. 332   13. 558   14. 395

Activity

1. $10 \times (5 + \frac{1}{5})$

     $10 \times 5 + 10 \times \frac{1}{5}$

     $50 + 2$

     52

2. $6 \times (50 + 4 + \frac{1}{5})$

     $6 \times 50 + 6 \times 4 + 6 \times \frac{1}{5}$

     $300 + 24 + \frac{6}{5}$

     $325\frac{1}{5}$

5   Simple Equations

1. $5 + y = 12$ 2. $n - 6 = 8$

3. $3 \times m = 12$ 4. $k \div 5 = 2$

5. $50 + 10$
     $60 - 20$
     40 Check: $40 + 20 = 60$
     40

6. $50 + 20$
     $70 \div 2$
     35 Check: $35 \times 2 = 70$
     35

7. $x + 3 - 3 = 12 - 3$
     9
     $9 + 3 = 12$

8. $7 \times n \div 7 = 28 \div 7$
     4
     $7 \times 4 = 28$

9. $m \div 2 \times 2 = 9 \times 2$
     18
     $18 \div 2 = 9$

10. $p - 9 + 9 = 26 + 9$
     35
     $35 - 9 = 26$

11. $q \times 5 \div 5 = 35 \div 5$
     7
     $7 \times 5 = 35$

12. $n \times 2 = 10; 5$ 13. $n \times 2 = 14; 7$

14. $n \times 2 = 18; 9$ 15. $n \times 2 = 36; 18$

16. $m \div 6 = 4; 24$ 17. $m \div 6 = 6; 36$

18. $m \div 6 = 8; 48$ 19. $m \div 6 = 9; 54$

20. $m \div 3 = 5$
     $m \div 3 \times 3 = 5 \times 3$
     15
     15 Check: $15 \div 3 = 5$

21. $p - 0.5 = 0.125$
     $p - 0.5 + 0.5 = 0.125 + 0.5$
     0.625
     0.625 Check: $0.625 - 0.5 = 0.125$

Activity

A, D

6   Time

1. 30   2. $\frac{1}{3}$

3. 90   4. 1 h 35 min

5. 100   6. 1 h 45 min

7. 110   8. 2 h 15 min

9. 65   10. 1 h 25 min

11. 4 h 10 min   12. 2 h 23 min   13. 0 h 40 min

14. 9:10   15. 2:47   16. 7:00

17. $5:00 - 1:05 = 3:55$; 3:55

18. $9:15 - 7:30 = 1:45$; 1 ; 45

Activity

1. 35 min   2. 12:50 p.m.   3. 3:45 p.m.

7   Area

	Height	Base	Area
1.	3	5	$7\frac{1}{2}$
2.	3	6	9
3.	3	3	$4\frac{1}{2}$
4.	3	3	9
5.	3	4	12
6.	2	3	6

7. 9, 7, 63   8. 10, 12, 120

9. 12.6, 5, 63   10. 8, 11.2, 89.6

11. 17, 5, 85   12. 12, 7, 42

13. 8, 6, 24   14. 3, 9, 13.5

15. 6, 2.4, 7.2   16. 6.4, 2, 6.4

17. 100, 35, 135

18. 48   19. 23

20. 48   21. 42

Activity

1. 21   2. 19

8 Directions

1. south
2. west
3. north
4. east
5. east
6. south, west
7. north-east
8. south-east
9. south-west
10. north-west
11. south-west
12. north-west

Activity

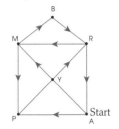

9 Graphs

1. 2,000 ; 1,000 ; 3,000 ; 3,000 ; 4,000 ; 5,000

2.

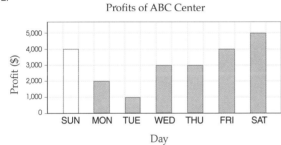

3. Saturday
4. Tuesday
5. 2
6. August
7. 3
8. 40,000
9. 2

Activity

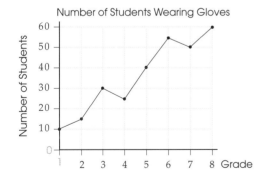

10 Factorization

1.

2. 199
3. prime
4. composite
5. prime
6. composite
7. composite
8. prime
9. 3 x 7, 3 x 7
10. 5 x 7, 5 x 7
11. 4
    2 x 2 x 7
    2 x 2 x 7
12. 5
    3 x 3 x 5
    3 x 3 x 5
13. 2 x 2 x 3 x 3
14. 2 x 3 x 3 x 3
15. 2 x 2 x 2 x 2 x 2 x 2
16. 2 x 2 x 2 x 3 x 3
17. 2 x 13
    3 x 13
    13
    13
18. 2 x 3 x 5
    3 x 3 x 5
    3, 5
    3 x 5 = 15
19. 2 x 2 x 7
    2 x 3 x 7
    2, 7
    2 x 7 = 14
20. 2 x 5 x 5
    3 x 5 x 5
    5, 5
    5 x 5 = 25
21. 4
22. 6
23. 20
24. 8
25. 2 x 2 x 3
    2 x 3 x 3
    2 x 2 x 3 x 3
    36
26. 3 x 5
    3 x 7
    3 x 5 x 7
    105
27. 30
28. 72
29. 48
30. 40

Activity

1. 199
2. 109

Midway Review

1. Twenty thousand six hundred eighty-one
2. Four hundred thirty-three thousand
3. 387,425 ; 387,245 ; 378,425 ; 378,245
4. 941,756 ; 941,576 ; 914,756 ; 914,576
5. 500,000   6. 1,000,000
7. $n + 6 = 15$ 8. $3 \times m = 18$ 9. $k - 5 = 9$

10. $y + 2 - 2 = 21 - 2$ 11. $m - 6 + 6 = 5 + 6$
    19   11

12. $4 \times n \div 4 = 24 \div 4$ 13. $p \div 9 \times 9 = 3 \times 9$
    6   27

14. 700,000 ; 900,000 ; 300,000 ; 200,000
15.

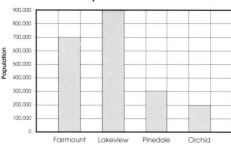

Population of Cities

16. 1,500   17. August   18. 7,000
19. 4,500   20. 1,500
21. 60   22. 77   23. 26
24. 12   25. 30   26. 38

27. $5\frac{1}{3}$ 28. $\frac{2}{7}$ 29. 14

30. 4   31. $1\frac{1}{2}$ 32. 1

33. $\frac{2}{3}$ 34. $\frac{1}{16}$ 35. $\frac{1}{2}$

36. $\frac{1}{2}$

37. $2 \times 3 \times 7$ 38. $2 \times 2 \times 2 \times 2$
    $2 \times 2 \times 2 \times 3 \times 3$ $2 \times 2 \times 2 \times 3$
    6   8

39. 3×5 40. $2 \times 2 \times 5$
    $3 \times 3 \times 5$ $2 \times 2 \times 2 \times 2 \times 2$
    15   4

41. $2 \times 2 \times 7$ 42. $2 \times 3 \times 3$
    5×7 $2 \times 2 \times 5$
    140   180

43. $2 \times 2 \times 2 \times 3$ 44. $2 \times 3 \times 5$
    $2 \times 2 \times 3 \times 3$ $2 \times 2 \times 2 \times 5$
    72   120

45. north-east   46. south   47. south-west
48. Library   49. 100   50. 1 ; 35
51. 11:10

11 Inverse Proportion

1. 12   2. $24 \div 3 = 8$
3. $24 \div 4 = 6$ 4. $24 \div 6 = 4$
5. $24 \div 8 = 3$ 6. $24 \div 12 = 2$
7. $60 \times 3 \div 6 = 30$ 8. $60 \times 3 \div 9 = 20$
   30   20
9. No. of groups: 6, 8, 12
   No. of people: 24, 16, 12

Activity

1. 10   2. 12   3. 15
4. 20   5. 30   6. 60

12 Decimals and Fractions

1. 16.25   2. 14.062   3. 15.2
4. 13.424   5. 17.07
6. 0.03   7. 0.005
8. 0.006   9. 10

10. $16\frac{3}{10}$ 11. $18\frac{1}{5}$ 12. $19\frac{2}{5}$

13. $13\frac{4}{25}$ 14. $13\frac{3}{4}$ 15. $18\frac{1}{50}$

16. $18\frac{1}{40}$ 17. $14\frac{433}{500}$ 18. $9\frac{21}{200}$

19. 25; 0.25   20. 12; 0.12

21. 0.625   22. 0.35   23. 0.36
24. 1.2   25. 2.15   26. 12.192
27. A. 0.5   B. 1.25   C. 2.13
    D. 3.57   E. 4.17   F. 6.07
    G. 9.85
28. 2.08   29. 6.30
30. 1.116   31. 1.2150

32.
$$\begin{array}{r} 1.3 \\ \times\ 1.9 \\ \hline 117 \\ 130 \\ \hline 2.47 \end{array}$$

33.
$$\begin{array}{r} 3.06 \\ \times\ 1.4 \\ \hline 1224 \\ 3060 \\ \hline 4.284 \end{array}$$

34.
$$\begin{array}{r} 0.06 \\ \times\ 0.12 \\ \hline 12 \\ 60 \\ \hline 0.0072 \end{array}$$

35. 0.868   36. 1.488
37. 0.75   38. 2.106
39. 1.236   40. 0.609

41.
```
      1.47
  6 / 8.82
      6
      2 8
      2 4
        42
        42
```

42.
```
       0.111
  18 / 1.998
       18
        19
        18
         18
         18
```

43.
```
       2.13
  7 / 14.91
      14
        9
        7
        21
        21
```

44.
```
       0.46
  12 / 5.52
       4 8
         72
         72
```

45.
```
       3.47
  8 / 27.76
      24
       3 7
       3 2
         56
         56
```

46.
```
       3.65
  9 / 32.85
      27
       5 8
       5 4
         45
         45
```

47. 5.51   48. 1.22
49. 0.45   50. 1.36
51. 0.85   52. 3.29
53. 2.73   54. 12.44
55. 3.14
56. 2.59; 2.59
57. $3.78 \div 6 = 0.63$ 58. $8.62 \div 2 = 4.31$
    0.63   4.31

Activity

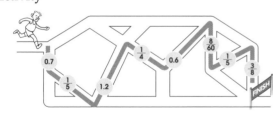

13 More about Simple Equations

1. $50 + 2 \times k - 50 = 90 - 50$
   $2 \times k = 40$
   $2 \times k \div 2 = 40 \div 2$
   20
   20

2. $3 \times p + 12 - 12 = 48 - 12$
   $3 \times p = 36$
   $3 \times p \div 3 = 36 \div 3$
   12

3. $9 \times q - 16 + 16 = 29 + 16$
   $9 \times q = 45$
   $9 \times q \div 9 = 45 \div 9$
   5

4. $m \div 4 + 13 - 13 = 19 - 13$
   $m \div 4 = 6$
   $m \div 4 \times 4 = 6 \times 4$
   24

5. $n \div 5 - 12 + 12 = 8 + 12$
   $n \div 5 = 20$
   $n \div 5 \times 5 = 20 \times 5$
   100

6. $2y - 9 = 3$, $y = 6$ 7. $4m \div 2 = 6$, $m = 3$
8. $2p + 5 = 7$, $p = 1$

Activity

1. a. 40   b. 30
2. a. 10   b. 70

14 Percents

1. $\frac{46}{100}$; 0.46; 46   2. $\frac{18}{100}$; 0.18; 18

3. 13%   4. 9%   5. 80%

6. 35%   7. 75%   8. 32%

9. 50%   10. $\frac{19}{50}$ 11. $\frac{3}{5}$

12. $\frac{2}{25}$ 13. $\frac{1}{25}$ 14. $1\frac{7}{20}$

15. $2\frac{17}{20}$ 16. $\frac{80}{100}$; 80   17. $\frac{76}{100}$; 76

18. $\frac{70}{100}$; 70   19. a, d, e, f, h, i, j; $\frac{7}{10}$; 70

20. 55   21. 25
22. 20   23. 25
24. 55   25. 20

26.

0.16	0.45	0.25	1.2	1.34
16%	45%	25%	120%	134%
$\frac{4}{25}$	$\frac{9}{20}$	$\frac{1}{4}$	$1\frac{1}{5}$	$1\frac{17}{50}$

27. $1 - 60\%$
    $100\% - 60\%$
    40%
    40

28. $1 - 30\% - 25\%$
    $100\% - 30\% - 25\%$
    45%
    45

Activity

1. Baseball
2. a. 30   b. 50   c. 20

15 More about Time

1. 04:30   2. 23:45
3. 18:15   4. 21:20
5. 3:35 p.m.   6. 9:28 a.m.

7. 9:19 p.m.   8. 1:06 p.m.

9. 6:55 a.m.   10. 12:05 p.m.

11. 8:25 p.m.   12. 8:57 a.m.

13. 1:40 p.m.   14. 8:00 a.m.

15. 1:25   16. 3:00

17. 80   18. 45

19. 50

Activity

1. C   2. E   3. A

4. D   5. B

16 Circles

1. a. diameter   b. radius   c. circumference

   d. center

2. 6   3. 3   4. 3

5. 5   6. 2   7. AOB

8. 1 in   9. 3 in   10. 3

Activity

2. a. many   b. bigger

17 Volume and Surface Area

1. 8   2. 4   · 3. 10

4. 12   5. 14

6. a. 12   b. 6   c. 4

   d. 12 x 6 x 4 = 288

7. a. 7   b. 5   c. 9

   d. 7 x 5 x 9 = 315

8. 12.5 x 2.2 x 2 = 55   9. 0.75 x 0.6 x 1.7 = 0.765

10. 36; 36   11. 50; 50   12. 25; 25

13. (2,400 + 800 +1,200) x 2

    4,400 x 2

    8,800

14. (20 x 30 +20 x 15 + 15 x 30) x 2

    (600 +300 + 450) x 2

    1,350 x 2

    2,700

15. (20 x 50 + 20 x 30 + 30 x 50) x 2

    3,000

Activity

1. 128   2. 1,000,000

18 Line Graphs

1. 3   2. 6

3. 20   4. 28

5. 40   6. 40, 35, 25, 20, 15

7.

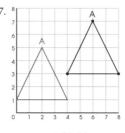

Tony's Savings

8. 2   9. 5

10. 35   11. 10

Activity

1. 2005   2. Tony

19 Transformations and Coordinates

1. Reflection   2. Translation   3. Rotation

4. Rotation   5. Reflection   6. Translation

7.   8.

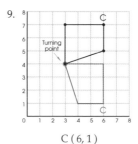

A (2, 5)   B (3, 6)

9.

C (6, 1)

Activity

1. (3,2)   2. (4, 1)   3. (2, 3)

20 Money

1. 40.04; 4.96   2. 44.88; 5.12   3. 76.11; 90.00

4. 56.01; 70.00   5. 61.95   6. 142.54

7. 3,350   8. 2,500   9. 4,650

10.

11. 10, 20, 100, 400   12. 5, 10, 50, 200

Activity

8

21 Probability

1. Blue
2. Yellow
3. No
4. unlikely
5. Blue
6. Yellow
7. $\frac{4}{8} = \frac{1}{2}$
8. $\frac{1}{8}$
9.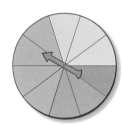
10.
11. $\frac{7}{8}$
12. $\frac{5}{8}$

Activity
(Suggested answer)

Final Review

1. 8, 6, 4, 3
2. No. of hours: 8, 12
   No. of days: 24, 16
3. 14.267
4. 5.42
5. 10.025
6. 0.002
7. 0.86
8. 1.4
9. 3.83
10. 2.56
11. 3.68
12. 1.4355
13. 0.0186
14. 0.426
15. 0.1436
16. 206
17. 14.1
18. 47
19. 90

20. $2 \times q + 6 - 6 = 10 - 6$
    $2 \times q = 4$
    $2 \times q \div 2 = 4 \div 2$
    2

21. $5 \times k - 2 + 2 = 18 + 2$
    $5 \times k = 20$
    $5 \times k \div 5 = 20 \div 5$
    4

22. $3 \times p + 1 - 1 = 10 - 1$
    $3 \times p = 9$
    $3 \times p \div 3 = 9 \div 3$
    3

23. $m \div 4 + 3 - 3 = 5 - 3$
    $m \div 4 = 2$
    $m \div 4 \times 4 = 2 \times 4$
    8

24. diameter
25. center
26. radius
27. circumference
28. 1, 2
29. 2.5, 5
30. $\frac{43}{100}$; 0.43; 43%

31. $\frac{67}{100}$; 0.67; 67%
32. $\frac{4}{12} = \frac{1}{4}$
33. $\frac{6}{12} = \frac{1}{2}$
34. $\frac{2}{12} = \frac{1}{6}$
35. 32
36. 34
37. 34
38. 32
39. 68
40. 10:30 a.m.
41. 4:40 p.m.
42. The Journey
43. Rumble
44. 4:07 p.m.
45. 88
46. 34.85
47. 31.24
48. 25
49. 100
50. 2.50
51. 50
52. 11
53. 14
54. 120
55. 36
56. 256
57. 112
58. 516

59.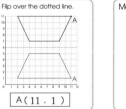
    Flip over the dotted line.
    A (11 , 1)

60.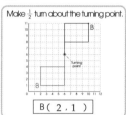
    Make $\frac{1}{2}$ turn about the turning point.
    B (2 , 1)

61.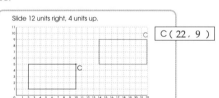
    Slide 12 units right, 4 units up.
    C (22 , 9)

1 Multiplication and Division of Whole Numbers

1. No. of pencils : 28 x 3 = 84   84
2. No. of books : 28 x 5 = 140   Difference : 140 – 84 = 56
   There are 56 more books than pencils given out at the beginning of the year.
3. No. of chairs : 28 + 2 = 30   No. of stacks : 30 ÷ 5 = 6
   There would be 6 stacks of chairs.
4. No. of pencils belonging to girls : 21 x (3 – 2) = 21
   There would be 21 pencils belonging to the girls.
5. No. of rows : 28 ÷ 7 = 4   There would be 4 rows of chairs.
6. No. of panes of glass : 9 x 8 = 72
   There were 72 panes of glass in the doors.
7. No. of panes of glass in the windows : 19 x 2 = 38
   Total no. of panes of glass : 72 + 38 = 110
   There were 110 panes of glass in the house.
8. Cost : 72 ÷ 2 x 3 = 108
   It would cost $108 to clean the panes of glass in the doors.
9. Cost : 38 x 5 + 108 = 298
   It would cost $298 to clean all the glass in the house.
10. Value : 11 x 34 = 374
    The value of Sally's pennies was 374¢ ($3.74).
11. Value : 135 ÷ 9 = 15   Each nickel was worth 15¢.
12. Value : 14 x 31 = 434
    The value of her collection of dimes was 434¢ ($4.34).
13. Value : 116 x 5 + 76 x (19 – 5) = 1,644
    The value of her quarters was 1,644¢ ($16.44).
14. Value : 374 + 135 + 434 + 1,644 = 2,587
    The value of her collection was 2,587¢ ($25.87).
15. Value : 25 x (34 + 9 + 31 + 19) = 2,325 (2,325 < 2,587)
    No, it would not be a good idea.
16. No. of hours : 30 x 2 = 60
    She spent 60 hours on doing homework in September.
17. No. of hours : 30 x 2 x 17 = 1,020
    The girls spent 1,020 hours on doing homework in September.
18. No. of hours : 60 ÷ 20 = 3
    3 hours of homework would be assigned each school day.
19. No. of hours : 25 x (30 ÷ 15) = 50
    Wanda would do 50 hours of homework in September.
20. No. of hours : 50 x 17 = 850
    All the girls would do 850 hours of homework in September.
21. Money spent : 4 x (7 x 3 ÷ 2) = 42
    Lisa spends $42 each week on long-distance phone calls.
22. No. of phone calls : 4 x 31 = 124
    She would make 124 long-distance phone calls in January.
23. Cost : 4 x (31 x 3 ÷ 2) = 186
    Her long-distance phone calls would cost $186 in October.
24. Money saved : 4 ÷ 2 x 300 – 4 x 39 = 444
    She could save 444¢ ($4.44).
25. Money saved : 4,200 – 500 x 7 = 700
    She will save 700¢ ($7) each week.
26. Time taken : 936 x 36 = 33,696
    It takes 33,696 seconds to dust all the paperback books.
27. Time taken : 882 x 36 = 31,752
    It takes 31,752 seconds to dust all the hardcover books.
28. No. of shelves : 936 ÷ 26 = 36
    There are 36 shelves of paperback books.
29. No. of shelves : 882 ÷ 21 = 42
    There are 42 shelves of hardcover books.
30. No. of books : 936 + 882 = 1,818
    No. of books in each box : 1,818 ÷ 6 = 303
    There are 303 books in each box.
31. Weight : 1,242 ÷ 6 = 207
    There are 207 grams of raisins in each bag.
32. Weight : 1,896 ÷ 8 = 237
    There are 237 grams of peanuts in each serving.
33. Weight : 63 x 4 x 3 = 756   Allan's figs weigh 756 ounces.
34. No. of days : (5 x 32) ÷ (4 x 2) = 20   Allan's apricots will last 20 days.
35. No. of cookies : 486 ÷ 6 = 81   Each person will get 81 cookies.
36. In bags of 5 : 486 ÷ 5 = 97...1   In bags of 7 : 486 ÷ 7 = 69...3
    To put in bags of 7.
37. No. of figs : 63 x 4 ÷ 3 = 84   Difference : 84 – 63 = 21
    Each bag will hold 21 more figs than before.
38. No. of bags : 1,896 ÷ 25 = 75...21   He will need 76 bags.
39. No. of portions of 18 grams : 1,242 ÷ 18 = 69
    Cost : 69 x 12 = 828   Allan's raisins cost 828¢ ($8.28).
40. No. of pinecones : 308 ÷ 4 = 77
    She would have to carry 77 pinecones each day.
41. Time spent : 17 x 4 x 1 x 12 = 816
    He would spend 816 hours in a year listening to the CDs.
42. No. of shelves : 1,648 ÷ 24 = 68...16
    He would need 69 shelves.
43. No. of plants : 35 x 23 = 805   Peter needed 805 plants.
44. Amount of water : 45 x 31 = 1,395   Peter will use 1,395 quarts of water.

Challenge

Day	Mon	Tue	Wed	Thu
No. of ants	100	200	400	800

x2   x2   x2

There might be 800 ants on Thursday.

2 Operations with Whole Numbers

1. Difference : 19 – 18 = 1   1 yard
2. Total distance : 12 + 18 + 14 + 19 + 16 = 79
   They threw 79 yards altogether.
3. Mario & Jimmy : 12 + 19 = 31   Sandy & Dolores : 18 + 16 = 34
   Sandy & Dolores threw the ball farther.
4. Danny : 14 + 14 = 28   Difference : 34 – 28 = 6
   The winning team threw 6 yards farther than Danny did.
5. Jimmy : 19 x 5 = 95   Sandy : 18 x 3 = 54
   Dolores : 16 x 1 = 16
   Jimmy got the highest number. The number is 95.
6. No. of days : 31 + 29 + 31 + 30 + 31 + 30 + 31 + 31 + 30 + 31 + 30 + 31 = 366   There are 366 days in a leap year.
7. No. of marbles : 56 x 6 = 336   Frank would have 336 marbles.
8. No. of people : 47 x 12 = 564   564 people will fill 12 rows.
9. No. of packages : 1,371 ÷ 250 = 5...121
   He must buy 6 packages of paper.
10. Total time : 60 + 20 = 80   No. of times : 80 ÷ 4 = 20
    He can ride around the park 20 times.
11. No. of stamps : 482 + 561 + 398 = 1,441
    She has 1,441 stamps in all.
12. Cost : 75 x 2 + 34 x 3 = 252   He should pay $252.
13. No. of pieces of lumber : 2,352 + 598 + 28 = 2,978
    There were 2,978 pieces of lumber in the lumberyard altogether.
14. Difference : 2,352 – 28 = 2,324
    There were 2,324 more pieces of pine than maple in the lumberyard.
15. Difference : 2,352 – 598 = 1,754
    There were 1,754 more pieces of pine than oak in the lumberyard.
16. Length : 2,978 x 2 = 5,956
    There were 5,956 yards of lumber in the lumber yard.
17. Length : (598 – 269) x 2 = 658
    658 yards of oak would be left to sell.
18.

No. of days	1	2	3
Length of pine sold (yard)	1,568	3,136	4,704

It would take 3 days to sell all the pine pieces.

19. No. of pieces of oak left : 414 ÷ 2 = 207
No. of pieces of oak sold : 598 − 207 = 391
391 pieces of oak were sold.

20. Money earned : 2 x 9 x 5 = 90   She earned $90.

21. Time taken : 25 + 17 + 28 = 70; (70 minutes = 1 hour 10 minutes)
He finished at 5:10 p.m.

22. Cost : 15 + 18 = 33
Money Mario had : 20 + 10 + 5 = 35 (35 > 33)   Yes, he could.

23. Time saved : (20 − 14) x 2 x 5 = 60
She can save 60 minutes each week.

24. There are 3 7 years in 21 years.   No. of times : 2 x 2 x 2 = 8
It should be worth 8 times its present value in 21 years.

Challenge

1. There are 2 leap years and 9 years.
No. of days : 366 x 2 + 365 x 9 = 732 + 3,285 = 4,017
He is 4,017 days old.

2. There are 3 quarters in 9 months.   Charge : 158,920 x 3 = 476,760
The client would pay them $476,760.

3   Comparing and Ordering Fractions

1. $6\frac{1}{2} = 6\frac{1 \times 4}{2 \times 4} = 6\frac{4}{8}$; $6\frac{4}{8} > 6\frac{3}{8}$ Peter

2. $\frac{1}{2}$ of an hour = 30 minutes (30 minutes < 42 minutes)
Mary read the chapter faster.

3. Douglas : 25 + 10 + 3 = 38   Jill : 10 + 30 + 1 = 41
Douglas had $\frac{38}{100}$ of a dollar; Jill had $\frac{41}{100}$ of a dollar. Jill had the larger fraction of a dollar.

4. Cake served : $\frac{2}{7} = \frac{2 \times 4}{7 \times 4} = \frac{8}{28}$
Cake kept : $\frac{1}{4} = \frac{1 \times 7}{4 \times 7} = \frac{7}{28}$
No, she didn't save more cake than she served.

5. Henry ate : $\frac{1}{3} = \frac{1 \times 5}{3 \times 5} = \frac{5}{15}$
Ann ate : $\frac{2}{5} = \frac{2 \times 3}{5 \times 3} = \frac{6}{15}$ ($\frac{6}{15} > \frac{5}{15}$)   Henry ate less.

6. ($1 = 100¢); She had $\frac{63}{100}$ of a dollar.

7. Money Dolores had : 100 + 25 x 7 = 275
(275¢ = $2\frac{75}{100}$ = $ 2\frac{3}{4}$) She had $2\frac{3}{4}$ of a dollar.

8. Money Milly had : 25 + 10 x 4 + 5 x 12 = 125
(125¢ = $1\frac{25}{100}$ = $ 1\frac{1}{4}$) She had $1\frac{1}{4}$ of a dollar.

9. Money Gerry had : 25 x 7 + 10 x 2 + 5 x 6 = 225
(225¢ = $2\frac{25}{100}$ = $ 2\frac{1}{4}$) He had $2\frac{1}{4}$ of a dollar.

10. Dolores raised the most money for charity.

11. Total amount : $\frac{63}{100} + 2\frac{75}{100} + 1\frac{25}{100} + 2\frac{25}{100} = 6\frac{88}{100} = 6\frac{22}{25}$
They raised $6\frac{22}{25}$ for charity in all.

Challenge

1. Sam : $\frac{21}{147} = \frac{1}{7}$ Hindy : $\frac{54}{216} = \frac{1}{4}$
Kelly : $\frac{28}{98} = \frac{2}{7}$ Oliver : $\frac{2}{166} = \frac{1}{83}$
Kelly had the largest fraction of valuable cards.

2. Sam had the second smallest fraction of valuable cards.

3. Kelly, Hindy, Sam, Oliver.

4   Addition and Subtraction of Fractions

1. Total time : $1\frac{5}{6} + 1\frac{4}{6} + \frac{1}{6} = 3\frac{2}{3}$; $3\frac{2}{3}$

2. Difference : $1\frac{4}{6} - \frac{1}{6} = 1\frac{1}{2}$
Dolores spent $1\frac{1}{2}$ hours more on the project than Mario.

3. Difference : $1\frac{4}{6} + 1\frac{5}{6} - \frac{1}{6} = 2\frac{9}{6} - \frac{1}{6} = 2\frac{8}{6} = 3\frac{1}{3}$
Ann and Dolores spent $3\frac{1}{3}$ hours more on the project than Mario.

4. No. of hours : $1\frac{5}{6} + \frac{1}{6} = 1\frac{6}{6} = 2$
Ann and Mario spent 2 hours on the project in all.

5. Time Dolores spent : $1\frac{4}{6}$ Time Ann and Mario spent : 2
Ann and Mario together spent more time on the project than Dolores.

6. Difference : $1\frac{5}{6} - \frac{1}{6} = 1\frac{2}{3}$
Mario would spend $1\frac{2}{3}$ hours more.

7. No. of bags : $\frac{3}{7} + \frac{5}{7} + \frac{1}{7} = \frac{9}{7} = 1\frac{2}{7}$
Harry collected $1\frac{2}{7}$ bags of bottles in all.

8. No. of bags : $\frac{5}{7} + \frac{3}{7} + \frac{2}{7} = \frac{10}{7} = 1\frac{3}{7}$
Barry collected $1\frac{3}{7}$ bags of bottles in all.

9. No. of bags : $\frac{6}{7} + \frac{6}{7} + 1 = \frac{12}{7} + 1 = 2\frac{5}{7}$
Mary collected $2\frac{5}{7}$ bags of bottles in all.

10. Mary collected the most bottles.

11. No. of bags : $1\frac{2}{7} + 1\frac{3}{7} + 2\frac{5}{7} = 5\frac{3}{7}$
The children collected $5\frac{3}{7}$ bags of bottles in all.

12. Difference : $2\frac{5}{7} - 1\frac{2}{7} = 1\frac{3}{7}$
Mary collected $1\frac{3}{7}$ more bags of bottles than Harry.

13. Difference : $2\frac{5}{7} - 1\frac{3}{7} = 1\frac{2}{7}$
Mary collected $1\frac{2}{7}$ more bags of bottles than Barry.

14. No. of bags : $2 - 1\frac{2}{7} = \frac{5}{7}$
He would need to collect $\frac{5}{7}$ of a bag of bottles more.

15. No. of bags : $3 - 1\frac{3}{7} = 1\frac{4}{7}$
He would need to collect $1\frac{4}{7}$ more bags of bottles.

16. No. of bags : $5 - 2\frac{5}{7} = 4\frac{7}{7} - 2\frac{5}{7} = 2\frac{2}{7}$
She would need to collect $2\frac{2}{7}$ more bags of bottles.

17. Total amount : $\frac{2}{5} + \frac{4}{5} + \frac{3}{5} = \frac{9}{5} = 1\frac{4}{5}$
He had $1\frac{4}{5}$ boxes of cereal in all.

18. Difference : $\frac{4}{5} - \frac{2}{5} = \frac{2}{5}$
He had $\frac{2}{5}$ of a box more bran flakes than corn flakes.

19. Difference : $\frac{3}{5} + \frac{2}{5} - \frac{4}{5} = \frac{5}{5} - \frac{4}{5} = \frac{1}{5}$
He had $\frac{1}{5}$ of a box more rice and corn flakes than bran flakes.

20. Amount of cereal left :
$(\frac{2}{5} - \frac{1}{5}) + (\frac{4}{5} - \frac{1}{5}) + (\frac{3}{5} - \frac{1}{5}) = 1\frac{1}{5}$
$1\frac{1}{5}$ boxes of cereal would be left.

21. Total amount : $1\frac{4}{5} + 1 - \frac{1}{5} = 2\frac{3}{5}$
He would have $2\frac{3}{5}$ boxes of cereal altogether.

22. Total distance : $2\frac{7}{20} + 3\frac{19}{20} + 2\frac{11}{20} + 5 = 13\frac{17}{20}$
They ran $13\frac{17}{20}$ kilometers in all.

23. Difference : $5 - 2\frac{7}{20} = 2\frac{13}{20}$ The person who ran the farthest distance ran $2\frac{13}{20}$ kilometers farther than the one who ran the shortest.

24. Total distance : $2\frac{7}{20} + 2\frac{11}{20} = 4\frac{9}{10}$ Their team ran $4\frac{9}{10}$ kilometers.

25. Distance : $3\frac{19}{20} + 2\frac{11}{20} = 6\frac{1}{2}$

They ran $6\frac{1}{2}$ kilometers in all.

26. Difference : $5 - 3\frac{19}{20} = 1\frac{1}{20}$ Toni ran $1\frac{1}{20}$ kilometers farther than Lori.

27. Difference : $2\frac{11}{20} - 2\frac{7}{20} = \frac{1}{5}$ Freda ran $\frac{1}{5}$ kilometer farther than Kim.

28. New magazines : $1 - (\frac{1}{19} + \frac{9}{19} + \frac{7}{19}) = \frac{19}{19} - \frac{17}{19} = \frac{2}{19}$

$\frac{2}{19}$ of his magazines are new.

29. Fraction of magazines : $\frac{7}{19} + \frac{2}{19} = \frac{9}{19}$

$\frac{9}{19}$ of his magazines were printed between 1980 and the present.

30. Fraction of magazines : $\frac{9}{19} + \frac{7}{19} = \frac{16}{19}$

$\frac{16}{19}$ of his magazines were printed between 1970 and 1990.

31. Fraction of magazines : $\frac{9}{19} + \frac{1}{19} = \frac{10}{19}$

$\frac{10}{19}$ of his magazines need protective envelopes.

32. Fraction of magazines : $1 - \frac{10}{19} = \frac{9}{19}$

$\frac{9}{19}$ of his magazines do not need protective envelopes.

33. Fraction of magazines left : $1 - \frac{3}{8} = \frac{5}{8}$

$\frac{5}{8}$ of his magazines will be left.

34. $\frac{113}{190}$ of his magazines are in English.

35. No. of French magazines : $190 - 113 = 77$

$\frac{77}{190}$ of his magazines are in French.

Challenge

$\frac{3}{13} + ? = \frac{9}{13} \longrightarrow ? = \frac{6}{13}$

The fraction under the chocolate stain is $\frac{6}{13}$.

5   Addition and Subtraction of Decimals

1. Weight : $0.75 + 0.007 + 1.28 + 0.95 + 0.01 = 2.997$; 2.997 kilograms
2. Weight : $4 - 2.997 = 1.003$

He could add 1.003 kilograms more to his dry ingredients.

3. Weight : $0.75 + 1.28 + 0.95 + 0.01 = 2.99$

This recipe requires 2.99 kilograms of vegetables.

4. Weight : $0.01 + 1.28 = 1.29$

This recipe requires 1.29 kilograms of herbs and spices.

5. Weight : $2.997 + 0.599 = 3.596$

The entire dish would weigh 3.596 kilograms before cooking.

6. Money saved : $7.5 - 3.49 - 1.78 - 2 = 0.23$

She saved $0.23 each week.

7. Money spent : $3.49 + 1.78 = 5.27$

She spent $5.27 for entertainment and snacks each week.

8. Difference : $3.49 - 2 = 1.49$ She spent $1.49 more for entertainment than transportation each week.

9. Money saved : $0.23 + 0.68 = 0.91$ She would save $0.91 each week.

10. Money left : $3.49 - (2.23 - 1.78) = 3.04$

She would have $3.04 left for entertainment.

Challenge

1. Distance : $5.78 \div 2 - 1.97 = 0.92$ He would have to go 0.92 mile farther.

2. Final balance : $15.02 + (5.78 - 0.15) + (1.99 - 0.15) - 3.14 - 0.15 - 2.67 - 0.15 = 16.38$ Her final balance was $16.38.

6   Multiplication and Division of Decimals

1. Money saved : $5.75 \times 12 = 69$ ($69 < 75.6$);   wouldn't

2. Difference : $75.6 - 69 = 6.6$ He would be short of $6.60.
3. Money saved : $6.45 \times 12 = 77.4$ ($77.4 > 75.6$)

Yes, that would allow him to buy the game on time.

4. He is short of $6.60. Extra money needed : $6.6 \div 12 = 0.55$

He would have to save an extra $0.55 each month.

5. Difference : $69 - 59.88 = 9.12$ Less money saved : $9.12 \div 12 = 0.76$

He would save $0.76 less each month.

6. Money spent : $2.16 \times 2 = 4.32$ She would spend $4.32 for pine.
7. Money spent : $0.3 \times 4.7 = 1.41$ She would spend $1.41 for oak.
8. Money spent : $2.4 \times 5.65 = 13.56$

She would spend $13.56 for walnut.

9. Money spent : $4.32 + 1.41 + 13.56 = 19.29$

She would spend $19.29 for wood altogether.

10. Total cost : $(2.16 + 0.3 + 2.4) \times 0.5 = 2.43$

The total cost would be $2.43.

11. Total cost : $19.29 + 2.43 = 21.72$

The total cost for the wood plus finishing was $21.72.

12. Amount each paid : $21.72 \div 3 = 7.24$ Each person would pay $7.24.
13. Length : $2.16 \div 3 = 0.72$ Each part would be 0.72 yard long.
14. Length : $(2.4 - 0.04) \div 4 = 0.59$ Each part would be 0.59 yard long.
15. No. of yards of pine : $16.5 \div 2 = 8.25$

I can buy 8.25 yards of pine.

16. Travel cost : $305 \times 0.06 = 18.3$ The travel cost on day 2 was $18.30.
17. Difference : $271 \times 0.04 - 186 \times 0.05 = 1.54$

The difference in travel cost was $1.54.

18. Day 1 : $271 \times 0.04 = 10.84$ Day 2 : $305 \times 0.06 = 18.30$

Day 3 : $652 \times 0.05 = 32.60$ Day 4 : $186 \times 0.05 = 9.30$

Day 5 : $395 \times 0.04 = 15.80$

The lowest travel cost was on day 4. It was $9.30.

19. Day 3 was the highest.   The cost was $32.60.
20. Day 5 : $15.80 > 12.00$ Yes, it would have exceeded his budget.
21. Day 2 : $18.30 > 12.00$ Day 3 : $32.60 > 12.00$

Day 5 : $15.80 > 12.00$ Days 2, 3, and 5 exceeded his travel budget.

22. Cost per mile : $4 \div 100 = 0.04$ The cost per mile would be $0.04.
23. Cost per mile : $(4 + 2) \div 100 = 0.06$ The actual cost per mile was $0.06.
24. Cost : $8.76 \div 4 = 2.19$ Each box of juice costs $2.19.
25. Capacity : $1.25 \div 5 = 0.25$ The capacity of each glass is 0.25 quart.
26. Capacity : $1.25 \times 7 = 8.75$ There is 8.75 quarts of juice in 7 boxes.
27. Regular size : $1.38 \div 2 = 0.69$ Jumbo size : $5.90 \div 10 = 0.59$

Jumbo size is the better buy.

28. Cost : $1.38 \times 8 = 11.04$ He should pay $11.04.
29. Amount of water : $1.75 \times 7 = 12.25$

He will drink 12.25 quarts of water in a week.

Challenge

Area : $16.8 \times 2.4 = 40.32$ Amount of paint : $40.32 \div 32 \times 2 = 2.52$

She will need 2.52 quarts of paint for the wall.

Midway Review

1. No. of helpers : $9 \times 4 + 12 \times 4 = 36 + 48 = 84$

There were 84 helpers.

2. No. of pieces of cake : $64 \times 8 = 512$ She made 512 pieces of cake.
3. Cost : $0.75 \times 8 = 6.00$ A cake cost $6.00.
4. Cost : $2.16 \times 64 = 138.24$

The total cost for baking all the cakes would be $138.24.

5. No. of doughnuts : $1,064 + 898 = 1,962$

There were 1,962 doughnuts in all.

6. No. of packages : $1,064 \div 4 = 266$

There were 266 packages of chocolate doughnuts.

7. No. of honey doughnuts sold : $898 - 159 = 739$

739 honey doughnuts had been sold.

8. Cost : $5.04 \div 8 = 0.63$ 1 honey doughnut cost $0.63.
9. No. of cookies : $4 \times 6 \times 15 = 360$ There were 360 cookies.
10. No. of cookies left : $360 - 218 = 142$ 142 cookies were left.
11. Weight : $17 \div 5 = 3.4$ 1 cookie weighed 3.4 ounces.

12. Amount of cake : $\frac{1}{8} + \frac{5}{8} = \frac{3}{4}$

They bought $\frac{3}{4}$ of the cake in all.

13. Difference : $\frac{5}{8} - \frac{1}{8} = \frac{1}{2}$

Sally bought $\frac{1}{2}$ more of the cake than Gary.

14. Change : 10 − 4.16 = 5.84   Her change was $5.84.

15. A bag of 5 bagels : 1.30 ÷ 5 = 0.26 $0.26 per bagel
A bag of 8 bagels : 1.76 ÷ 8 = 0.22 $0.22 per bagel
A bag of 8 bagels was a better buy.

16. Money collected : 459 x 8 = 3,672
The stalls collected $3,672 in all.

17. Money donated : 3,672 ÷ 2 = 1,836
Mr. Stanley donated $1,836 to the Children's Hospital.

18. Money Mr. Stanley had : $1,836 ($1,836 > $1,285)
Yes, he made a profit after the donation.

19. Profit : 1,836 − 1,285 = 551   He gained $551.

20. Amount of paint : 3.48 x 4 = 13.92
13.92 quarts of paint are needed for all the bedrooms.

21. No. of cans : 13.92 ÷ 4 = 3.48   She needs 4 cans.

22. No. of boxes of tiles needed : $1\frac{3}{5} + 1\frac{3}{5} + 1\frac{3}{5} = 4\frac{4}{5}$
$4\frac{4}{5}$ boxes of tiles are needed.

23. She needs to buy 5 boxes.

24. No. of boxes left : $5 - 4\frac{4}{5} = \frac{1}{5}$
$\frac{1}{5}$ of a box of tiles will be left over.

25. Money spent : 798.65 + 268.47 = 1,067.12
They spend $1,067.12 in all.

26. Store A : 102 x 6 = 612   Store B : 621 (621 > 612)
Stores A offers a better buy.

27. Cost : 1,295 + 612 = 1,907   She will pay $1,907.

28. B   29. C   30. D   31. A   32. C
33. A   34. D   35. C   36. A

7   Operations with Decimals

1. Cost : 12.37 x 3 + 14.62 = 51.73; $51.73

2. Amount saved : (19.99 − 14.62) x 5 = 26.85
She will save $26.85.

3. Cost : 12.37 + 227.36 = 239.73 (239.73 > 230)   No, he cannot.

4. Change : 150 − 67.99 x 2 = 14.02   Her change was $14.02.

5. Average price : (12.37 + 14.62 + 67.99) ÷ 3 = 31.66
The average price was $31.66.

6. Money spent : 5.88 + 3.35 + 4.32 + 8.37 = 21.92
They spent $21.92 in all.

7. Change : 50 − 21.92 = 28.08   They should receive $28.08 change.

8. Amount each paid : 21.92 ÷ 2 = 10.96
Each person should pay $10.96.

9. They spent $21.92; there were 2 ten dollars.
Cost : 21.92 − 1.05 x 2 = 19.82   They would have paid $19.82.

10. Cost : 5.88 ÷ 12 = 0.49   The cost of 1 pound of apples was $0.49.

11. Cost : 8.37 ÷ 3 = 2.79   The cost of 1 pound of candies was $2.79.

12. Cost : 3.35 ÷ 5 = 0.67   The cost of 1 head of lettuce was $0.67.

13. 5-pound bag : 6.45 ÷ 5 = 1.29   8-pound bag : 9.28 ÷ 8 = 1.16
An 8-pound bag is a better buy.

14. Distance : 0.3 x 1,000 = 300
Rachel lives the closest to the school. The distance is 300 meters.

15. Distance : 1,620 ÷ 1,000 = 1.62
The distance between Sandra's house and Paul's house is 1.62 kilometers.

16. Distance : 1.57 + 0.89 = 2.46
The distance from Debbie's house to the school is 2.46 kilometers.

17. Shortest distance : 0.93 + 1.35 = 2.28 (via Sandra's house)
The shortest distance from Debbie's house to the school is 2,280 meters.

18. Rachel → School → Virginia → Debbie : 0.3 + 0.89 + 1.57 = 2.76
Rachel → School → Sandra → Debbie : 0.3 + 1.35 + 0.93 = 2.58
The shortest distance is 2.58 kilometers.

19. Distance walked per minute : 1.35 ÷ 5 = 0.27
The average distance she walked per minute was 0.27 kilometer.

20. Distance traveled per minute : (1.57 + 0.89) ÷ 6 = 2.46 ÷ 6 = 0.41
The average distance she traveled per minute was 0.41 kilometer.

21. Distance traveled per minute : (2.82 + 1.32) ÷ 9 = 0.46
The average distance she traveled per minute was 0.46 kilometer.

22. Distance traveled : 1.35 x 4 x 5 = 27
She will travel 27 kilometers in 5 days.

23. Distance traveled : 0.89 + 1.35 + 0.3 x 2 = 2.84
They walk 2.84 kilometers in total.

24. Actual distance : 2.5 x 0.3 = 0.75   The actual distance is 0.75 kilometer.

Challenge

1. Cost : 3.75 x 25 + 6.90 = 93.75 + 6.90 = 100.65
They would have to pay $100.65 in total.

2. Cost : 3.75 x 35 − 12.60 = 118.65
They would have to pay $118.65 in total.

8   Two- Step Problems

1. No. of seats : 26 x 48 = 1,248
No. of empty seats : 1,248 − 952 = 296   296

2. Total amount from children's tickets : 2,475 − 462 x 4.5 = 396
No. of children's tickets : 396 ÷ 3 = 132
132 children's tickets were sold.

3. Amount each child paid : 3 + 2 = 5
Money collected : 1,248 x 5 = 6,240
$6,240 would be collected for that show.

4. Amount each adult paid : 4.5 + 2 = 6.5
Money collected : 1,248 x 6.5 = 8,112
$8,112 would be collected for that show.

5. She would have to buy 1 adult ticket, 4 children's tickets, and 3
popcorns. Cost : 4.5 + 3 x 4 + 2 x 3 = 22.5   She would pay $22.50 in all.

6. Cost : 9 + 14 = 23   He paid $23 for his purchases.

7. Cost : (18 ÷ 3 x 6 + 19) − 4 = 51   Change : 100 − 51 = 49
She would get $49 change.

8. Cost : (9 ÷ 2 x 4 + 18) − 4 = 32
Money needed : 32 − 20 − 10 = 2   She needed $2.

9. Cost : (14 x 2 + 9 + 2 x 4) − 4 = 42
He paid $42 for his purchases.

10. Cost : (18 ÷ 3 x 9 + 14 x 3) − 4 x 2 = 88
She paid $88 for her purchases.

11. Cost : 19 x 4 = 76   Money needed : 76 − 50 = 26
She would need to borrow $26.

12. Price of 6 blouses : 18 ÷ 3 x 6 − 4 = 32   Price of 4 dresses : 19 x 4 = 76
Difference : 76 − 32 = 44   The price difference was $44.

13. Amount spent on dresses : 71 − 14 = 57
No. of dresses : 57 ÷ 19 = 3   She bought 3 dresses.

14. No. of shirts : 128 + 224 = 352   No. of packages : 352 ÷ 4 = 88
He would make 88 packages of 4 in all.

15. No. of packages : 352 ÷ 3 = 117...1
He would make 117 packages of 3 in all.

16. Time for ads and music in an hour : 8 x 2 + 16 x 2 = 48
Time for talk : 60 − 48 = 12 There is 12 minutes of talk every hour.

17. There are 16 minutes of ads in an hour; 16 minutes have 32 30 seconds.
Cost : 120 x 32 = 3,840 The station will earn $3,840 per hour.

18. No. of songs in an hour : 16 x 2 ÷ 4 = 8
No. of songs between 4:00 p.m. and 9:00 p.m. : 8 x 5 = 40
40 songs can be played between 4:00 p.m. and 9:00 p.m.

19. Non-ad time in an hour : 60 − 8 x 2 = 44
Non-ad time in a day : 44 x 16 = 704
There are 704 minutes of non-ad time in a day.

20. There are 12 minutes of talk in an hour; there are 72 10 seconds in 12 minutes.   No. of words in an hour : 36 x 72 = 2,592
    He will say 2,592 words in each hour's talk time.
21. Cost : 0.39 x 4 = 1.56   Change : 5 – 1.56 = 3.44
    She got $3.52 change.
22. Cost for Anna's friends : (0.39 x 4) x 4 = 6.24
    Total cost : 0.39 x 4 + 6.24 = 7.80   They spend $7.80 in postage.
23.

1st chain	2nd chain

    1 —x4→ 4 —x4→ 16

    No. of people involved: 1 + 4 + 16 = 21
    21 people would be involved in the chain.
24. Cost : 85 x 0.39 = 33.15   They would pay $33.15 for postage.
25. Time each person spent on sending a letter : 6 + 2 = 8
    Total time spent : (4 + 16) x 8 = 160
    They would spend 160 minutes.

Challenge

1.

Day	Mon	Tue	Wed	Thu
No. of pages read	38	67	67	29

    No. of pages left : 249 – 38 – 67 – 67 – 29 = 48
    She would have 48 pages left to read on Thursday at noon.
2. Total amount for the payments : 92.6 x 24 = 2,222.4
    Difference : 2,222.4 – 2,120.5 = 101.9
    Wayne pays $101.90 more by purchasing it on the instalment plan.

9   Patterns

1. 1st : 4 + 2 = 6   2nd : 6 x 3 = 18   18
2. 1st : 6 + 2 = 8   2nd : 8 x 3 = 24   Dorothy would answer 24.
3. 1st : 5.5 + 2 = 7.5   2nd : 7.5 x 3 = 22.5
    Dorothy would answer 22.5.
4. A : 4 ÷ 2 = 2; 2 + 10 = 12 ✗   B : 4 x 6 = 24; 24 – 10 = 14 ✓
    C : 4 – 3 = 1; 1 x 10 = 10 ✗   D : 4 + 8 = 12; 12 ÷ 2 = 6 ✗
    B is correct.
5. 1st : 2.4 x 6 = 14.4   2nd : 14.4 – 10 = 4.4
    Gladys would answer 4.4.
6. Yes. He scored 2 more baskets each day.
7. 1 —+2→ 3 —+2→ 5 —+2→ 7 —+2→ 9
    The numbers increase by 2 each time.
8. Billy would score 11 baskets on the 6th day.
9.

6th	7th	8th	9th	10th

    11 —→ 13 —→ 15 —→ 17 —→ 19
    Billy would score 19 baskets on the 10th day.
10. Total no. of baskets : 1 + 3 = 4
    Billy scored 4 baskets in the first 2 days.
11. Total no. of baskets : 1 + 3 + 5 = 9
    Billy scored 9 baskets in the first 3 days.
12. Total no. of baskets : 1 + 3 + 5 + 7 = 16
    Billy scored 16 baskets in the first 4 days.
13. Total no. of baskets : 1 + 3 + 5 + 7 + 9 = 25
    Billy scored 25 baskets in the first 5 days.
14.

Day	1	2	3	4	5	6	7	8	9
No. of baskets in all	1	4	9	16	25	36	49	64	81

    Billy would score 81 baskets in the first 9 days.
15.

Day	9	10	11
No. of baskets in all	81	100	121

    Billy would take 11 days.
16. 1 —x3→ 3 —x3→ 9 —x3→ 27 —x3→ 81 —x3→ 243
    Each number is 3 times the previous number. The next 2 numbers are 81 and 243.

17. 1 —+0.9→ 1.9 —+0.9→ 2.8 —+0.9→ 3.7 —+0.9→ 4.6 —+0.9→ 5.5
    The numbers increase by 0.9. The next 2 numbers are 4.6 and 5.5.
18. a —b→ c —d e→ f —g h i→ j —k l m n→ o —p q r s t→ u
    The letters skip 1 more letter than before. The next 2 letters are o and u.
19. 3 —+3→ 6 —+4→ 10 —+5→ 15 —+6→ 21 —+7→ 28
    The numbers increase by 1 more each time. The next 2 numbers are 21 and 28.
20. 1, 1, 2, 2, 2, 4, 3, 3, 6, 4, 4, 8, 5, 5, 10
    3 numbers are in a group. The first 2 numbers in the group increase by 1, the last numbers increase by 2.
    The next 6 numbers are 4, 4, 8, 5, 5, and 10.
21.

    1+2 2+3 3+5 5+8 8+13 13+21 21+34
    1 , 2 , 3 , 5 , 8 , 13 , 21 , 34 , 55
    Each number is the sum of the previous 2 numbers.
    The next 2 numbers are 34 and 55.
22.

Day	1	2	3	4	5	6	7
Allowance	0.1	0.2	0.4	0.8	1.6	3.2	6.4

    Total allowance in a week :
    0.1 + 0.2 + 0.4 + 0.8 + 1.6 + 3.2 + 6.4 = 12.7 (12.7>12)
    To give $12.00 per week is a better deal for Hortense's parents.
23. Improvement : 58 – 52 = 6;   Final mark : 58 + 6 x 2 = 70
    Mr. Finley would give Karen 70 for her next test.
24.

Age	12	22	32	42	52	62	72
Value of bond	25	50	100	200	400	800	1,600

    It will be worth $1,600.00 when Jerry is 72 years old.

Challenge

1. 40   2. Subtraction   3. Addition

10   Using Patterns

1. 62.50, 125.00, 500.00, 2,000.00, 4,000.00
2.

Year	2000	2010	2020
Price ($)	4,000.00	8,000.00	16,000.00

    The price of the savings bond in 2020 will be $16,000.00.
3.

Year	2000	2010	2020	2030	2040
Price ($)	4,000.00	8,000.00	16,000.00	32,000.00	64,000.00

    It will be worth $64,000.00 in 2040.
4. 62.50 x 2 x 2 = 250
    No. of times : 2 x 2 = 4   It was 4 times more.
5. Money earned : 16,000 – 1,000 = 15,000
    I would earn $15,000.
6. 6, 5;   2.25, 3.60;   19, 24, 30, 38, 43
7.

Week	1	2	3	4	5	6	7	8	9
No. of cards	5	6	8	5	6	8	5	6	8

    He will buy 8 cards.
8.

Week	7	8	9	10
Money spent	2.25	2.70	3.60	2.25

    He will spend $2.25.
9. He will collect 19 cards.   10. He will collect 38 cards.
11.

Week	7	8	9
No. of cards bought	5	6	8
No. of cards in collection	43	49	57

    He will collect 57 cards.

12. No. of cards collected in 3 weeks : 5 + 6 + 8 = 19
No. of cards collected in 30 weeks : 19 x 10 = 190
He will collect 190 cards.

13. Following the pattern, Matthew should buy 6 cards next week.
He will buy 6 cards in week 23.

14. Total amount : 2.25 + 2.7 + 3.6 = 8.55   He will spend $8.55.

15. Money spent : (2.25 + 2.7 + 3.6) x 2 = 17.1
He will spend $17.10.

16. 14, 16, 18, 20, 22;   8, 11, 14, 17, 20

17. No. of yellow marbles : 22 + 2 = 24;   24

18. No. of blue marbles : 20 + 3 = 23
Tony will have 23 blue marbles on the 7th day.

19.

Day	6th	7th	8th	9th	10th	11th
No. of yellow marbles	22	24	26	28	30	32

Tony will take 11 days to have 32 yellow marbles.

20.

Day	6th	7th	8th	9th	10th
No. of blue marbles	20	23	26	29	32

Tony will take 10 days to have 32 blue marbles.

21.

Day	6th	7th	8th
No. of yellow marbles	22	24	26
No. of blue marbles	20	23	26

Tony will take 8 days to have the same number of yellow and blue marbles.

22. No. of marbles : 22 + 20 = 42
Tony will have 42 marbles in all in the first 6 days.

23. The number of yellow marbles increases by 2 each day. The number of blue marbles increases by 3 each day. The total number of marbles increases by 5 each day.

24. 0, 0;   6, 10;   4, 8, 12, 16, 24;   6, 12, 24, 30;
16, 24, 48;   40, 50

25. The numbers increase by 6 each time.
The next 3 numbers will be 36, 42, and 48.

26. The numbers increase by 4 each time.
The next 3 numbers will be 28, 32, and 36.

27. Column 5 has the same pattern as that in row 6.
The numbers increase by 10 each time.

28. Row 6 can show the counting pattern of Joe's cards.
He will have 50 cards after 5 days.

29. Row 5 can show the amount of money Raymond has spent.
He will have spend $32 after 4 days.

30. 4, 9, 14, 19, 24, 29   31. 2.50, 3.00, 3.50, 4.00, 4.50, 5.00

32.

Hour	6	7	8	9	10
Charge ($)	29	34	39	44	49

The charge was $49.

33. Charge : 19 + 3.5 = 22.5   The twins earned $22.50 for the service.

34. Cost : 4 + 2 x 4 = 12   Lily's bill was $12.

35. Charge for 8 hours of simple care : 29 + 5 + 5 = 39
Total bill : 39 + 39 x 2 = 117   Their total bill was $117.

36. $3.50, $4.50, $5.00

37. Cost : 12.50 + 12.00 + 0.75 x 6 = 29
His total bill was $29.

38. Charge for 7 hours' care : 17 + 4.5 + 4.5 + 4.5 = 30.5
Total bill : 30.5 + 10 = 40.5   Their total bill was $40.50.

Challenge

Hour	1	2	3	4	5
Charge ($) for children over 3	1	2.5	4	5.5	7
Charge ($) for children under 3	3	4.5	6	7.5	9

Cost : 7 + 9 = 16   Their bill would be $16.

Final Review

1. Area : 1.96 x 4 = 7.84   The area is 7.84 square miles.

2. Distance traveled : 1.4 x 3 = 4.2   She will walk 4.2 miles.

3. Distance traveled : 1.4 x 4 = 5.6   He will walk 5.6 miles.

4. Distance traveled : 1.4 x 3 x 2 = 8.4   They will travel 8.4 miles in all.

5. Difference : 1.4 x 2 – 1.86 = 0.94   She would have to walk 0.94 mile.

6. Distance traveled in 1 minute : 1.4 ÷ 5 = 0.28
He would travel 0.28 mile in 1 minute.

7. Difference : 1.4 ÷ 4 – 1.4 ÷ 5 = 0.35 – 0.28 = 0.07
Doris would walk 0.07 mile more than Bobby in 1 minute.

8. 5.6, 7, 8.4;   12, 15, 18

9. The time taken increases by 3 minutes.

10. The distance traveled increases by 1.4 miles.

11.

No. of blocks	6	7	8
Time (min)	18	21	24

He would take 24 minutes to travel 8 blocks.

12.

No. of blocks	6	7	8	9	10	11	12
Time (min)	18	21	24	27	30	33	36

He would pass 12 blocks.

13.

No. of blocks	6	7	8	9
Distance traveled (miles)	8.4	9.8	11.2	12.6

He would travel 12.6 miles.

14.

Time (min)	15	30	45	60	75
Water drunk (qt)	$\frac{1}{4}$	$\frac{2}{4}$	$\frac{3}{4}$	1	$1\frac{1}{4}$

He would drink $1\frac{1}{4}$ quarts of water.

15.

Time (min)	75	90	105
Water drunk (qt)	$1\frac{1}{4}$	$1\frac{2}{4}$	$1\frac{3}{4}$

He would have traveled 105 minutes (1 hour 45 minutes) on his bike.

16. Cost : 29.45 – 7.15 = 22.3   I have to pay $22.30.

17. Price : 53.25 + 15.5 = 68.75   Its price was $68.75.

18. Cost : 10.8 x 3 = 32.4   He can save $7.15.

19. Cost before discount : 15.99 x 2 = 31.98
Cost after discount : 31.98 – 7.15 = 24.83   He will pay $24.83.

20. Cost before discount : 22.99 x 2 = 45.98
Change : 50 – (45.98 – 15.5) = 19.52   He will get $19.52 change.

21. Cost before discount : 59.99 + 3.99 = 63.98
Change : 60 – (63.98 – 15.5) = 11.52   She will get $11.52 change.

22. Cost after discount : 19.87 – 3.25 = 16.62
Money Gary has : 10 + 1 x 6 + 0.25 x 3 = 16.75 (16.75 > 16.62)
Yes. He will have enough money to buy a box of chocolates.

23. No. of male customers : 329 – 251 = 78
There will be 78 male customers.

24. Money collected : 215 x 5 = 1,075
$1,075 can be collected from 215 customers.

25. Sweater A : 34.87 – 7.15 = 27.72
Sweater B : 40.05 – 15.5 = 24.55
Difference : 27.72 – 24.55 = 3.17
The price difference between sweater A and sweater B after the discount is $3.17.

26. Ray should buy sweater B because it is cheaper after the discount.

27. B   28. C   29. A   30. B   31. C   32. C

33. B   34. A   35. B   36. D   37. C   38. B

39. B   40. D   41. D

1 Operations with Money

1. Cost : 4.98 + 12.49 = 17.47 $17.47
2. Cost : 20.18 + 5.39 = 25.57   His bill would be $25.57.
3. Cost : 4.98 + 2.84 + 12.49 + 20.18 – 4.5 = 35.99
   His bill would be $35.99.
4. Change : 100 – 35.99 = 64.01   He would get $64.01 change.
5. Raking leaves : 23.02 – 4.98 = 18.04 ✗
   Sweeping sidewalks : 23.02 – 2.84 = 20.18 (cleaning garage) ✓
   He swept Mrs. Winter's sidewalk and cleaned her garage.
6. Change : 50 – 23.02 = 26.98   She would get $26.98 change.
7. Amount earned per hour : 20.18 ÷ 2 = 10.09
   Ben would earn $10.09 per hour.
8. Amount after donation : (37.65 + 35.94 + 31.53) – (37.65 + 35.94
   + 31.53) ÷ 4 = 78.84   Ben would have $78.84 after his donation.
9. Change : 100 – (82.97 – 8 x 1.5) = 29.03   Ann's change is $29.03.
10. Change : 100 – (120.45 – 12 x (1.5 + 0.3)) = 1.15
    Tim's change is $1.15.
11. Cost : 16.99 x 3 = 50.97 ; Rebate : 5 x 1.5 = 7.5
    Change : 50 – (50.97 –7.5) = 6.53   Ray's change is $6.53.
12. Rebate for buying separately : 1.5 x 9 x 2 = 27
    Rebate for buying together : (1.5 + 0.3) x 9 x 2 = 32.4
    Sally can get more rebate by buying them together.
13. Jacket A : 98.27 – (9 x 1.5) = 84.77
    Jacket B : 102.95 – 10 x (1.5 + 0.3) = 84.95
    Eric should buy Jacket A.
14. Cost of 12 lollipops : 0.97 x 12 = 11.64 ;
    Money saved : 11.64 – 10.8 = 0.84   Donna would save $0.84.
15. Change : 25 – (10.8 x 2) = 3.4   Donna's change was $3.40.
16. Cost of 1 package : 3.24 ÷ 6 = 0.54   1 package cost $0.54.
17. Change : 20 – (0.54 x 18) = 10.28   His change was $10.28.
18. Money spent on jellybeans : 23.76 – 10.8 = 12.96

No. of boxes of jellybeans	1	2	3	4
Cost ($)	3.24	6.48	9.72	12.96

   Ted bought 4 boxes of jellybeans.
19. Average cost : (1.26 x 2) ÷ 3 = 0.84
    Each chocolate bar cost $0.84 on average.
20. Cost : 1.26 x 6 = 7.56   Alexander paid $7.56.
21. Cost of 3 jars of candies : 12.96 x 3 = 38.88   (40 > 38.88)
    Yes, Jeffrey would have enough money to buy 3 jars of candies.
22. Money left : 40 – (12.96 x 2) = 14.08
    Jeffrey would have $14.08 left.
23. $570.75 ; five hundred seventy dollars and seventy-five cents
24. $461.20 ; four hundred sixty-one dollars and twenty cents
25. $415.40 ; four hundred fifteen dollars and forty cents
26. $520.23 ; five hundred twenty dollars and twenty-three cents
27. week 1, week 4, week 2, week 3

Challenge

1. Amount : 20.94 x 12 = 251.28   Mr. Tiff will get $251.28.
2. Gain : 251.28 – 187.2 = 64.08   He will gain $64.08.

2 Perimeter and Area

1. Perimeter : 1.8 + 2.1 + 3 + 2 + 2.5 = 11.4   11.4 centimeters
2. Perimeter : 3.4 + 3.6 + 1 + 1.8 + 3.4 = 13.2
   Its perimeter is 13.2 centimeters.
3. Perimeter : 2.5 + 2.5 + 1.3 + 1.2 + 1.2 +1.3 = 10
   Its perimeter is 10 centimeters.
4. Perimeter : 2.5 + 3.8 + 2.5 + 1.5 + 1.1 + 1.3 + 1.1 + 1 = 14.8
   Its perimeter is 14.8 centimeters.
5. Perimeter : (3.4 + 2) x 2 = 10.8   Its perimeter is 10.8 centimeters.
6. Perimeter : 2.2 x 4 = 8.8   Its perimeter is 8.8 centimeters.
7. 11.4 meters, 13.2 meters, 10 meters, 14.8 meters, 10.8 meters, 8.8 meters
8. Actual perimeter : (4 + 3 + 6) x 100 = 1,300

The actual perimeter is 1,300 centimeters (13 meters).
9. Actual perimeter : (4 + 2 +3.5 + 4) x 100 = 1,350
   The actual perimeter is 1,350 centimeters (13.5 meters).
10. Actual perimeter : (2 + 3 + 2 + 3) x 100 = 1,000
    The actual perimeter is 1,000 centimeters (10 meters).
11. Actual perimeter : (3 + 4 + 5) x 100 = 1,200
    The actual perimeter is 1,200 centimeters (12 meters).
12. Actual perimeter : (6 + 4 + 3.5 + 3) x 100 = 1,650
    The actual perimeter is 1,650 centimeters (16.5 meters).
13. T, Q, P, S, R
14. Area : 5 x 6.5 = 32.5   Its area is 32.5 square yards.
15. Area : 3 x 7.3 = 21.9   Its area is 21.9 square yards.
16. Area : 7.9 x 7.9 = 62.41   Its area is 62.41 square yards.
17. No. of times : (5 x 13) ÷ (2.6 x 5) = 5
    The area of the dining room is 5 times that of the washroom.
18. Area : (13 + 6.4) x (7.9 + 5) = 250.26   The area is 250.26 square yards.
19. Area : (7.9 x 7.9) + (5 x 6.5) = 94.91
    94.91 square yards of carpet would cover the living room and the library.
20. Cost : 94.91 x 2 = 189.82   He needs to pay $189.82 for the carpet.
21. Amount of paint : (5 x 2.8 + 6.4 x 2.8) ÷ 4 = 7.98
    7.98 quarts of paint are needed for the 2 walls.
22. No. of cans : 7.98 ÷ 2 = 3.99   He needs to buy 4 cans.
23. Perimeter : (2.5 + 1.2) x 2 = 7.4   Area : 2.5 x 1.2 = 3
    Its perimeter is 7.4 yards and its area is 3 square yards.
24. Perimeter : 30 x 4 = 120 ;   Area : 30 x 30 = 900
    Its perimeter is 120 inches and its area is 900 square inches.
25. Length : 12 ÷ 4 = 3   Each side is 3 feet long.
26. Width : 450 ÷ 25 = 18   Its width is 18 yards.
27. Length : (45 ÷ 2) – 5 = 17.5   Area : 17.5 x 5 = 87.5
    Its area is 87.5 square inches.

Challenge

1. Length : 20 – (1 x 2) = 18   Width : 12 – (1 x 2) = 10
   The length is 18 inches and the width is 10 inches.
2. Area : 18 x 10 = 180 ;   Perimeter : (18 + 10) x 2 = 56
   Its area is 180 square inches and its perimeter is 56 inches.

3 Time

1. Time : 9 h 40 min + 57 min = 10 h 37 min   10:37 a.m.
2. Time : 10 h 37 min + 40 min = 11 h 17 min
   They left the park at 11:17 a.m.
3. Time : 11 h 17 min + 32 min = 11 h 49 min
   They reached the convenience store at 11:49 a.m.
4. Time : 11 h 49 min + 35 min = 12 h 24 min
   They left the store at 12:24 p.m.
5. Time taken : 12 h 42 min – 12 h 24 min = 18 min
   It took them 18 minutes.
6. Time : 1 h 17 min – 26 min = 0 h 51 min
   She started at 12: 51 p.m.
7. No. of days : 29 – 3 = 26   Larry has 26 days.
8. Time taken : (12 h 0 min – 8 h 16 min) + 4 h 5 min = 7 h 49 min
   He has worked for 7 hours 49 minutes.
9. Time : 5 h 32 min – 2 h 20 min = 3 h 12 min
   He started at 3: 12 p.m.
10. Time : 1 h 48 min + 23 min = 2 h 11 min (2:11 p.m.)
    Yes, she will be there on time.
11. Time : 11 h 45 min + 1 h 35 min = 13 h 20 min
    It will be over at 1:20 p.m.
12. Time movie A finishes :   Time movie B finishes :
    11 h 45 min + 1 h 43 min   12 h 10 min + 1 h 16 min
    = 13 h 28 min (1:28 p.m.)   = 13 h 26 min (1:26 p.m.)
    Movie B finishes first.
13. No. of days = 170 ÷ 24 = 7...2   He spent 7 days and 2 hours.

14. Time : 11 h 26 min + 37 min + 16 min = 12 h 19 min
    He reached the theater at 12:19 p.m.

Challenge

Time Flight A arrives :   Time Flight B departs :
11 h 55 min + 2 h 16 min   2 h 11 min – 1 h 45 min
= 14 h 11 min (2:11 p.m.)   = 0 h 26 min (12:26 p.m.)
Flight B must leave at 12:26 p.m.

4 Speed

1. Time : 400 ÷ 40 = 10   10 hours
2. Time : 550 ÷ 50 = 11   It would take 11 hours.
3. Average speed : 480 ÷ 10 = 48   Their average speed was 48 mph.
4. Time : 480 ÷ 40 = 12   It would take 12 hours.
5. Time : (400 + 550 + 480) ÷ 50 = 28.6   It would take 28.6 hours.
6. Average speed : (400 + 550 + 480) ÷ 20 = 71.5
   The average speed was 71.5 mph.
7. Time taken : (4 x 2) ÷ 20 = 0.4   She will take 0.4 hour (24 minutes).
8. Time taken : 2.4 ÷ 12 = 0.2   She will take 0.2 hour (12 minutes).
9. Time saved : (2.4 ÷ 12 – 2.4 ÷ 20) x 60 = 4.8
   She will save 4.8 minutes.
10. Time taken : 3.6 ÷ 20 x 60 = 10.8   She will take 10.8 minutes.
11. Speed : 3.6 ÷ 15 = 0.24   Her cycling speed was 0.24 mile per minute.
12. Speed : 0.24 x 60 = 14.4   Her cycling speed was 14.4 miles per hour.

Challenge

No. of days Ricky takes : 180 ÷ 20 = 9
No. of days Raymond takes : 180 ÷ (36 ÷ 2) = 10
No. of days Sam takes : 180 ÷ (15 x 2) = 6
Ricky will take 9 days. Raymond will take 10 days. Sam will take 6 days. Sam will finish first.

5 Volume and Surface Area

1. Volume of air : 25 x 10 x 15 = 3,750   It was 3,750 cubic inches.
2. 3,750 cubic inches of water would be needed.
3. Volume of water: 25 x 10 x 4 = 1,000   It was 1,000 cubic inches.
4. Increase in volume : 25 x 10 x (8 – 4) = 1,000
   The increase was 1,000 cubic inches.
5. Volume of air : 25 x 10 x (15 – 12) = 750   It was 750 cubic inches.
6. Volume of the fish: 25 x 10 x (13 – 12) = 250
   Volume of the fish was 250 cubic inches.
7. Volume : 30 x 16 x 20 = 9,600   It is 9,600 cubic inches.
8. No. of times: 9,600 ÷ 320 = 30   The tank can hold 30 times of the volume of water held by the pail.
9. 30 pailfuls of water are required to empty the tank.
10. Volume : 320 x 8 = 2,560
    2,560 cubic inches of water has been removed.
11. Water remained : 9,600 – 2,560 = 7,040
    7,040 cubic inches of water will remain in the tank.
12. Pailfuls of water : (9,600 ÷ 2) ÷ 320 = 15
    15 pailfuls of water must be removed.
13. Height : 9,600 ÷ (4 x 12 x 20) = 10
    It would be 10 inches high.
14. Volume : 320 ÷ 5 = 64   It is 64 cubic inches.
15. Surface area: 4 x 4 x 6 = 96   Its surface area is 96 square inches.
16. Volume : 100 x 50 x 60 = 300,000
    It's volume is 300,000 cubic centimeters (0.3 cubic meter).
17. Volume : 60 x 50 x 60 = 180,000
    It's volume is 180,000 cubic centimeters (0.18 cubic meter).
18. Difference : 300,000 – 180,000 = 120,000
    The volume of the big aquarium is 120,000 cubic centimeters (0.12 cubic meter) larger than that of the small one.
19. No. of cubes : 180,000 ÷ (10 x 10 x 10) = 180
    It can hold 180 cubes.

20. No. of cubes : 300,000 ÷ (10 x 10 x 10) = 300
    It can hold 300 cubes.
21. Rate of water flow : 300,000 ÷ 30 = 10,000
    Time taken: 180,000 ÷ 10,000 = 18
    It will take her 18 minutes to fill up the small aquarium.
22. Volume : 5.6 x 8.6 x 3 = 144.48
    There is 144.48 cubic meters of air in the living room.
23. Volume : 8 x 7 x 3 = 168   There is 168 cubic meters of air in bedroom 2.
24. Difference : (4 x 7 x 3) – (2.3 x 2.8 x 3) = 64.68
    There is 64.68 cubic meters more air in bedroom 1 than in the washroom.
25. Volume : (4 x 5 x 3) ÷ 8 = 7.5   It is 7.5 cubic meters.
26. Volume : (400 x 500 x 300) ÷ 8 = 7,500,000
    It is 7,500,000 cubic centimeters.

Challenge

1. 5 x 4 x 3 = 60 ;   (5 x 3 + 4 x 3 + 5 x 4) x 2 = 94
2. 5 x 2 x 6 = 60 ;   (5 x 6 + 2 x 6 + 5 x 2) x 2 = 104

6 Coordinate Systems

1.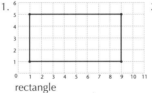
rectangle

2.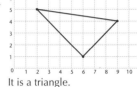
It is a triangle.

3.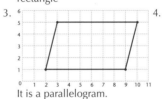
It is a parallelogram.

4.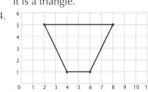
It is a trapezoid.

5. a.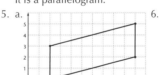
b. It is (10, 5).
c. It is a parallelogram.

6. a.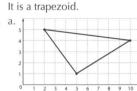
b. It is (2, 5).
c. It is a triangle.

7. a.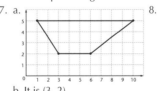
b. It is (3, 2).
c. It is a trapezoid.

8. a.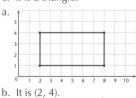
b. It is (2, 4).
c. It is a rectangle.

9. (0, 0)
10. (12, 2)
11. (2, 4)
12. (4, 9)
13. (8, 5)
14. (12, 10)
15.
16. 12 ; 2
17. 7 ; 2; 3
18. up ; right
19. right ; down
20. right ; up ; right
21. (Suggested answers)
    1 ; 10 ; 11

22.

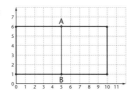

2	George	Mary	Michael	Lori	John	Daisy
1	Susan	Ray	Alvin	Emily	Jessica	Matthew
0	Leon	Amy	Elaine	Gary	Sarah	Jerry
	0	1	2	3	4	5

23. (0, 2)   24. (0, 1)   25. (2, 0)
26. (2, 1)   27. (4, 1)   28. (1, 2)

Challenge

The possible coordinates for the other two vertices are (0, 1) and (0, 6) or (10, 1) and (10, 6).

Midway Review

1. Time taken : 11 h 11 min – 10 h 47 min = 24 min
   She took 24 minutes to go from her home to the mall.
2. Distance : 30 x (24 ÷ 60) = 12
   The mall was 12 miles from her house.
3. Time : 11 h 11 min + 2 h 18 min + 45 min
   = 14 h 14 min (2:14 p.m.)   She left the mall at 2:14 p.m.
4. Time taken : (12 ÷ 24) x 60 = 30
   Time : 2 h 14 min + 30 min = 2 h 44 min
   She reached home at 2:44 p.m.
5. Change : 100 – 18.27 – 52.49 = 29.24   Her change was $29.24.
6. Difference : 52.49 – 18.27 = 34.22
   It cost $34.22 more than the box.
7. Area : 20 x 24 = 480   She would need 480 square inches of felt.
8. Length : (20 + 24) x 2 = 8   Her border would be 8 inches.
9. Volume : 20 x 24 x 20 = 9,600   It was 9,600 cubic inches.
10. No. of boxes : 3 x 4 x 5 = 60   It could hold 60 boxes of tissues.
11. Volume of water: 8 x 16 x 12 = 1,536
    It could hold 1,536 cubic inches of water.
12. Time taken : 4 h 34 min – 4 h 29 min = 0 h 5 min
    It took 5 minutes.
13. Volume : 8 x 16 x (12 – 2) = 1,280
    It was 1,280 cubic inches.
14. Volume : (8 x 16 x 0.5) ÷ 8 = 8
    On average, each pebble was 8 cubic inches.

15.

16. (1, 2)
17. (0, 4)
18. (5, 4)
19. (2, 0)
20. (4, 0)
21. (3, 3)

22. Distance : 30 x (15 ÷ 60) = 7.5
    The mall is 7.5 miles from the bus stop.
23. Time : 11 h 56 min + 15 min = 12 h 11 min
    She will arrive at 12:11 p.m.
24. Money saved : (1.28 x 10) – 10.4 = 2.4   She will save $2.40.
25. Cost : 10.40 + (2 x 1.28) = 12.96   She pays $12.96.
26. Total amount : 12.84 + 31.39 = 44.23   She spends $44.23 in all.
27. Money she had : 32.97 + 22.81 = 55.78
    She had $55.78 at the beginning.
28. C   29. B   30. A   31. C
32. D   33. D   34. B   35. A

7 Transformations

1. a.   b. c.

2. a.  b.   c.

3. a.   b. c.

4. a. b. c.

5. a. 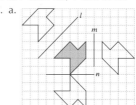 b.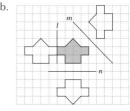

   $\frac{1}{2}$ turn clockwise $\frac{3}{4}$ turn clockwise

6. a. 7 units left, 1 unit down   b. 7 units right, 2 units up

7. a. b.

8.   9.   10.   11.

12. It will be (8, 2).   13. It will be (2, 6).
14. He moves it 6 units left and 2 units down.
15. It will be (20, 8).   16. It will be (17, 8).
17. She moves it 1 unit right and 4 units up.
18. It will be (22, 5).

Challenge

   C

8 Line Graphs

1. 80
2. 70 toy cars were produced last Friday.
3. Difference : 85 – 40 = 45
   45 more toy cars were produced on Wednesday than on Thursday.
4. It happened on Thursday because the production dropped that day.
5. It was closed on Saturday and Sunday because there was no production in those two days.
6. No. of toy cars : (80 + 75 + 85 + 40 + 70) ÷ 5 = 70
   70 toy cars were produced each working day.
7. 2,000 sports cars were produced.
8. 4,000 vans were produced.
9. 7,000 Jeeps were produced.
10. Difference : 2,000 – 1,000 = 1,000
    1,000 more vans were produced.
11. Total no. of Jeeps : 7,000 + 6,000 + 7,000 + 6,000 = 26,000
    26,000 Jeeps were produced.
12. Total no. of vehicles : 6,000 + 6,000 + 2,000 = 14,000
    14,000 vehicles were produced in the 4th quarter.
13. In the 4th quarter.

14. In the 2nd quarter.
15. It indicated a continuous increase in the production of sports cars.
16. Vans should be cut because there was a continuous decrease in the production of vans.

17.
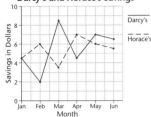

Darcy's and Horace's Savings

18. Difference : 8.5 – 3.5 = 5
    Darcy saved $5.00 more than Horace in March.
19. Difference : 6 – 2 = 4
    Horace saved $4.00 more than Darcy in February.
20. Darcy saved more than Horace in March, May, and June.
21. Darcy's savings were more than Horace's in three months.
22. Their savings were the same in January.
23. Amount saved : 4.5 + 2 + 8.5 + 4.5 + 7 + 6.5 = 33
    Darcy saved $33.00 in the six months.
24. Amount saved : 4.5 + 6 + 3.5 + 7 + 6 + 5.5 = 32.5
    Horace saved $32.50 in the six months.
25. Total : 33 + 32.5 = 65.5   (65.5 > 65.39)
    Yes, they would have enough money to buy it.

26.
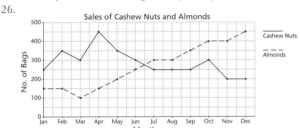

Sales of Cashew Nuts and Almonds

27. Difference : 450 – 150 = 300
    300 more bags of cashew nuts were sold than almonds in April.
28. Difference : 350 – 250 = 100
    100 more bags of almonds were sold than cashew nuts in September.
29. Bags of nuts sold : 300 + 250 = 550
    She sold 550 bags of nuts in June.
30. The sales of cashew nuts increased the most in April.

Challenge

The sales of cashew nuts decreased, but the sales of almonds increased.

9 Circle Graphs

1. apples
2.
3. Karin spent the least money on grapes.
4.

Karin's Spending on Fruit

5. Spending on pears : 100 ÷ 4 = 25
   She would spend $25 on pears.
6. Apples, bananas, pears, grapes
7. Group 4 had the most As.
8. Group 3 had the fewest As.
9. 6 students with an A were in Group 4.
10. 3 students with an A were in Group 1.
11. No. of students in Group 4 : 6 x 2 = 12
    There were 12 students in Group 4.
12. No. of students : 12 x 4 = 48   48 students took the test.

13.
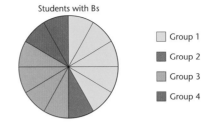

Students with Bs

14. Mario's group raised the second most money.
15. Lori's group raised the least money.
16. Shirley, Mario, John, Lori.
17. Money raised : 24 x 2 = 48   Mario's group raised $48.
18. Money raised : 24 x 4 = 96   Shirley's group raised $96.
19. Money raised : 24 ÷ 2 = 12   Lori's group raised $12.
20. Money raised : 12 + 24 + 48 + 96 = 180
    They raised $180 altogether.
21. Shirley's group sold the most number of apples because they raised the most money.
22. Mario's group sold the second most number of apples because they raised the second most money.
23. He spent the most time on video games on Saturday.
24. He spent the second most time on video games on Sunday.
25. He did not play video games on Tuesday and Thursday.
26. Time spent : 1 x 2 = 2
    He played video games for 2 hours on Monday.
27. Time spent : 1 x 3 = 3
    He played video games for 3 hours on Saturday.
28. Difference : 2.5 – 0.5 = 2
    He played 2 more hours on Sunday than on Wednesday.

Challenge

B ; Circle graph B shows that Katie spent the most money on clothing, the second most money on entertainment, the second least money on transportation, and the least money on food.

10 Mean and Mode

1. Mean : (127+117+120+105+110+105+100) ÷ 7 = 112   112
2. Mean : (110+126+112+104+108+110+121) ÷ 7 = 113
   Her mean running time was 113 seconds.
3. Mean : (124+106+98+110+106+106+106) ÷ 7 = 108
   Her mean running time was 108 seconds.
4. Mean : (100+125+105+104+100+104+104) ÷ 7 = 106
   Her mean running time was 106 seconds.
5. Her mode running time in the 3rd week was 106 seconds.
6. Her mode running time in the 4th week was 104 seconds.
7. Amy had the highest allowance in the class.
8. Wayne had the lowest allowance in the class.
9. Mean : (5 + 6.75 + 5.37 + 5) ÷ 4 = 5.53
   Their mean allowance was $5.53.
10. Mean : (3.83 + 7.37 + 3.83) ÷ 3 = 5.01
    Their mean allowance was $5.01.
11. Mean allowance of group B :
    (6.8 + 9.15 + 4.16 + 4.16 + 4.18) ÷ 5 = 5.69
    Mean allowance of group D :
    (4.75 + 8.13 + 4.75 + 4.75 + 8.13 + 0.69) ÷ 6 = 5.2
    Yes, the mean allowance received by the students in group B was higher than that in group D.
12. The mode allowance in group B was $4.16.
13. The mode allowance in group D was $4.75.
14. Mean : (5 + 6.75 + 5.37 + 5 + 4.18) ÷ 5 = 5.26
    Their mean allowance would be $5.26.

15. By systematic trial :
Mean (Lily in group C) :   Mean (Donny in group C) :
$(3.83 + 7.37 + 3.83 + 4.75) \div 4$ $(3.83 + 7.37 + 3.83 + 8.13) \div 4$
$= 4.945$ (not 5.79) ✗ $= 5.79$ ✓
Donny and Mark were the possible students.

16. Mean : $(258 + 426 + 426 + 678) \div 4 = 447$
The mean number of cards was 447.

17. No. of cards : 258, 426, 426, 678
The mode number of cards was 426.

18. Mean : $((258 + 126) + 426 + 426 + (678 – 126)) \div 4 = 447$
The mean number of cards would be 447.

19. No. of cards : 384, 426, 426, 552
The mode number of cards was 426.

20. Mean : $(258 + (426 – 252) + (426 + 252) + 678) \div 4 = 447$
The mean number of cards would be 447.

21. No. of cards : 258, 174, 678, 678
The mode number of cards would be 678.

22. Mean : $((258 – 40) + (426 + 60) + (426 – 60) + (678 + 40)) \div 4 = 447$
The mean number of cards was 447.

23. Mean : $((258 + 120) + (426 + 28) + 426 + 678) \div 4 = 484$
The mean number of cards would be 484.

24. Mean : $(258 + 426 + 426 + (678 – 88)) \div 4 = 425$
The mean number of cards would be 425.

25. Mean : $((258 + 426 + 426 + 678) – 160) \div 4 = 407$
Their mean number of cards would be 407.

26. Mean : $((258 + 12) + 426 + (426 – 48) + 678) \div 4 = 438$
The mean number of cards would be 438.

27. By systematic trial :
Average : $(110 + 150 + 120 + 130) \div 4 = 127.5$ ✗
Average : $(110 + 120 + 130 + 180) \div 4 = 135$ ✓
He has boxes A, C, D, and E.

28. Mean : $(110 + 150 + 120 + 130 + 180) \div 5 = 138$
The mean number of cards would be 138.

29. By systematic trial :
Average : $(10.68 + 12.37 + 13.25 + 11.89) \div 4 = 12.05$ ✗
Average : $(10.68 + 12.37 + 11.89 + 14.46) \div 4 = 12.35$ ✓
She has bags A, B, D, and E.

30. Mean : $(10.68 + 12.37 + 13.25 + 11.89 + 14.46) \div 5 = 12.53$
The mean amount in each bag would be 12.53 kilograms.

Challenge

1. Mark : $(76 \times 5) – 78 – 86 – 92 – 68 = 56$
His mark in math was 56.

2. Mark : $(77 \times 5) – 78 – 86 – 92 – 68 = 61$
He would have to get 61 in math.

11 Probability

1.
No. of Times Each Outcome Occurred

2. No. of times of spinning : 100
No. of times stopped on 'ice cream' : 40
Fraction of times : $\frac{40}{100} = \frac{2}{5}$ It was $\frac{2}{5}$.

3. No. of times stopped on 'pop' : 10
Fraction of times : $\frac{10}{100} = \frac{1}{10}$ It was $\frac{1}{10}$.

4. No. of times stopped on 'lollipop' : 30
Fraction of times : $\frac{30}{100} = \frac{3}{10}$ It was $\frac{3}{10}$.

5. It is least likely to stop on 'pop'.

6. It is most likely to stop on 'ice cream'.

7. There are 8 marbles altogether; 5 out of 8 marbles are red.
The probability is $\frac{5}{8}$.

8. There are 10 marbles altogether; 4 out of 10 marbles are blue.
The probability is $\frac{4}{10}$ ($\frac{2}{5}$).

9. There are 12 marbles altogether; 4 out of 12 marbles are green.
The probability is $\frac{4}{12}$ ($\frac{1}{3}$).

10. There are 9 marbles altogether; 0 out of 9 marbles are yellow.
The probability is 0.

11. There are 18 marbles altogether; 4 out of 18 marbles are blue.
The probability is $\frac{4}{18}$ ($\frac{2}{9}$).

12. No, because there are more blue marbles than red marbles. The most likely marble is blue.

13. 1 out of 4 sections is 'Hamburger'. The probability is $\frac{1}{4}$.

14. 2 out of 6 sections are 'Sandwich'. The probability is $\frac{2}{6}$ ($\frac{1}{3}$).

15. 1 out of 8 sections is 'Pop'. The probability is $\frac{1}{8}$.

16. 3 out of 8 sections are 'Hot Dog'. The probability is $\frac{3}{8}$.

17. Spinner A : 1 out of 4 sections
Spinner B : 1 out of 6 sections
Spinner C : 3 out of 8 sections ($\frac{3}{8} > \frac{1}{4} > \frac{1}{6}$)
Spinner C has the greatest probability.

18. Spinner A : 1 out of 4 sections
Spinner B : 1 out of 6 sections
Spinner C : 1 out of 8 sections ($\frac{1}{8} < \frac{1}{6} < \frac{1}{4}$)
Spinner C has the least probability.

19. $20.08 has two tens. Michael can spin 2 times.

20. He should spin Spinner C because it has the greatest probability that the spinner will stop on 'Hot Dog'.

21. The probability is 1.

22. The probability is 0.

23.
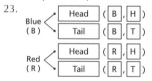

24. There are 6 possible outcomes.

25. They have 1 chance out of 6 to get a red marble and a head.
The probability is $\frac{1}{6}$.

26. They have 1 chance out of 6 to get a blue marble and a tail.
The probability is $\frac{1}{6}$.

27. No, it is because both have a probability of $\frac{1}{6}$.

28. They have 1 chance out of 6 to get a yellow marble and a head.
No. of times : $60 \div 6 = 10$
They would get a yellow marble and a head about 10 times.

Challenge

Spinner A :
$P(A) = \frac{2}{12} = \frac{1}{6}$ $P(B) = \frac{4}{12} = \frac{1}{3}$
$P(C) = \frac{2}{12} = \frac{1}{6}$ $P(D) = \frac{4}{12} = \frac{1}{3}$

Spinner B :
$P(A) = \frac{2}{8} = \frac{1}{4}$ $P(B) = \frac{3}{8}$
$P(C) = \frac{1}{8}$ $P(D) = \frac{2}{8} = \frac{1}{4}$

Spinner C :

$P(A) = \dfrac{1}{6}$ $P(B) = \dfrac{2}{6} = \dfrac{1}{3}$

$P(C) = \dfrac{1}{6}$ $P(D) = \dfrac{2}{6} = \dfrac{1}{3}$

Spinner D :

$P(A) = \dfrac{3}{8}$ $P(B) = \dfrac{1}{8}$

$P(C) = \dfrac{1}{8}$ $P(D) = \dfrac{3}{8}$

Spinner A and Spinner C show the same probability of getting each letter.

Final Review

1. Volume : 20 x 60 x 90 = 108,000
   The volume of the carton was 108,000 cubic centimeters.
2. No. of boxes : 4 x 3 x 4 = 48
   It would hold 48 boxes of cereal.
3. Cost : 2.99 x 48 = 143.52
   It would cost $143.52.
4. Boxes of granola : 48 – 18 – 8 – 10 = 12
   There were 12 boxes of granola.
5. 8 out of 48 boxes of cereal were rice flakes.
   The probability was $\dfrac{8}{48}$ ($\dfrac{1}{6}$).
6. 38 out of 48 boxes of cereal were not corn flakes.
   The probability was $\dfrac{38}{48}$ ($\dfrac{19}{24}$).
7. Bran flakes had the greatest probability because they had the most number.
8.

Number of Boxes of Cereal

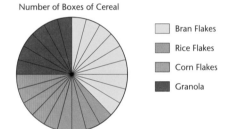

- Bran Flakes
- Rice Flakes
- Corn Flakes
- Granola

9.

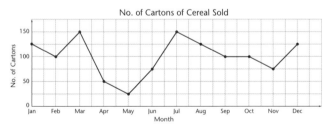

No. of Cartons of Cereal Sold

10. Difference : 125 – 25 = 100
    100 more cartons were sold.
11. Average : (125 + 100 + 150 + 50 + 25 + 75 + 150 + 125 + 100 + 100 + 75 + 125) ÷ 12 = 100
    On average, 100 cartons were sold each month.
12. Charge : 0.25 x 75 = 18.75
    The cost of delivery in November would be $18.75.
13. Mean : (80 + 86 + 86 + 75 + 79 + 86) ÷ 6 = 82
    Sarah's mean mark was 82.
14. Mean : (78 + 91 + 78 + 65 + 85 + 89) ÷ 6 = 81
    Molly's mean mark was 81.
15. Mean : (76 + 88 + 97 + 72 + 76 + 83) ÷ 6 = 82
    Stanley's mean mark was 82.
16. Mean : (82 + 97 + 69 + 96 + 80 + 80) ÷ 6 = 84
    Elaine's mean mark was 84.
17. Sarah's mode mark was 86.
18. Molly, Stanley, and Elaine had their mean mark higher than their mode mark.
19. Mean : (80 + 78 + 76 +82) ÷ 4 = 79
    It was 79.
20. Mean : (86 + 89 + 83 + 80) ÷ 4 = 84.5
    It was 84.5.
21. 1 out of 4 cards was Elaine's. The probability was $\dfrac{1}{4}$.
22. 3 out of 4 cards were not Molly's. The probability was $\dfrac{3}{4}$.
23. No. of times : 40 ÷ 4 = 10
    He would get his own card about 10 times.
24. C   25. D   26. B   27. A
28. D   29. D   30. C   31. B
32. A   33. A   34. C   35. D
36. B   37. D